May Crommelin

ORANGE LILY

By May Crommelin
(also including the stories *The Witch of Windy Hill*
and *An Old Maid's Marriage*)

edited, with an introduction by
Philip Robinson

Ullans Press

FOR THE ULSTER-SCOTS LANGUAGE SOCIETY

First published by Harper & Brothers, New York, 1879. This
new edition published by Ullans Press, Belfast, 2017.

Introduction and other additional material © the authors

ISBN 978-1-905281-31-2

This book has been published as part of an ongoing project by
the Ulster-Scots Academy.

www.ulsterscotsacademy.com

Cover image is taken from an old postcard of Main Street,
Carrowdore, County Down, courtesy of Desmond Rainey.

ACKNOWLEDGEMENTS

The publisher would like to thank all those who helped in the publication of this book: The United Ulster History Forum, The Ulster-Scots Academy, Ballywalter and District Historical Society, and Books Ulster, for financial support; Philip Robinson (editing, transcription and written contribution); Derek Rowlinson (transription, digitisation and set-up); Mark Thompson (illustrations, advice and written contribution); Desmond Rainey (permission to reproduce images from his collection of old Carrowdore postcards); Billy Carlile (promotion and fund-raising); Laura Spence (sourcing illustrations), and many others who have advised, encouraged and provided practical support. Without the enthusiastic assistance of all, the Ulster-Scots Language Society would not have able to republish this important work.

CONTENTS

INTRODUCTION

When Nicholas Delacherois-Crommelin (May Crommelin's grandfather) built Carrowdore Castle in 1819, he had the date '1690' boldly inscribed on one of its stones. Similarly, when May Crommelin began her literary career in the 1870s, one of the first of her prolific output of novels was *Orange Lily*—a nostalgic celebration of Carrowdore life in which she blended the local Ulster-Scots and Williamite traditions, not to mention castle society-life and cottage folk-life, in a tight, inextricable weave. But more of the reasons behind this strong family identification with King William III later.

Maria Henrietta Delacherois-Crommelin (1849–1930), known as 'May' Crommelin, was born on 30th August, 1849, daughter to Samuel Arthur Hill Delacherois-Crommelin (1817–85) of Carrowdore Castle. She was the author of numerous books, short stories and magazine articles, and became widely known as a travel writer as well as a novelist. May Crommelin continued to live, for at least part of the year, in Carrowdore Castle until the 1880s when, after her father died in 1885, she took up semi-permanent residence in London. Her 1930 gravestone in England records

"MARIA HENRIETTA   F.R.G.S.   AUTHORESS
    second daughter of S. de la Cherois CROMMELIN
    of Carrowdore Castle, Co. Down Ireland".

The first book by May Crommelin was published anonymously in 1874 when she was only 24 years of age. *Queenie. A novel* was a 3-volume romance, as was her second novel *My Love She's But a Lassie*, published in 1875. These were set in Canada, England, and Ireland, but without much local reference or description, and largely restricted to high society. Her next three books had an unmistakably Ulster backdrop: *A Jewel of a Girl*, (1877), based

INTRODUCTION

around Cushendun and north Antrim; *Orange Lily,* (1879), set in the area of Carrowdore in the Ards Peninsula of east Down, and *Black Abbey*, (1880) located at Greyabbey, near Carrowdore.

The 1879 first edition of *Orange Lily* was published in New York (with American spellings of words like 'favor' and 'neighbor'), and that version provides the basis for the current republication. However, the second edition published in London in 1880 (*Orange Lily, and Other Tales*), as the title suggests, contained several other short stories, two of which were set in the Ards Peninsula and are included in this new edition.

Between 1880 and 1924, May Crommelin published more than 40 other books, but only a few were of particular Ulster interest. In 1899 *'Divil May Care'; Alias Richard Burke, sometime Adjutant of the Black Northerners*, was dedicated 'To All Ulster Friends', and is set in county Antrim, where an officer home on sick leave from India gets embroiled in a series of humorous adventures. *The Golden Bow*, again set in Ulster, appeared in 1912 and is a story, peppered with Ulster-Scots dialogue, of a poor but pretty girl tracing an unhappy childhood to a joyous engagement. *The Luck of the Lowland Laddie* (1900) has a Scottish setting, with a wealth of lowland Scots dialogue throughout.

Orange Lily is the story of Lily Keag ('Or'nge Lily'), the young Carrowdore daughter of a local farmer, and Tom Coulter ('Tammas Cowltert') her childhood school friend and then farm-servant sweetheart. Their romance was disapproved of because of their different social backgrounds; but plot apart, the novel is particularly rich in historical and cultural content. The strength of the Williamite sympathies of the author for the Orange dimension of local folk-culture is perhaps surprising, coming, as it does, from a 'gentry' perspective. But Maria Delacherois-Crommelin's family background did not have the usual Anglo-Irish or Scottish-Laird credentials. In fact, both the Delacherois and the Crommelin sides of her ancestry were French Huguenot in origin.

INTRODUCTION

In the late 17th century, Louis Crommelin, from whom May was descended, was living in Holland as a leading member of the French Huguenot refugee colony there. In common with the Duke of Schomberg and most of the other Huguenots in the Netherlands, he had pledged support to Prince William of Orange in the religious wars in Europe leading up to the Glorious Revolution of 1688 in England and the 1690 Battle of the Boyne in Ireland. After the events of 1688–1691, Louis Crommelin received a personal invitation and a royal grant from King William III to lead a Huguenot colony of 70 French-speaking families, including two of Louis' brothers, three sisters and some cousins, in establishing the linen industry on the Dutch model in Lisburn in 1698. More than 1,000 looms and 'Dutch' spinning wheels were imported from Holland. In consideration of Louis Crommelin having spent £10,000 on the venture, William III also conferred a pension of £200 a year on Louis' son.

In the winter of 1689/90 a French pastor, Jean Dubourdieu, had acted as chaplain to the Huguenot regiments in the Lisburn area, and by 1711 the Huguenot colony had grown to 120 familes with its own French-speaking pastor and church. Despite the Huguenots being originally Calvinists, they conformed to the established Church of Ireland right from the start in response to their royal patronage. Many of the early Crommelins are buried in Lisburn Cathedral, including May Crommelin's ancestor Louis Crommelin.

But May's full surname was Delacherois-Crommelin, as she was equally descended from another first-generation member of the Williamite Huguenot colony at Lisburn—Nicholas De la Cherois. Daniel De la Cherois, a brother of Nicholas, arrived in Lisburn in 1699 after having married Marie Angelique Crommelin (a cousin of Louis Crommelin) in London. Nicholas had also got married before coming, in his case to Mary Crommelin, a sister of Louis. Nicholas and Mary's grandson Samuel De la Cherois then adopted the composite name Delacherois-Crommelin in accordance with the conditions of the will of his cousin, Nicholas Crommelin of Lisburn. Both Nicholas senior and his brother Daniel De la Cherois fought at the Battle of the Boyne in 1690.

In 1689 King William III had formed two regiments of French Huguenots which he brought to England from Holland. In the first of these, Nicholas De la Cherois (May's great, great, great-grandfather) was appointed major, his brother Daniel De la Cherois a captain, and yet another brother, Bourjonval De la Cherois, a lieutenant. They all landed in Ireland at Groomsport in 1689, and accompanied King William from Carrickfergus on his march south to face King James in 1690. Major Nicholas De la Cherois distinguished himself at the Battle of the Boyne. Afterwards, with only a small band of men, he made 1,500 of King James's men lay down their arms, and was presented with a large reward of 1,500 crowns for this action. Bourjonval De la Cherois was killed at Dungannon by rebels in the aftermath of the battle, and Daniel De la Cherois was rewarded for his actions by being appointed governor of Pondieberry in the East Indies.

With such strong family ties to the Williamite cause, it is hardly surprising that May Delacherois-Crommelin would wear her colours on her sleeve in *Orange Lily*. In the Public Record Office of Northern Ireland is an unpublished manuscript: "Louis Crommelin, His life, His Ancestors, His People, His Descendents" written by "Miss May Crommelin, of Carrowdore Castle". It contains not only a full account of the family connections with William of Orange, but also an unabridged and detailed account of the atrocities suffered by her Protestant Huguenot ancestors in France. In 1900, May's brother Frederick had at Carrowdore Castle a silver toothpick case that had been brought to Ireland by Major Nicholas De la Cherois in 1689 when with the Williamite army, and a rosette reputedly worn by King William at the Boyne.

Although May Crommelin completed and published *Orange Lily* in 1879, the main part of the story is set in the 1860s when

INTRODUCTION

the author was a young girl in Carrowdore and when the entire county of Down was in a state of high political unrest. There were serious 'faction fights' and skirmishes following Orange parades in county Down, such as that at Dolly's Brae in 1849. A Party Processions Act of 1850, reinforced by a Party Emblems Act of 1860, prohibited Orangemen assembling and marching together in procession using banners, emblems and flags and from playing music tending "to provoke animosity". May Crommelin's grandfather, Nicholas Delacherois-Crommelin, who was a leading Orangeman in this period, having been County Grand Master for 30 years, and her uncle (Nicholas Crommelin) were both prominent in the organisation of opposition to the parades ban.

In 1867, William Johnston of Ballykilbeg, supported by Nicholas Crommelin of Carrowdore Castle, organised an illegal Orange Order parade from Bangor to Newtownards in County Down in protest at the Party Procession Act. The parade took place on 12th July, 1867, and about 30,000 took part. Johnston was sentenced to a short term in prison the next year for his actions that day. He was then elected as Member of Parliament for Belfast in 1868. When as a result, the Party Processions Act was eventually repealed in 1872, and the local 'Twelfth' came to Carrowdore in a subsequent year, the event was a special occasion for the Crommelins and, apparently, for 'Orange Lily' too! It is not only recorded in *Orange Lily*, but also in a contemporary Orange ballad called "The Hills o Carrowdore", which includes the following lines referring to 'Mr. Crommelin':

> *Now the speeches from the platform sounded in our ear*
> *And first was Mr Crommelin who occupied the chair.*
> *He told us of our forefathers who did King William join*
> *Who fought and gained the victory at the Battle of the Boyne*
> *So here's to Mr Crommelin for giving us the ground*
> *A splendid platform he put up—it cost him many a pound.*

INTRODUCTION

The opening paragraph of *Orange Lily* informs us that Lily Keag, the story's principal character, was the daughter of a small farmer, Mr. James Keag, whom the brethren had, years ago, made 'Master of the Ballyboly Orange Lodge'. Lily Keag was dubbed 'Or'nge Lily' at school, partly because of her reddish hair, but also because of her father's prominent position in the local Orange lodge. This name has entered contemporary tradition, with a gaily bedecked parody of 'Orange Lily' appearing in Belfast and other parades almost as often as the figure of 'King Billy' himself. But the model for the original 'Orange Lily' was a sophisticated and real-life person in the guise of Maria Henrietta Delacherois-Crommelin of Carrowdore Castle.

Orange Lily takes the exuberant and colourful political and religious traditions of the Carrowdore community in the 1860s and blends them with the quiet and reserved Ulster-Scots linguistic and cultural traditions of the same people. Simulanteously, the author creates an interesting fictional interplay between the main 'local' characters and the world of her own aristocratic family life at Carrowdore Castle.

In this story, May Crommelin displays (and records for posterity) a convincing insight into the vernacular 'voice' of these *'Scotch-speaking descendants of Scotch-bred colonists'*, as even a glance at the descriptive glossary at the end of this edition will confirm.

Philip Robinson

ORANGE LILY

CHAPTER I

"Here came the brown Phoenician,
　　The man of trade and toil—
Here came the proud Milesian,
　　A hungering for spoil;
And the Firbolg and the Comry,
　　And the hard, enduring Dane.
And the iron Lords of Normandy,
　　With the Saxons in their train."

DAVIES.

"She's not a dull or cold land;
No! she's a warm and bold land,
Oh! she's a true and old land—
　　This native land of mine."

DAVIES.

LILY KEAG was the eldest-born child of Mr. James Keag, of the parish of Ballyboly[1], in the county of Down. A worthy, quiet man was the latter in character; by occupation, a small farmer; and as to worldly honor, the brethren had, years ago, made him Master of the Ballyboly Orange Lodge.

"Boys—O!" her friend Tom Coulter, of eight years' experience in the world, used to exclaim to Lily, who was herself then only aged six. "Boys—O! but it's grand to see yer da riding on the ould gray mare on the Twalfth of July; with all the lodges marching and the flags and drums beating, and him with the scarlet cloak about him like King William himself."

And Lily would reply, with brightening eyes and head raised erect.

"Ay, Tom; *it is that!*"

---

[1] Carrowdore (the Ballyboly village of this book) is actually in Donagh-adee Parish.

1

For, all through the few summers she remembered, her small mind had been brimming over with pride in, and reverence for, her father's great position. When the May nights grew to be warm, and the "boys" began to drum along the lanes practising for the Twelfth, she, however tiny, had always run after them with the older children till her little legs failed for weariness. Then some evening idler often carried home the Master's small lass in his arms, praising her as "a grand wee Orangewoman, already."

But on the night before the great Twelfth itself, she would lie hours awake with excitement, to be roused again by the beat of the drums[2] practising in the gray fresh dawn long before the sun was up. Then later, when the morning was well on, the whole countryside would turn out of doors to see their own lodge defile[3] gayly down the road, its three flags flying and their own men just marvels in scarfs and cockades like yearly glorified grubs, marching to join more lodges, and go in procession to the meeting-place for that year. All the grown-up lasses went with the Orangemen, too, in new dresses, most with orange and blue ribbons on their bonnets; only the steady-minded folk and the "childer" stayed behind.

Hey! but Lily was proud and glad that there had once been a battle of the Boyne. She had a vague idea that her father must have been at it, but was shame-faced when she once inquired about it, he had laughed so much. She asked Tom Coulter's opinion, but he didn't know either; only he was certain sure the great King William was "da" to our Queen Victoria.

Our little lass's real name, as her father told most folks, was

---

[2] 'Lambeg' drums. These were extremely large drums beaten on both sides with curved malacca canes. They were usually played in pairs accompanied by a single fifer, and were ubiquitous in Orange parades of the 19th century.

[3] march in a 'file' of a single line or 'by files'.

ORANGE LILY

Lily-un or Lily-ann, just whichever way you liked to pronounce it; and he was justly proud that it was "so entirely oncommon." For many of the Ballyboly farmers had been decidedly studious, and had clubbed together to buy papers from London, with pictures of the most bloody murders and stories of the very highest life, the writers of which scorned to touch with their pens any one beneath a baronet. In one of these, Lilian was the name of a duchess in her own right, whom a mad marquis tried to marry, then murder in a dozen different ways, till she was triumphantly rescued by a Prince of the Blood, whom she had stooped to love in the disguise of a common earl. And this Duchess Lilian may be justly considered our Lily's god-mother, since the honest farmer's fancy was so taken with her history that he at once named his new-born child after her.

Lily wasn't pretty. She had a shock of yellow-reddish hair, a wide mouth, and freckles; but her hair was neatly combed, her face smiling, and her skin, as Mistress Keag declared, "if you rightly took note to it between the freckles, was as white as milk, and her cheeks as red as strawberries." And, though her mother had died early in her young life, was still merry, since her step-mother was a hearty soul, a trifle untidy, "out-of-the-common" kindly; whilst Lily had been born with the knack of fitting her soft temper to everybody else's sharp mind.

The child toddled all day by her father's side in early summer, when the long grass fell in swathes under the mower's scythe and shared amply at noon his dinner of potato-bread and butter-milk. Again, in the summer, she would stand prattling to him, while the farm-men, and women too, were pulling the flax that grew higher than her waist, of so fresh a green that the very color was enough to praise God for. She would pluck herself a posy of its tiny blue lint-flowers, and press them to her breast, chuckling because "they were so bonny." And when the strong backs ached with stooping, the sun glared, her child's laugh made many a hard face in the field smile; so she unwittingly did her part already for good. But best she liked the harvest-time when her da reaped ahead of his men, and she pretended to bind to him or played hide and seek in the stooks. Then the yearly night-dance in the barn, when the fields were bare, and the turkeys wandered through the stubble! How her life was changeful and pleasant!

Tom Coulter, or "Tammy Cowltert," as his name was generally pronounced by those who spoke as broad as their Scotch ancestors did, was her dearest companion. He was an impudent, pleasant, but unfortunately a dirty boy, so her step-mother considered him a vulgar acquaintance for Lily; besides, his father was a poor cottager and ne'er-do-well, sometimes driven to break stones for a livelihood. But the friendship had begun this wise: One day wee Lily was going to see him when she met Tom limping painfully along, with a wry face, yet glancing black eyes that were searching for old birds' nests in the hedge, bees' nests in the ditch—for I verily believe in those days he would have tried to kill flies if he had been dying, and have wished to possess the death-worm that ticked for himself as a nice curiosity in beasties.

"What's wrang wi' ye, Tom?" cried out the affrighted child; for his jacket was off, his shirt torn, and his shoulders finely tattooed with bruises.

"Da whaled me," replied Tom, short and careless as any young Spartan. Then, to her shocked reiterated questions, he deigned to explain that the baby in their cottage, which Tom evidently considered an impertinent late intruder into his home, spoiling his pleasure in many ways, had died; and as it was a sickly thing, Tom, being a very small boy then, thought "a good riddance too." "But," he now went on to explain, with the air of a practical man aggrieved and injured by a sentimental section of society, "father he took to the cryin'; and mother *she* took to the cryin'; and Aunt Marget and Uncle William-Thomas they fell to the cryin'. But deed I couldna cry, for I saw naething to cry aboot; so da just took the big stick and threshed me *till make me cry!*"

And with a diabolical grin, Tom proceeded to frighten Lily's tender mind by making a cut on his arm bleed again, and displaying some of the welts made by the whacking that had been meant to relieve the paternal grief and arouse tender feelings in the body, at least, of this unnatural child.

Lily's eyes filled up with pity, her little breast heaved, and with a loud sob she wailed—

"Och, anee! anee! anee!"

"Oh, and now *you're* at the cryin' too!" exclaimed Tom in dismay. "Then I'll be off. I'll take to the cryin' for no man!"

Nevertheless, with all his hardihood, he only limped away two paces, and allowed himself to be appeased by a tearful assurance from Lily that she wouldn't cry no more if he'd stop making the nasty blood come. He even accepted half of the big farl of buttered oatcake, which was already nicked all round by her teeth, and said she was a nice wee gurl.

When school was over, Lily, tripping back with small-booted feet up the lonely lane, found the solitary little sufferer paddling his toes, that were always bare, in the cows' water-hole; and was persuaded by him to do likewise, and to eat unripe blackberries and haws, and had pains that night in consequence. "They played theirselves finely," in fact, as Mistress Keag severely remarked when Lily came in well muddied that night—she that was the pattern small lass of a mile around for her tidiness, always wore boots, and had been even known to cry when her "pinny" for school was not clean. Verily, a marvel of a wee girl in that country of unkempt, bare-toed childer; but then her mother had been a maid, and once in service in England, and the English were over-any-thing particular, folk here heard tell, so perhaps hers was an inherited peculiarity.

CHAPTER II

"A country fellow at the pleugh,
  His acre's till'd, he's right eneugh;
A country girl at her wheel,
  Her dizzen's done, she's unco weel;
But gentlemen, an' ladies warst,
  Wi' ev'ndown want o' wark are curst.
  ....
Their days insipid, dull, and tasteless,
Their nights unquiet, lang, an' restless."

BURNS.

"And it is not impossible that, amidst the infinite disorders of the world, there may be exceptions to the happiness of virtue, even with regard to those persons whose course of life, from their youth up, has been blameless."—*Analogy of Religion.*

MISS ALICE and Miss Edith Alexander lived up at the Castle, that crowned the woods beyond Ballyboly. They were gentle, middle-aged, twin ladies, in whom the thought had begun to glimmer that if a woman has neither husband nor family she should search out some work on which to expend the natural abilities for good God gave her, or these, for want of being used, will likely sour; so they gently strove to make all the poor in Ballyboly happy.

But, having lingered through many winters, so to say, with their toes on a fender, and many summers sat shading their complexions in the Castle garden, they could not nowadays be energetic even in God's service. Slowly they would walk down together into Ballyboly village, that consisted of a handful of cottages and three public-houses[4]; would visit, because God's word bade them, the

---

[4] Ballyboly (Carrowdore). Although there is a townland of Ballyboley which adjoins Carrowdore village to the west (the village itself is in the townland of Ballyrawer), BALLYBOLY is the fictional name given in this book to Carrowdore.

sick and widowed, feeling heavy-hearted for days after the sight of such sorrow, not knowing what comfort to give. They would see sores and skin-diseases displayed without flinching, though the poor ladies inwardly felt very sick; would murmur with painful effort a few words of sympathy, mourning because they could say no better; then with some relief give money, and wearily go back to the Castle to sip their afternoon tea, wishing ruefully they could like better this "doing good," in which yet, because they believed it to be their duty, they steadily continued to persevere.

Folk say there is a mysterious connection between twins, bodily and spiritual; it seemed so with these, they were so much alike. Each had delicate health and little spirits. Neither had ever known the strong joy of living a full life; either had felt, as it were, half of the other. In youth both gentle souls had gone out together into society; in middle age they were still together, but living lonely at the Castle, more fearful, more tender-minded; recalling their past life in the gay world at moments with a sort of frightened pleasure, as might two simple country souls who, having spent a summer's day in the noise and heat and hurlyburly of a great town, congratulate themselves at eventide on having escaped its temptations—secretly ashamed that they enjoyed seeing a little of its wickedness, but feeling that now they, too, have eaten fruit of the tree of knowledge of good and evil.

All their relations were dead, except a wild young step-brother in London. They kept the old house warmed till he should marry and come back; then they meant to leave it together. Their lives were like a gray November sky from its dawn, towards afternoon, God be thanked, to be brightened in the West by a band of yellow light, deepening and broadening till the sun set; but not yet.

Life was no enjoyment to them. They felt of no use in it; yet dreaded death for its physical pain and the awful possibilities of the after-life. The more this great mystery pressed on them the unhappier they grew; then, having all thoughts in common, sought for comfort in their religion with feeble crying and groping—but at first found no light in the darkness. Yet, having read that faith without works is void, they sought to do good works with all their weak powers in the parish; but many a night literally watered their couch with tears because they believed they had not got the faith "necessary to salvation;" because they believed they did not love their Lord God, nor their poor neighbors. They knew that they would gladly suffer hunger or thirst, heat or cold, to do the latter a kindness; "but that is not love," they said. It was because simply they could not bear not to do so, even to their enemies. So they bewailed their own hard-heartedness, and examined themselves continually with doubts and torments. Meanwhile, the poor often blessed them behind their backs for their Christian love. Verily, I think these were wisest.

The sisters struggled on thus, doing good deeds and reading religious books, vaguely hoping thereby, if might be, to *save themselves;* an unchristian idea (but even that they thought this was not clear to their own minds). But sorest-troubled were they thinking they grew luke-warmer, in charity cold-hearted, till their consciences became a daily torture, hourly examined, hourly doubted. Then, one day, one read this passage in good Bishop Butler's "Analogy of Religion":

"Let a man set himself to attend to, inquire out, and relieve distressed persons, and he cannot but grow less and less sensibly affected with the various miseries of life, with which he must become acquainted; when yet, at the same time, benevolence considered not as a passion, but as a practical principle of action, will strengthen; and whilst he passively compassionates the distressed less, he will acquire a greater aptitude actively to assist and befriend them."

She softly showed this to her sister, who sat down beside her to study it; and after a while they looked up in each other's faces and felt somewhat comforted. They had the most delicate respect for the poor, as poor. They almost envied them, thinking, "How hard it will be for us rich to enter into the kingdom of heaven—easier for a camel to go through a needle's eye." And, if they entered an untidy house with dirty children and a cross mother, they could sooner have washed the floor on their knees than have taken advantage of their superior station to reprove her, thinking only, "Poor soul! She gets on somehow—in her place we should have lain down and died. Very likely she will sit high above us in the kingdom of heaven."

Unhappily, from their having been unaccustomed to going among the peasants in early life, poor folk often could not understand their excessive timidity and reserve, and thought these coldness and pride. And more than one woman, seeing them gather their silken skirts together on sitting down in her cottage, felt huffed, supposing they dreaded dirtying their gowns. They would have cried at being so wronged had they known it; the feeling that prompted them having been shame at wearing rich dresses whilst their sisters were in rags. "Yet is it not our duty to keep up trade?" the poor ladies asked each other, bewildered. However, the time came when the Ballyboly people got to understand them and feel protectingly towards them, even tenderly. It was almost laughable to see how their natural positions became reversed; yet pitiful too.

The Misses Alexander often visited Ballyboly school-house[5], and tried to lure thither the ragged truants about the lanes, by saying "how nice it was" in that stuffy and unenticing room; not to mention the bit of play-ground, all mud in winter and dust in summer. But indeed the Ballyboly children needed little pressing. What with their mingled Scotch and Irish breeding, they were as sharp

[5] There were two school-houses in Carrowdore in the 1830s: one on the Main Street, and one on the western outskirts, in the townland of Ballyboley. It seems that the school described here is the one in the village.

9

as needles to learn; and some of them, like Lily, would roar lustily if kept from "schuil." (This, however, involving potato-picking in wet plough fields or such-like work, unpleasing to the youthful mind, is not to be so much wondered at.) And then the playground supplied mud-pies in winter and a grand marbles-court in summer, thick dust being just the thing to trace rings in.

For weeks and weeks honest little Lily, who tramped most praiseworthily to her lessons, tried to persuade vulgar Tommy "Cowltert" to come too.

"It was 'hooray, boys!' the day she got him to go," said her father in Ballyboly dialect. "She was quare and proud!"

Likewise, finding Tom's religious instruction neglected, she took that also in hand, and asked him every morning carefully, "Did ye say your prayers last night?" and once or twice, at first, when Tom said "No," was so bitterly grieved that he repented; and this became a daily attention on her part of which Tom resented any neglect.

For the first week at school Lily nodded at Tom encouragingly; then, one fine day, her under-lip lengthened horribly, and her face would have frightened a bachelor, such crying preparations being alarming to look at—for "Tommy had got ahead of her."

"It's owre ocht—it's beyant the beyants!' she gurgled; forgetting the schoolmaster's withering sarcasms upon "broad pronuncia-tion, and "beyond the beyonds" being quite too tame in sound to express her sharp and bitter grief. The truth was that Tom was clever beyond most of his clever race, whilst she was only a poor tortoise in learning.

"Hould yer whisht! here's the quality!" whispered Tom, as Miss Alice and Miss Edith entered. "I've a black-ball" (a hard sweetie as big as a young cannon-ball) "in my pocket; I've only suckit the half o't, and I'll bestow *that* upon ye."

And, like a just reward of Providence for his generosity, up came Miss Alice to them both.

"Well, little boy, and where do you stand?" quoth she, mildly.

Tom giggled and sniggled; shuffled his muddy bare toes to the very edge of a circle painted for each class on the floor, thinking maybe he had been in a wrong position; and wished within his soul (being a vulgar boy) that the quality would not speak so softly, as if they had flour in their mouths.

"Are you at the head or bottom of your class?" chimed in Miss Edith.

"*I'm at the heid!*" burst from Tom, shyness suddenly overborne, and words coming in an explosion; while gentle murmurs of approval ensued from both the sisters, as from a couple of gray-clad doves.

"And how many more are in your class?" they inquired, admiringly, while Tom gazed up at them with a bold air, as who should say, "See what a good boy am I!" But no answer came from the modest youth. "How many more?" they encouragingly repeated, thinking they had found a model boy at last, and smiling down upon him.

Tom replied, sturdily, "*There's just me and a lassie.*" And Lily hung her head, for she was the lassie; that particular class only boasting two small human specimens just then. "And who is this little girl?" now asked Miss Alice, pleasantly. She had a more inquiring mind than Miss Edith.

"This is Mrs. Keag's wee lass," replied the schoolmistress, putting one hand under Lily's chin and turning up her face for inspection, till her eyes goggled at the ceiling—an ordeal any of the scholars who attracted attention were playfully put through, and actually supposed to like. "Lily-yun is her proper name, but they call her Lill or Lily for short."[6]

---

[6] The parody of Lillian / Lill / Lily that still appears as a brightly bedecked woman with orange hair in present-day 12 July parades is known just as often 'Orange Lill' as 'Orange Lily'.

ORANGE LILY

"*Lily!*" murmured Miss Edith, who was somewhat reflective, smiling curiously on the little freckled face, and the reddish pate that, neatly combed and thick, was what is termed by proud mothers a fine head of hair. "Orange Lily, I think, would be a better name," and she moved away to hear a class of bigger children go in turns through the curious gabble they called reading aloud. But, behind her, ensued choked giggles, sniffles, nudgings, and whispers, which, if listened to by the down-bent ear of a big person, resolved themselves into repetitions by all the children of "Or'nge Lily! Or'nge Lily!"

Poor Lily! that seemed the bitterest hour of her little life. Surpassed, laughed at, she bent her curly head over her slate; but, when the tears plumped down on it, she smeared them round with her palm, and tried to make believe it was a new way she had of cleaning out her last sum.

"Tom! Tom Coulter," called the master.

It was Tom's turn to read aloud, so he quickly licked his finger to turn the pages better, and uplifted his voice, as usual, in a doleful chant; never drawing breath save where there wasn't a comma, or when he collected himself in front of a big word, like young Captain Alexander's hunter before leaping a fence.

"Saint John th*a* Bap-tist was a good man an' a; p-r-o-pro; p-h-e-t … pro-phet an' he; pre-a-c-h-e-d-ched … pre-ched in *tha* wil-der-ness of Ju-de-a-an'; his meat was l-o-c-u-s-t-s—locusts an'; his r-a-i-rai-ment was a—a … ah—ah—ah! …"

"Leathern girdle," promptly uttered poor Miss Edith, to end the torture she had undergone till Tom came at last to that stop. "And what did that mean, little boy? He wore, it, you know, instead of his coat. Come now" (encouragingly), "what was it?"

"'Twas a *griddle!* burst out Tom, who hated feeling nagged at.

"Well, yes. And what does that mean?"

"It means just a griddle—what *folks bakes breid on!*" retorted Tom, now defiant, and apparently thinking Miss Edith a fool; for that poor lady stood stock still, with her lips slightly parted, quite bewildered by the suggestion that the Baptist's clothing consisted of a kitchen utensil like a lipless frying-pan, slung somehow about his waist. She retired discomposed, leaving explanations to the schoolmaster, and thereby rescued Miss Alice from still deeper despair. For that excellent middle-aged maiden had been ill-advised enough to assist at a display of what sums the small fry could reckon up in "mental arithmetic"; she who never *could* tell: If a herring and a half cost three half-pence, how many do you get for a shilling?

Breathlessly she had listened to such questions as, "A man is hired to break stones at seven pence per day. Find what that pay amounts to in the year, omitting Sundays." Little children, who seemed mere babes to her undiscriminating eyes, gabbled fluent answers in their trebles. A biggish boy reduced 2½ to an improper fraction in a jiffy. At last Lily Keag, one of the smallest there, told rapidly how many fourths there were in thirteen apples, and fifths in six cakes, almost as soon as she was asked; and the master, turning with a bland smile, requested Miss Alice to say whether their answers had been correct or not. How the poor woman evaded that awful test by ladylike *finesse;* how she seized her sister's arm, and got out of the school without betraying her ignorance, she never knew.

"But it has cured me of putting questions to them, for many a long day," she murmured to Miss Edith, with a sigh of exhaustion, when they neared their lodge gate. And both good women felt vastly relieved that conscience would not prick them to revisit that school now, for nearly one whole restful fortnight.

Little Lily, however, after running the gauntlet of her schoolmates' jeers, when lessons were done, crept home along their own lane in tears; and so appearing over the farmhouse threshold considerably surprised her family, with whom her good temper was a matter of course they had grown accustomed to. (Tom Coulter often mused whether it *answered well* to be so good-humored, like Lily, that folk "put upon her," and were amazed if she ever showed any ill-temper like their own; for he himself found a character for naughtiness most useful, seeing his misdeeds surprised nobody.)

"She cried so sorely, ye could have heard her down at the lint-hole," said Mistress Keag, late after supper, to her husband, who had been busy all day pulling his steeped flax-bundles out of the stagnant water-holes which they made most unsavory. And Lily had been utterly dumb as to what ailed her. Her little step-brothers had wondered at, then pitied her without effect; even the baby had howled on seeing her woful face. (The boys had been given the common work-a-day names of Hans and Henry-Thomas, it may be here remarked; but Farmer Keag had gratified his taste for the beautiful in his daughters, and the baby rejoiced in the appellation of Osilla, found, like that of Lilian, "in a book.")

"Come to yer da, my daughter, and tell him what ails ye," called Keag, cheerily; and lifting the little maid on his knee, he succeeded, by coaxing, in extracting from her the troubles of the day. "Called ye Orange Lily, did they? Weel, and yon's a very purty name, I think; for isn't it the handsomest flower that ever blows? Ye'll be my own wee Orange Lily, and I'll think a heap more of ye than ever I did; and every twelfth of July ye shall wear a flower of it in your breast."

And so indeed the child ever after did; and her father's assurances of fancying the name "above onything" not only comforted the little lass then, but made her proud of being thus known after a while. For, seeing that her father was such an enthusiastic Orangeman, and Master of the Ballyboly Lodge, the nickname first used by her teasing playfellows stuck to his child the more readily; and thenceforth she was often spoken of through all Ballyboly, where *sobriquets* were favorite and undying humor-ticklers, as Orange Lily.

CHAPTER III

"A cottar howkin in a sheugh,
  Wi' dirty stanes biggin a dyke,
  Baring a quarry and sic like,
  Himself, a wife, he thus sustains,
  A smytrie o' wee duddie weans,
  An' nought but his han' darg to keep
  Them right and tight in thack an' rape."
                                    BURNS.

Alas! they had been friends in youth,
  But whispering tongues can poison truth.

AND what happens to any human pair, must have happened to
many such a pair, since men and women multiplied on earth;
thus was it with our little Lily and Tom.

For some of the other school children, prompted thereunto by
the naughty feelings that spring up, the devil best knows how! in
the hearts of all human dwellers on the green earth, partly invented
and much magnified the tale, that "Tommy Cowltert had bragged
about beating Lily Keag in class." The little story-tellers did not
thereby mean to do harm. Half the wrong-doers in the world
mean to do no harm, bless you! Either their deeds diverge quite
unaccountably from the uprightness of their intentions, or else
folk interpret things unkindly; but still—"no harm was meant!"

Well, the Keags' farm-house lay on a hill-slope, half a mile from
Ballyboly village, with very few neighbors' houses around, and
none near but that of the Coulters. This lay still further from the
village, and was a big cottage in some disrepair, down in a bit of
marsh-ground, full of meadow-sweet in summer, and of snipes
in season. It will therefore be seen that Tom and Lily had
no other children near to play with; and, when the former took
himself off to the village in search of fun, he got so skelped by

his mother and clouted by his father, who were only unanimous in such very necessary attentions towards their offspring, that he decided it "answered best" to work after school hours. It was one of his duties to bring up the cow at milking time; and then Lily had been accustomed to trot down the hill to the end of her father's big meadow that marched with the Coulters' one small field, and have a talk with Tom across the gap or the thorn bushes that generally supplied the place of gates in Ballyboly parish. Sometimes Tom hauled these aside, and she crept through and tasted the delights of usefulness by "shooing" at the old cow too.

One evening Lily did not come. It was on that morning she had heard of Tom's ingratitude to his mentor—to her who had coaxed him to school; and her little heart felt queer and sore. Tom felt only lonely that evening. But, next morning, as he came along by their marsh, or "quaw," as he delighted in calling it to Lily, who considered it vulgar to say such "broad " words, he was startled to see her trotting far ahead on the straight, lonely causeway through the bog which lay between the village and the grass land about their own homes. She gone on! who had daily waited for him at the corner where the Keags' private lane and his own marsh-path met. It was curious!

"What for did ye not stop a wee while for me this morning?" he asked simply, when, after three o'clock, they were released from school and he joined her, as usual. "I cried on ye, all my able. Did ye no hear?"

"Ay! but why should I be late at school for the likes of you?"

Lily's cross answer died away in a sort of frightened whisper, its bitterness shocking herself; her eyes filled with tears. Tom was silent with utter amazement, but he, too, felt queer now and sore. They trotted along silently for a long time, then he suggested—

"I'm feared ye've taken the sulks."

"I never have them; it's yourself," said Lily, with an angry sob.

"Them that has them never acknowledges till them. I'm sorry

for ye," was the young Pharisee's calm reply in tones of pitying superiority. Then, parrot-like, mimicking a sentence much used by his uncle by marriage towards his aunt, which he kept stored in his memory like mental ammunition, awaiting a good occasion for discharging it with effect, he added, "I'm thankful the Lord never made me one of yer sulkers—like wimmen! *I* get in a tearing rage, and then it's over."

Lily piously pursed up her lips, shocked at his presumption in impugning the work of Providence in her person.

"I suppose the Lord made me the way he wanted me. Perhaps he was tired of tearing-ragers!"

On and on they trotted along the black bog causeways in bitter silence. The little girl's heart was bursting at the boy's accusation, all the more that conscience could not excuse her. She only knew that it was burning pain to her to be in a real rage with anybody; it made her feel, in her horrified penitence afterwards, as if she was an utterly hopeless sinner. She loved her playfellow, Tom, too well to take his supposed ill-treatment lightly; but was too sensitive to reproach him for his reported jeers about her. There was the situation.

This quarrel proved to be the thin end of the wedge that parted these small friends during the wet, windy winter following—a dull time to both. Not that Lily's good temper in the main, and Tom's latent generosity might not have made all straight again, had they met. But there it was! Like older folks, chance, and the wishes of others, kept them asunder. First Tom's mother took poorly, and kept him many weeks from school to do odd jobs in the cottage; then Lily and her little brothers got the chin-cough, which was prevalent through the country, and had measles after that again, so stayed at home at the farm till nearly spring-time. This was chance; the persons who helped on fate were their respective mothers. Lily's step-mother honestly and openly rejoiced that the wean ran about less with that wee boy of the Cowlterts'; who she was sure—because he belonged to *them ones*—could never come to good. Tom's amiable parent objected to his "diverting himself with thon wee lass of Mr. Keag's," on the broad principle that opposition to his every childish wish kept him in his place finely—and afforded herself an unnatural satisfaction. During those weeks Tom got more whalings, skelpings, scoldings, and stray clouts on the side of the head than during all his short life before, when he had generally escaped from home all day, or, of late, gone to school. But, now, being deprived of the schooling was, curiously enough, what most troubled his mind; and that really did so.

One day, Tom's mother, being up near the Castle, made so free as to ask Miss Alice for some jam for her cold in the head—a sovereign recipe. And she not only got a pot of preserved black currants, but also a diffidently gracious offer that the ladies would come and visit her some day, as she was ailing.

The day on which the ladies went down to the marsh was keen and windy, yet the cottage door stood wide open; for the chimney smoked so badly that breathing without such means would have been impossible. Therefore, as both stood gently on the threshold, feebly tapping on the doorposts, and asking, "Is Mrs. Coulter in?" while gazing at her back as she crouched over the fire, they had the full benefit of a loud monologue from Tom, who was violently rocking the cradle, in which lay his baby sister a few weeks old. Thump! bump! went the cradle. "E-m-b-a-r—r-a-s-s-e-d; embarrass'd!" shouted Tom, by way of impressing the spelling forcibly on his memory; while his dirty finger travelled down the lines of his "spells" to the next biggest word in his school-book. Bump! thump! went the cradle again. He was seated on the damp mud floor, in a shirt and ragged corduroy breeches, bare-toed and shock-headed. Miss Alice and Miss Edith knew mildly what embarrassed meant, when they could not make themselves heard.

"Hould yer whisht, Tom! Here's the ladies," called his mother, then, from one side of the fireplace; and his father added from the other, where he, too, was stooping over the peat-embers—

"Don't ye see the quality? A body can't hear theirselves speak with the tongue of ye."

"But is the poor little boy learning his lessons for school?—that is very nice!" mildly put in both sisters, seating themselves on the dirty chairs, to which Tom's mother, being "a proud body," never condescended to give the usual apron wipe.

"Och! we have to keep him at home because *she's* weakly," dully observed the father. "But he's terrible fond of the schooling. He's always for learning his spells or his joggraphy by himself."

"He's that cross at missing the school that many's the day I have to beat him," snappishly interrupted the mother; "but, now that he has till mind the wean, he's quieter."

"And do you like the baby?" asked Miss Edith, bending down to the boy with interest.

Tom only said, "Ay." But he had a manner of saying that which made people believe him thoroughly.

Out of kindness to him, both ladies changed the conversation, perceiving that Tom's fondness for learning was considered either vanity or impudence at home; but they bore it in mind none the less.

"I am glad to see you are looking a little better to-day," said one of the twins to Mrs. Coulter.

The latter sniffed, and was manifestly annoyed.

"Och, och! the dear knows but I am far worse," quoth she, rocking herself to and fro. "Pains in me head, an' me arms, an' me body; an' a blast of wind in me chest that comes out under me shouldher."

"Oh, dear me, how strange!" murmured both spinsters, utterly amazed at this strange complaint; and perceiving too late that Tom's mother, like her neighbors, felt insulted at any one taking away the distinction given her through illness by supposing her better.

"Ach, she's no better. Shure ye can see it in her face," now broke in Coulter himself, slowly; for he, too, felt his wife had a right to expect much sympathy from visitors—else why did they come?—and sympathy meant enlarging on her sufferings. "She'll never be better," he added, groaning.

"Never! never!" echoed his wife.

"Ye're dying, woman, dear—ye're dying!" added the husband, uttering his black-cap sentence with a sort of cheerful decision, meant to compose his wife's wounded feelings, that left the Castle ladies gazing at each other, stricken dumb.

"And he has no been well himself this time past," said the wife, after a pause: thinking it due now to let Coulter share her dignity. "He has pains too."

"Rheumatism, no doubt—he looks old enough for it," observed Miss Alice, with a vigor that startled herself. "Since they like hearing disagreeable things, I'll gratify them," she had inwardly declared. But she had made a mistake.

"Deed he's not so to say horrid old; though he is horrid bad for certain—horrid bad!" answered the sick woman, with some asperity.

The sisters secretly wondered whether she alluded to his character or his complaint.

"The doctor from Maghrenagh" (the best doctor thereabouts), "he said I had dispepshyur," went on Coulter; pleased with the opportunity of detailing his symptoms. "But the Ballykillycocky doctor" (a mere licensed man-slayer), "he said it was cowld in me chest; and ordered me a linseed poultice and mustard every morning. Ochone—ochone!"

"Doesn't it make you better?" asked Miss Alice, touched by his groan, as the gaunt man raised himself from cowering over the white peat ashes, and looked at her with a gray face.

"I'm aye sicker after each while I takes it."

"Perhaps you put it on wrong," suggested Miss Edith, anxiously, who mostly thought whilst her sister spoke.

"Wrong—!" interrupted Mrs. Coulter, jealous for her conjugal care of him. "Och, shure, don't I give it him meself after his breakfast, reg'lar, as the doctor said he be'd to have it; and mixes up the linseed nicely in a tumbler o' warm water wi' the mustard, and he drinks it all down—but it disagrees wi' him awful every time!"

"Drink his poultice! and when he has dyspepsia!" exclaimed the horrified sisters, and began both at once a duet of lectures and warnings. Nor, indeed, did these fail; for the Ballyboly faith in "the skill" of ladies of quality who meddled with medicines either transported the mind to feudal ages, or argued great things for lady-doctors hereafter practising in that district; if so be always that the Ballybolyites knew what family these had come of; otherwise they would be simply reduced to the same vaguely suspicious level as the doctors around, from no-one knew where.

"Och, it was the workin' through the wet ploughed fields that done it on me," ended Coulter at last, with a shake of his head. "They tell me Providence sends us only what's best for us; but troth, I wonder it doesn't know better than to send us such bad weather."

"It is wick—yes, it is wicked to say that. Providence does all things in kindness," retorted Miss Alice, growing pink-complexioned; for he had really roused what fire there was in her mild nature.

"Weel, *maybe*," retorted Coulter, slowly.

"But it seems queer kindness o' the Almichty to rain on the fields till they're champit up like a bran-mash! … Is yon good for us, will ye tell me? Doesn't that hurt the likes of us poor folk?"

The women, both gentle and simple, were for a moment silent; not that they had nothing to say, but the poor one was too conscious of poverty's sufferings, the ladies too sorrowfully conscious of the immunity of the rich from such harm, to know how best to frame the answer of patient womanhood to impatient man. A childish treble broke the silence.

"Da," said Tom, in a coaxing aside, as he stood leaning against his father's shoulder, who treated him far more affectionately than did his mother, "when ye gi'ed me a hiding yesterday, because I hadn't snedded" (cut the tops off) "enough turnips, it hurted me; and when I cried on ye to give over, ye said it was for my good."

The boy's voice had dropped to a frightened whisper, perceiving, to his alarm, that the great ladies and his mother were listening. At home he only trusted to male sympathy, begotten by fellow-suffering.

"Weel; and what'll ye be wanting?" responded the father, speaking likewise aside, with a grim smile; for these two understood and a good deal loved each other.

"Och, dinny hurt me for my good again!" roguishly murmured the little lad, putting his lips near his father's ear; "for I don't like it, and ye said yersel', just now, no more do ye."

The father swore a big oath.

"The wee fallow has more wit nor any one of us," said he, "and a more releegious way of explainin' the ways of Providence."

Then the Misses Alexander rose and came away, with a last look at the smoky, windy kitchen; the black pile of turf in one corner; the hollows in the mud floor, used to keep food in for the fowl that ran in and out at will; the barrel that held, not meal, but a clucking hen on her eggs. And as they went the black-haired boy was again resignedly rocking the cradle with a thump and a bump, having cowered nearer the dull peat-embers on the flat hearthstone to get a "wee-thing" warmer.

"A fine little lad!" murmured Miss Edith, reflectingly. "If she does die (and she seems distressingly ill), I must see to his schooling. He might turn out a—a remarkable man."

And the good lady tried to review in her dim mind the names of the many Northern Irishmen who, despite low birth, arduously rose to high estate. But their histories were hazy to her. "We must read them again, too," she sighed. Then the sisters passed the marsh, with its rank grass and melancholy rustling reeds, and starting snipe; and went up the hill meadows by Farmer Keag's untidy but comfortable-looking home, meaning to pass down his lane. But Mistress Keag met them, with floury hands, on her threshold, crying out lustily,

"Och! och! ladies, but I'm glad to see you. You're not often visitors."

In truth the sisters had never called there before; had only come by as a short cut; and, though willing enough to enter in, were too shy to like doing so for the first time without some pretext. Mistress Keag had a shrewd notion of this when she so ably intercepted them; and therefore beamed upon them with her broadest smiles, to put the poor souls at their ease.

"Ye'd rather step into the room?" she cried, in interrogative persuasion; only just refraining from clapping them on the back, as she afterwards told her husband, "they looked so timorsome."

"The room," or parlor, opened off the kitchen, and contained two testered beds, a table, a picture of King William III. (adorned with spangles about the coat), and six new chairs in its narrow compass. It was further set out with two samplers, three orange and blue bead mats, and five antimacassars, all owing their origin to Lily's busy fingers and longing, poor child, to "have things pretty."

"It is very nice," said the sisters, gazing round it and shivering, being chilly souls. "But the kitchen looks so cheerful we would rather sit there and see the children—if you don't much mind."

"Mind!" quoth Mistress Keag, hooting the idea; and returning there, she planted two chairs right before a glowing peat-fire on the hearth, above which swung a griddleful of mixed bread, made of potatoes and oat-meal, that had an excellent smell. The sisters glanced round at the cheerful though somewhat untidy room; the dresser full of crockery; the baking-board covered with dough; the children crowding round Orange Lily, each eating a buttered cake fresh from the griddle, while the latter herself kept them all in order, besides rocking Osilla, the baby, on her knee, keeping time with one foot on the ground like any grandmother.

"We never could have done the like," flashed through both the sisters' minds with a sort of envy. They loved children too, in their tenderly dreamy manner of doing most things in life; but if ever either took a baby in her arms it felt like a lump of jelly, and, with an awful conviction that its neck meant to break, she was fain to return it hastily to safer hands. What a contrast between this home and that poor cottage in the hollow below; yet in both a child taught them silent lessons. Their lonely hearts felt somehow drawn to little Orange Lily and Tom, and comforted, they knew not how, for—they could hardly have told what.

> "Some there be that shadows kiss.
> These have but a shadow's bliss."

And so both Lily and Tom did good to others also that day, unwittingly. In ran some chickens by the open door; up jumped the little boys at Lily's bidding to shoo them out. Another difference betwixt farm and cottage.

"But are they not hungry, poor things? I noticed their bills were wide open," said gentle Miss Edith.

"He! he! he!" laughed Mistress Keag, vastly tickled, and no wonder. Even Lily hid her smiling face on the babe's downy head. "Hungry! It's the *gapes* they have! Hungry! … Oh! he! he! he! Excuse my making so very free, ladies dear, but I can't keep from the laughing. Shure, it's a disease amongst fowl, and then they aye keep their bills open."

"Then I'd tie them up," cried Miss Alice, quite eagerly and cheerfully; for the moral atmosphere of the farm invigorated her. "Cord might hurt them, but I could bring you some old ribbon shoe-string that would just do. Ah! … that is to say, if you have none by you just at present."

She had caught a glance from her sister, meaning, "You will offend them by offering your shoe strings, as if they were paupers." There came a fresh burst of laughter from Mrs. Keag, who first held her sides, then clapped her knees, in an ecstasy of mirth.

"Tie them up! … O! ladies darling, but it's worth the world to hear ye! Dear, my! but it does me good to be cheered up to a laugh!" and so on, till the sisters, perceiving they had, unawares, delighted her heart, laughed too, and felt happier and more at home than in any other farm-house or cottage round the country-side.

Suddenly one of the little boys cried—

"Lily, a feather!"

Up jumped Lily, ran outside, and, coming back with a bit of gray down just dropped from a goose, put it solemnly into a little bag hanging by the window. Her step-mother laughed heartily.

"The dear, oh! but that is the queer, careful child," said she, in answer to the ladies' inquiries. "She just heard me tell once how my grandmother picked up, like that, every blessed feather in her own bed, and bequeathed it to my mother, who bestowed it upon me when she died; and a darlin' bed it is, and travelled with me to America and back."

"What! the feather-bed?"

"Oh! every foot of the way," cried Mrs. Keag, exultant at the recollection. "'Woman dear,' says my brother to me, when our ones was thinking of flitting over the water—and a lump of a girl I was then—'would ye trail a feather-mattress into the ship, and up to Chicago?' 'Ay,' says I, I *would that!* Ye may flit by yourselves, and desert me behind, but me and my feather-bed'll no be parted.' So out we both went; and after awhile, when my brother got married on an American woman, and I began to think long" (feel homesick), "back me and it came together. And James Keag was looking out for a wife at the time, to mind Lily and the house, and I'd always thought a heap of him for a decent, quiet man, so we just took up with one another.—Wean, dear" (to Lily), "you'll be having your own ready by the time you're forty."

The little maid seemed nowise discomposed at this, but smiled soberly. To her steady mind, impatience to attain her goal was a rare and disturbing feeling. The Castle ladies looked wonderingly at her; so young, yet unmoved by idle words; while themselves swayed like willows to every breath, even of the foolishest human opinion.

The talk now turned upon a sort of ague prevalent around, and the visitors found, to their discomposure, that Mistress Keag knew, to a farthing's worth, of all the relief they had ever given through the parish; but after each enumeration she cried, with such heartiness, "O! ye done well!" or, "The Lord reward you!" that their timid souls felt warmed within them. So much so, indeed, that Miss Alice almost impulsively was drawn to disemburden her soul of a grief that had lain there heavily since some days, and began—

"Do you know a most miserable old woman in the mud cabin down there, Mrs. Keag? For we went to give her some money, poor soul; but she—she shut the door in our faces, and called out that she would throw *water* at us."

The speaker had lowered her voice to a shocked whisper, and eyed her more reticent sister guiltily. Both twins flushed all over their pale cheeks at the painful remembrance. Mrs. Keag threw up her hands in boisterous indignation.

"Dear!—ah dear!—ah dear!—but I am affronted to hear that!"

"The coachman drove over a duck one day," went on Miss Edith, taking up the recital. "We stopped the carriage at once, and—and spoke *severely* to him; but he said, 'Indeed, ladies, I have been trying to drive over ducks all my life; and I never thought till now it was possible.' So next day we heard it was hers, and were much grieved, and went to her with money—but, as we tell you—"

"It was all on account of *that* duck. She told me her heart was broken," interrupted Lily, with eager eyes and warm cheeks.

The ladies looked round surprised; but James Keag, who had come in a little while before, and stood silently by, patted his child's head.

"I'll warrant ye, ladies, my wee girl can insense you into the rights of it. Many a bite and sup she carries down to thon old witch; who wouldn't let another livin' soul inside her door."

"She called it Betty; and it slept with her, and ate out of her hand," explained Lily, in a shy voice; frightened at the novel attention bestowed upon herself; "and it knew its name, oh! as well—and she said, excepting me, it was the only living thing that cared for her."

The two poor ladies looked ready to weep.

"We know money would never repay her; but we *could* not help it," murmured Miss Alice, miserably.

"I told her so—and how good you were to everybody—and that she was very unkind to be so unmannerly," stammered Orange Lily.

"You did, child? And what did she say?"

"First, she was fit to kill me; but then she cried, and said I spoke God's truth, and that maybe *she had been as much in the muck as the ladies were in the mire.*"

The little peacemaker blushed deeply as she spoke, being ashamed to mention the Misses Alexander's names in such a vulgar manner; but, to her intense relief, the ladies smiled quite warmly upon her. They told her she had best be their almsgiver in future to the bereaved old crone; as Keag advised them. And they looked wistfully at this child who had found the secret of comforting a miserable human soul, as they themselves could never do.

"We were not angry; we were only hurt, you know," explained Miss Edith to James Keag, with a gentleness painful to witness; and there were tears in her eyes. "For we try ourselves to be respectful to *everybody*."

"Oh! faith, ye do that."

"And I often think that the poor ought to remember how much will be expected of the rich; and that it will be easier for a camel to pass through a needle's eye than for us to enter into the Kingdom of Heaven," the poor lady went on low, making a great effort to say, if only for once, what was in her heart; although it was pain, almost desecration, to do so. "And even if we do gain it, doubtless they will be placed high above us; yet there we shall certainly feel no envy."

There was a silence around. But the farmer wagged his head dubiously at the beginning of her last sentence, muttering, "I'm thinking that will depend upon their conduck;" and eying Miss Edith with a sort of curious reverence, as if she were a psychological study the like of which he had never known before.

"It is just a little painful to be misunderstood, you know," ended their timorous rich guest, more cheerfully, but with a sad moonlight smile.

"Ah! weel," replied James Keag, with strong emphasis, "there's one place where none of us will misunderstand the other; so bide that time, ladies. It will be when we meet in the city that lieth four square, of gold and of glass, and full of light; ay, verily!" Therewith he took up his hat, and stepped out to his ploughing again.

When the ladies left the farm that day it was with hearts gladdened in a manner they did not understand; but, in truth, it was by the hearty, healthy atmosphere of family life, so different from their own indoors existence of solitary self-consciousness.

CHAPTER IV

"Bogs, purgatory, wolves, and ease, by fame
Are counted Ireland's earth, mistake, curse, shame."
BARTEN HOLYDAY.

"It was a lad and a little lass,
    And they went to school together;
Blow high, blow low, in shine or snow,
    In fair or stormy weather.

"They spell'd their words from the self-same book,
    Like sister and like brother;
They shared their seat, they shared the rod,
    And learn'd—to love each other."

THE winter passed with such rains that down by the marsh Coulter the elder believed that he and his would be rotted off the face of the earth; and took, poor soul, to whiskey-drinking to put some warmth in him in his damp, miserable abode.

Before Christmas-time, his wife had dutifully fulfilled his prophecy, and been laid in the wet churchyard. A few days later her babe died too, and that cost two coffins; worse luck! If it had gone to a better place at the same time as its mother, one would have served "the pair of them," said the sympathizing neighbors.

Then March came, with wilder winds than had almost ever blown within memory of old John McConnel, who was one hundred and four years old; and had shouldered a pike (on the wrong side) in the Rebellion.

"It's remar-r-kable weather, ladies! The coarsest *ever* I recollect—most remar-r-kable!" said Keag one of those days to the Alexander ladies, meeting them on the high-road. "Verily, it is." (From this last trick of speech, and that of rolling his r's as if he relished the taste of them, he had gained the nick-name of Verily James.)

"We hope you have not suffered from the wind," said Miss Edith, with grave politeness. She did not use the pronoun in a royal sense, but as one to whom duality, implying herself and her sister, was a more natural form of thought than singularity of consciousness.

"Well, no, ladies, the Lord be thankit—though, verily, it was a wunner I didn't catch the cowld," said Keag, with hearty reverence, yet a humorous twinkle in his eye. "For I had to rise from bed, with but little clothes on, saving yer ladyship's presence, and sit all the night through i' the roof o' my cow-house *houlding it on!*"

"Holding it on—the roof?"

"Ay, verily—that same; for the wind was so remar-r-kable, I thought it would have blown the both of us clean and clever across till Scotland, sure-lie! But it is a new roof, and good; and, more by token, har'ly finished. So, says I, we'll no be parted till we're better acquent; and holds on by her, as if she was a sweet-heart—like deith."

Knowing he always spoke the truth, but not knowing exactly how much he dressed it out for company, the Misses Alexander gazed at him with bewildered eyes, till a gust of wind almost blew both the feeble women down—the storm, indeed, being tremendous.

"Och!—och!—och!" exclaimed Keag, fearing it would be "making too free" to "take a good grup of them both," much as his kind heart prompted him thereto. Then came a lull, and he added—"Go home, ladies dear; go home. For there was a wum-mun yesterday that the wind just took and cowpit" (threw down), "and broke her leg—clean and clever."

"You don't say so! Has she had a doctor?" asked the sisters, in one breath, roused to hear of any fresh case in which they could "do good."

"Och, no! Shure, I misdoubt that it was *fairly* broken; though she let on" (yelled) "as much as if it was," said Keag, afraid that his love of talk might mislead them. "She's, at best, a poor body."

"Poor! We'll go and see her."

"Aw, verily, ladies dear, ye'd not think much of her; a wee, miserable creature, always picking and stealing. One day I caught her, and she down on her two knees before me. 'Och, bloody murder! Keag darlin', forgive me,' says she. *For it's all because I'm desolate orphant!*"

"Poor little thing! How old is she?" cried the sisters.

"She's better than sixty," replied Keag, and could not restrain a grin.

There was a moment's silence; then Miss Edith said—

"No matter if she is a humbug. She is poor, and miserable, and old. We will go to see her." And, after asking where she lived, they beat down the road to windward, like a couple of feeble rooks. James Keag looked after them.

"I mind a missionary preaching once," he meditated, "and he told us of Indian beggars that, the dirtier and poorer they were, the holier folk thought them. And I'm feared our ladies is that ways inclined."

Since his mother and the baby died, Tom went regularly to school; at the express request of his new patronesses, the Castle ladies. He had another companion along the lonesome bog road now. Some old people living in a big, untidy farm on the far side of Keag's hill had a grandson on a visit with them, Daniel Gilhorn by name, to which young man, of eleven years, our Tom conceived a deep aversion. It was not only that "the fallow" had carroty hair, pig-eyes, and a disgusting trick of sniggering whenever Tom made mistakes in class; not only that he would push Tom unawares when going along the bogs, and nearer than usual one or other of the deep water-courses that yawned on either side of their way, so that Tom would "get a start," and with reason—more than one person having perished within even his memory in those black, sluggish peat-waters. Tom did as much and more to him. It was

31

not all this alone; but it was just—that they disliked one another.

One windy morning—"Hooroo, boys!" cried Tom—didn't he see Orange Lily herself, hale and recovered, and in a tidier dress than ever, trotting to school in front of him. It was the first day for many weeks that she had been allowed to go to school. Alongside of her was Daniel Gilhorn. This was a few days after that one on which Keag met the Misses Alexander. The wind had abated between whiles, but this day blew fiercer than ever, as if rested. That was remembered, long afterwards, as the Spring-day of the Big Storm.

"Hi!—hi!—Danny, wait upon me, bellowed Tom down the wind; making a speaking-trumpet of his fists. Lily looked back, and hesitated. Little Gilhorn pulled her on. "Wait upon me, I tell ye," howled our hero, losing his temper.

"The fallow" looked behind, and was plainly making faces at his rival; uglier even, thought Tom, than his own ugly one.

"None of us wants ye—ye beggar."

"*Bad scran to ye!*" roared the virtuous-feeling Tom, now in a furious passion, and he seized a stone to clod therewith the dastard. But, bethinking himself that it might chance to hit and hurt wee Lily instead, he dropped it; contenting himself with using abusive language as he trotted behind them—too proud to go nearer.

How it blew! Every other minute Tom had to clap his hand to his cap to keep it on; had at last to hold it thus permanently, and put his head down to bore his way sidelong against the nor'-easter which smote them on the left. Had he been in better humor, he would have laughed out to feel the strong blast, which seemed tempting him to leave his footing on mother earth, and be whirled on its breast away above fields and hedges. But Lily, in front, was staggering, buffeted about by the gale; for her petticoats acted as a sail, and her broad straw hat was almost carried away, though she clung by it persistently. Dear little lass, she could hardly breathe at moments, and felt as if she would be lifted off her booted feet—bare toes cling better.

Then came a narrow piece of road all broken away at the sides. A stronger blast than any previous one howled across the dark waste around; past black peat-stacks and blacker intersecting water-courses. An agonized shriek, a boy's yell, rang through the chill airs up to the cold gray sky. Wee Lily—she knew not how—was blown over the edge of the road, and clinging desperately by a projecting stump of an old bog-oak down the side of the bank, below which the deepest bog-ditch lay.

"Help me, Danny, Danny, *Danny!*" the child screamed. But the boy stood still, and only howled at the top of his voice. Lily was slipping into the awful black water below; going—gone! Her boots slid slowly from their treacherous hold on the bank; she felt the cold flood rise up to her breast; her little hands still clutched the jagged oak-stump, but more feebly now. Tom behind saw all … saw her waver on the brink … totter over … disappear from his horrified gaze.

"Coward! Hould on till her," he yelled, seeing his little fellow-being—his dear friend—going down alive into the black grave before his eyes: the while his legs flew under him he knew not how—but as if they must cover all the intervening yards at every stride.

The other boy turned and rushed along the causeway, calling wildly for help—too frightened even to look back.

Then Tom had reached the spot, and battling, himself, against the wind, peered over trembling, expecting either to see some drowning struggles, or, maybe, to see—nothing. A small white face gazed up at him beseechingly, just above the thick dark peat-waters; its lips parted, but no sound came.

"Hould on—hould on till I grip ye!" was all Tom could utter as, squatting on the bank edge, he carefully and bravely slid down; calculating that the old stump would come between his legs, and thus hold him up also, just above her. So it indeed happened.

Next moment, he had grasped the little lass's arms, and held them with all his might: they should come out of their sockets before he let her go.

"I'm sorry till hurt ye, Lily," he said, after a few breathless moments; with a wonderful gentleness, newly come to him. "Dinna fear—but keep hold a wee-thing longer, till your da comes—till people comes."

"My feet is on a wee something that keeps them up—but I'm feared it'll break from under me soon," gasped the child. "Tom! Tom! ... dinna let me go!"

"I'll not let ye go; we'll both go in thegether first."

Tom set his teeth hard. The boy's muscles were being terribly strained, and always more. He knew that Lily's toes, which she must have dug desperately into the bank, were slowly slipping from that treacherous footing. She knew it too; but neither dared waste their breath. Instinct told them some strength would go from them therewith. O, the long moments! O, the terrible long-drawn moments! And each seemed to those children only charged with the thought, "Hould on, hould—hould!" or else, "Slip ... slip ... slip!"

Then the bairn gave a wee moan, no louder than that of a dying mouse. It was almost over with her. Tom wriggled himself well-nigh over the edge of the stump, gaining thus an inch of nearness; and lying back along it, managed to put his toes under the little one's armpits, so low was she under him. A few more moments, and by the pain in his muscles, both of legs and arms, he knew her weight would pull him down into death with her. But yet he only thought of holding on while both could; the idea that he could save himself and leave her never even embodied itself—though the knowledge that it was possible to do so was existing in his mind.

"Oh, God!" poor little Lily gasped, noiselessly; for her breath could hardly fill her lungs, and no longer issue in sound.

"Oh, God, please—*please* pull me out—and Tom too!"

A halloo came down the wind. Another, and nearer; fresh strength came to both the trembling children.

"Yer da, Lily," muttered Tom, well-nigh spent, and setting his teeth closer.

It was so, indeed. Warned by Danny Gilhorn's shrieks, the father had left his work in the field beyond the moss[7], and, followed by a neighbor, was running like a madman through the bog, leaping drains and dykes, as if nothing could stop him. A few seconds more, and he came up to the strugglers, and that only just in time, for then Tom's strength vanished clean away, and he slipped plump in beside Lily. But nevertheless, one hardly knew how, the children were grasped by their hair and clothes, dragged out, and soon carried towards Keag's farm.

"For I'll take him too. Ay! ay! It's nearer hand," cried the good man.

So to the farm Tom was carried and well dried at the fire by the hands of the friendly neighbor who had helped to save him; and soon recovered himself enough to partake of the lunches of bread and the noonday tea brewed all expressly for himself to "warm his inside," so soon as anxiety about Lily a little abated. For both father, mother, and servant-girl had much ado for a while, trying to take the chill out of her body; she having been so much longer in the water than Tom. Yet all that evening the little maid was still fearful and shivering, though flushed with fever; and continually kept crying, as her mind wandered—

"Save me from the water, Tom! … Oh, it's deep!—it's deep!"

"I'll never forget it till ye, wee Tom Cowltert; never," said the father, with tears in his eyes and a moved voice, as he shook the little lad's childish hand in his own hard fist. And he said that again on meeting Tom a week later, when Lily was running about

---

[7] moss = peat-bog

again, quite well.

The former suffered no further harm than a frightful night-mare in the testered-bed he shared with his father. He imagined himself bobbing again up and down in the foul peat-waters that filled his mouth as he gurgled—"Lily is off the kash[8]! Lily's in the shough[9]!" while Danny Gilhom and all Tom's *un*-friends gibbered and danced on the bank. Then suddenly the scene changed to the school-house again, and Lily was observing with grave contempt—"You do speak so broad, Tom; say path, not kash." Whereupon the Misses Alexander, the schoolmaster, and all the children gave full chase after Tom, crying out—"Spell kash! spell kash!" and jumping the forms and desks, ran round and round unendingly like mad, with such a whullabaloo … !

"Wake up, my sonny," said his father's voice in the darkness. "I'm feared ye're something ill, ye're crying and jumping that much. Give over, dear, give over; ye're safe." And he pulled the thin coverlet better about his little lad, and put his arm protectingly round him.

---

8 kash, or kesh = causeway through a bog.
9 shough, or sheuch = water-filled drain or ditch.

CHAPTER V

"There is a nameless air
Of sweet revival over all which fills
The earth and sky with life;
....
Already above the dewy clover
The soaring lark begins to hover
Over his mate's low nest;
And soon from childhood's early rest
In hall and cottage to the casement rise
The little ones with their fresh morning eyes,
And gaze on the old Earth which still grows new,
And see the tranquil Heaven's unclouded blue;
And since as yet no sight nor sound of toil
The fair-spread, peaceful picture comes to soil,
Look from their young and steadfast eyes
With such an artless sweet surprise
As Adam knew when first on either hand
He saw the virgin landscapes of the morning land."
Songs of Two Worlds.

THE saving of Orange Lily's life was the beginning of a happier
one for Tom Coulter. Daily he trotted to school with his little
friend all that windy spring; all the warmer summer through,
cooled by constant sea-breezes; through all the pleasant, wind-
less autumn. How, after school-hours, they played together till
late in the gloaming! First, the wild winds lulled somewhat; and
the whole land grew green and blossomed into a great Garden
of the Lord, with wee wild-flowers laughing and nodding up in
the sun's face. Windwafts of scent blew over the country from
the hawthorn-hedges, that made a great network over hills and
hollows. The little brown birds began to sing. The butterflies and
all manner of insects seemed to start into life; and the swallows
flew back from over the sea. The cuckoos, too, and the corncrakes

reappeared; but where from none knew—excepting those who agreed with James Keag that they had lain asleep at the bottom of the horse-ponds all winter.

"For no man need go for to tell me that corncrakes could fly three or four and twenty miles over till Scotland, at neardest. Them as can hardly rise above a hedge at the best of times, and are that weighty on the wing," quoth he one spring twilight to an assenting audience loitering like himself on the white road. "And, as to the cuckoos, I don't misdoubt but they *may* go to Africa. Only I have neither read nor yet heerd tell of any yun[10] as seen them there for certain."

After which speech, he would have been foolish who doubted that Keag was a sensible, temperate-minded man; so dispassionately did he nod his head, so thoughtfully did he wrinkle his sunburnt brow, striving fairly to consider all that could be adduced in favor of the new-fangled notion of the migration of corncrakes and cuckoos.

While Keag and his men-neighbors thus discoursed beside some gate, you would only have to go a "bit further along" the road to find Tom and Orange Lily, with the little Keag children, quietly diverting themselves with some self-invented game or other. For our sonsie little maiden was carefully kept from consorting with the wilder-mannered village children; and Tom (bar an occasional outbreak with kindred spirits) liked her company, and all the delights of farm-visiting it involved, hugely.

And a "piece further on" one would surely come upon a Jack and Jill sitting courting under the hedge; with many more pairs all along to the village. The road was thus the common meeting-place for all after the sun had set and the day's work was done. Then, a few weeks later, when the two drums were got out and the Orange lads began to practise beforehand for the Twelfth of July and the

---

[10] yun, or yin = one

great Orange meeting, how excited were Tom and Lily! How, long after they were both in their beds, one in the comfortable farm-house, one in the bare cottage, they listened to the tum-tum-ming round the lanes; and fell asleep with the brave strains of Protestant Boys in their ears.

Soon after that day, to be remembered much by Tom, of the great wind, Keag had come down to the Coulters' cottage, and had offered most kindly to take Tom, after school hours, as a job-boy, so to say, about the farm; secretly prompted by the wish to give the poor little lad his fill to eat, in return for saving the good man's dearly-loved eldest-born. So Tom gleefully did his best to stable the horses, feed the pigs, fetch in the cows, or herd the turkeys, from afternoon till six; had his supper like the two farm-servants; and might then play with his ideal of all that was nice in a wee gurl, his little mistress in some ways, his small sweetheart in others, but always his fast friend—Lily Keag.

In social position Tom was, of course, much Lill's inferior; but at her tender age neither father nor step-mother heeded this friendship enough to interfere with it. One was busy indoors, the other out of doors, all the day, and much of the evening; they were good-humored, rather "throughother," careless folk. So the pleasant play-hours of the children in barn or byre, stack-yard or lane, would be by them remembered gladly to their lives' end, and seem the principal part of their young years; while the parents might barely recall that the children had been much together— and be utterly amazed to guess how to each the other's figure was associated with almost every dear memory of their sweet human springtime. Well, too, for Tom that, besides the gratitude owed him, his home was far from the village, and the contamination, in Mrs. Keag's eyes, of the small inhabitants thereof. He did not use bad language, was a biddable enough boy in her eyes; a "verily remar-r-kable smart wee chap" in those of her husband. Then his father, though poor, was always allowed through the country to be on the whole a decent, quiet man.

"And that sometimes means a footherin fool, that has neither the wit nor spirit to get into mischief," quoth James Keag. But it likewise means one as goes his own road in peace, and lets others go theirs; does harm to none, and mostly leaves the whiskey alone—and that's Cowltert for ye."

It was agreed universally that father and son did just as well without the late Mrs. Coulter; a sharp-tongued, unthrifty woman, with whom there could be no peace in the house. Now a spinster aunt of Tom's came to keep house for her brother: and, by degrees, an air of comparative comfort began to appear in the cottage by the marsh. First, a big clock was bought; then the dresser was covered with crockery; the bare four-post beds testered, to keep out draughts. And, most important of all, in Tom's opinion, a new crane was hung. Hitherto they had made shift with a broken one; which, as his appetite well knew, supported meagre pots indeed. Till then, dinner often meant to him a broken brown teapot put to draw among the peat embers; no milk or sugar on the table; not always butter on the gritty oatmeal cakes. This should not have been. Smaller cottages, without land attached, poorer inmates, were to be found in Ballyboly village, who swung full pots on the bools (or pot-hooks), which fasten these to the crane.

But truth will out, so it must be told at last that Tom's mother, besides other faults, had a craving for drink; so what else could you expect but that her home should be a wretched, throughother dwelling? Ah well! those bad days were past. Let the poor soul's sins be buried under the churchyard mould that hid her coffin; forgotten by others as the two who suffered most from her yet loved her best—Tom and his father—forgot them. That summer, and just when all the grass was cut, and tiny hay lap-cocks dotted the meadows, came a pair of visitors to tea at the Keags' farm, whom Lily minded well in later years; for they gave her henceforth fresh pleasure in her simple little life. These were old Hans Majempsy and his wife, from their handsome farm by the sea; a now childless couple, as old friends of James Keag, almost, as himself was aged in years. And at tea it was naturally related, when the children were discussed, how near-hand wee Lily there—who sat up so nice and pretty—had been to drowning in the moss (bog).

"Och and och! … child dear—och and och!" exclaimed white-haired Mrs. Majempsy at intervals; regarding the little girl with brimming eyes, fed from a full heart, whose love went out to all other weans now her own were grown, and gone to heaven before her. "And this is the wee boy as saved ye? Hans! Hans!—Man dear! … but he's like our darlin' son that's now drowned, when he was the same age." And the good old farmer's wife suddenly burst out weeping.

Everybody was sorry, and tried to comfort her. The men clacked their tongues on the roofs of their mouths, and stared at the big fireplace glowing with hot turf. Osilla, the baby, gave a sympathetic howl. Tom, in utter terror of the woe his face had wrought, ducked under the table, pretending he had dropped his buttered farl of potato-bread, and stayed there. Mistress Keag urged hospitably—

"Take another wee drop of tea, Mistress Majempsy—poor soul! Ochone! now, a bit more bread; and just this wee taste of butter to comfort ye. Dear-ah-dear! to think of your son lying down at the bottom of the sea this blessed minute! … A sore end he came by, surely."

But Lily, who sat beside the old woman, kept softly stroking her hand. Suddenly the latter turned and kissed the child's brow, to everybody's surprise, saying—

"Bless you, daughter! You have done my heart more good than any of them."

When the visitors left on that evening in the scented summer twilight, the wife solemnly invited little Lily to pay her a visit "come August," when school-holidays began; adding, with

41

a hungering look towards lower-born Tom Coulter—

"And let him come too, to mind her, Mistress Keag: if I may make that request."

"Ay, ay. She might drown herself in the sea otherwise—she has such a fancy that way, it appears," laughed the old husband, as assent was given.

CHAPTER VI

"The morning's fair, the lusty sun
With ruddy cheeks begins to run;
And early birds that wing the skies,
Sweetly sing to see him rise.
   I am resolved, this charming day,
In the open field to stray,
And have no roof above my head,
But that whereon the gods do tread.
Before the yellow barn I see
A beautiful variety
Of strutting cocks, advancing stout,
And flirting empty chaff about.
Hens, ducks, and geese, and all their brood,
And turkeys gobbling for their food;
While rustics thrash the wealthy floor,
And tempt all to crowd the door.
   What a fair face does Nature show!
Augusta, wipe thy dusty brow."—DYER.

HEY! how our two little friends were excited on that August morning. They hardly slept the night before. Fine children might have laughed at the little peasants, fine folks have envied them. Lily had on her Sunday clothes, and her father fondly stuck the last orange lily from their flower-pot in the blue ribbon round her straw hat.

As young Tom eyed his little mistress's hair, that he called golden, and that was really of a pleasant enough reddish-yellow, her shining eyes, like small blue skies with suns in them that morning, his heart swelled, and he thought her beautiful. He himself was gloriously uncomfortable in new boots and a Scotch cap[11]; for his father's pride had been roused on this great occasion. But Lily's

---

[11] Scotch cap. A plain glengarry or 'blue bonnet' as worn in the district into the 20th century.

pride, as she gazed at him, was still greater.

"O, Tom, you look so nice!" she ejaculated to her humble but faithful squire.

"You're nicer," gruffly responded the flattered Tom.

Then they took hands, and ran downhill together.

"You forgot to ask me if I said my prayer last night," said Tom, when they slackened their pace to breathe. For this old habit was still kept up between them, if not daily, yet often; and Tom still resented any prolonged omission thereof on Lily's part, as implying lessening interest in himself.

"Oh, but," said Lily, affectionately, "I had no call to ask, for I know you did. You must have been so happy!"

Away, for three miles, they could see the whole flat country up and down the coast; with its neat little fields utterly bare of trees, save just around the whitewashed homesteads dotted on all the slight rises.

A mile in front stretched the broad blue setting of the land— the home of the herrings both children ate so greedily those summer days; the highway for the ships they watched now sail by afar 'twixt them and Scotland. After a mile of almost deserted lane came a slight hill, just above the white sands. This was crowned by the farmhouse; twice as big as even Lily's home, three times as handsome; for it was brand new and of "an elegant in-and-out shape," had two stories, and was whitewashed blindingly. A fairly big garden faced the sea, and what Tom called a real carriage-road led to the door; trees and farm-buildings surrounded it. Inside, there was a staircase of varnished pine, with rooms upstairs; no mere ladders and lofts. And, besides the kitchen, there was such a parlor for state occasions with mahogany chairs set round it, and tables with handsome oil-cloth covers, and a bunch of wax flowers, just like life, that surely nothing in the Castle was finer, thought our children, when Mistress Majempsy led the big-eyed pair in a sight-seeing procession over her dwelling, after a hearty reception. Then they were given the run of the place; and Tom made acquaintance with every corner of it, to the very inside of the dog's house, in a jiffy; while Lily dutifully and soberly trotted after him, a beaming smile on her face. Here, as guests, they were both equal—the boy, indeed, the most favored, perhaps. Orange Lily was all the happier for that in her heart; since it was a standing grief to her that her friend had always less dinner than herself, and such an ugly house for his home.

"They're ram-stamming everywhere—bless them! Such a pair as they are!" cried the old woman to her goodman, as she awaited him at her sunny back-door when he came home at noonday. Then the aged couple peeped cautiously into the stable and espied Tom slapping the carthorses on the ribs, and standing back with his legs wide apart and his lips pursed to admire them.

"Them's the sort!" quoth he, sturdily, with the nod of a judge.

"Ours is as nice," put in Lily, jealous for the old gray mare which her father rode every Twelfth of July, because King William had ridden a white steed at the Boyne; also for their young colt, which smashed everything to smithereens, and therefore had gained the old Irish epithet of "that Tory." Tom looked calmly round on the defender of these absent beasts of burden, and reduced her to utter insignificance for a moment by the one syllable—"Hutt!"

"That is a most knowledgable little lad now; that is!" whispered the old farmer to his wife. And she, smiling, went to blow the horn that called the men from the far fields to dinner.

"Mr. Majempsy," quoth Tom, perceiving his host, "who built this house?"

"Well, my sonny, it was me built it," said the old man, sadly. "But our boy, it was, that sent home the money for it from Australia; and died on his way back, just as we had it fitted out for him. Well, well! He is gone to wait for us in a finer house in heaven, instead of us waiting on him here."

Tom was silent a few moments, and then said, very gravely,

"I'd like to buy this one, well, when I grow up to be a man. Will ye sell it then to me?"

"Dear, dear," said old Majempsy as he looked down at the sturdy little lad, and softly laughed like one whose heart is far away. We'll be dead and gone to a far better home by that time, I'm thinking, my wee man. Still I'd like well to know you able to have it. Come in, weans dear, to dinner."

O, how bravely the children were fed! The peace and plenty most impressed Tom. The good order, and pretty things, as Lily called the furniture, most stirred her feminine mind. But best of all was their play on the sea-shore that long, sunny summer day. How they pulled off boots and socks and crumpled their toes with pleasure on feeling the sands' warmth. How they paddled in the translucent shallow tide that so lazily lipped the wide strand, as if uncertain whether to ebb or not. How they searched for shells and cockles; trembled lest a big crab should steal out from under the red seaweed clumps and nip their toes; admired their feet because they looked so white and pretty under the water. That was an afternoon they would remember with a smile and a stir of pleasure at their hearts, if even they lived to be very old. No little prince or princess was ever happier than were Orange Lily and Tom Coulter that white day by the sea. Then at evening they were given tea, with so many kinds of bread and sweet cakes that, at last, even Tom paused from making these his own.

"Can ye do no more, my wee son?" asked the old farmer, sympathizingly.

"I'm feared not—I feel too fat!" replied Tom, with truthful regret.

Then, when the sky paled after sunset, and the big low moon rose, gleaming in the tender evening sky, and the trees looked as if they were happed up for the night in dark shadows, the good old Majempsys strolled down the deserted lane. A hundred others led inland like it, but this one went straight towards Keag's Hill and the marsh below it. When they had "put the wee ones a piece on their way," the worthy old couple turned back; and the children alone set their faces homewards, feeling full with the day's pleasure and satisfied into happy quiet.

At a pleasant corner they sat down at last to rest, and looked once more at the treasures in their pockets. The furze grew so high above them that they could only see the sky overhead and one star, and the grassy path at their feet. Moved by the sense of nearness, of being alone together in a deserted summer-night world, of past pleasures enjoyed together begetting sympathy—their little hearts grew so softened that they pressed their cowries and dulse on each other's acceptance. Then Tom at last produced silently from his most sacred pocket something—at sight of which Lill gave a little covetous exclamation. The object was only a limpet-shell, with its centre knocked out, leaving a ring; but she thought it beautiful.

"O! Tom," she said, "will ye bestow that upon me?"

"Ay! It was for you I kept it," said Tom solemnly. "But if I do—ye must promise to marry me when I grow big."

"O—!" said Lily.

"Ye must *that*," pursued Tom, sturdily. "I like ye a heap better nor any other wee gurl I know; and if ye go and take up with any other boy, I'll—I'll flit the country, and ye'll never see me no more."

"O! Tom—don't, Tom!" ejaculated his small sweetheart, appalled at this awful threat; neither considering that, under those supposed circumstances, she might be glad to get rid of him.

"Never no more," repeated he, gloomily.

"But I'd *like* to marry you; only I wouldn't like to live in your house, because it's so ugly," objected poor Lill, in a much troubled voice.

"Of course not! I'll tell ye what I thought on, this very day. I'll buy Mister Majempsy's house from him, and we'll live there!" replied Tom, with a triumph at his own prudent foresight, which impressed Lily with no less admiration; not a doubt shadowing their clear minds that, after having thought it out, such a magnificent idea could fail of accomplishment.

"Will ye really?" said the little girl.

"I will so," said the little boy. Then he stuck his limpet ring on the rosy finger she held out to him, and said, "It's just as bonny as the gold rings grown ones gives their sweethearts."

Lily, who never gainsaid him since he had saved her life in the bogs, because she hardly ever could find it in her mind to differ from him, heartily agreed; and, putting up her lips, gave him a butterfly kiss in simple thanks, saying,

"I'll always keep it."

"And ye'll marry me—that's a bargain," quoth Tom.

"As sure as I'm livin'!" answered the little lass; mimicking, but with awe, the most solemn assurance she could remember of her step-mother's; and gravely wagging her head.

Then they started homewards again through the gloaming; and the moon seemed broadly laughing at them, and the little stars smiling. O! but it was a bonny night; and O! but it had been a happy day!

CHAPTER VII

"Th' expectant *wee things*, toddlin, stacher through,
　　To meet their Dad, wi' flichterin noise and glee,
His wee bit ingle blinkin' bonnilie.
　　His clean hearth-stane. his thrifty Wifie's smile,
The lisping infant prattling on his knee,
　　Does a' his weary kiaugh and care beguile,
　　　...
Belyve, the elder bairns come drapping in,
　　At service out, amang the farmers roun';
Some ca' the pleugh, some herd, some tentie rin
　　A cannie errand to a neebor town."
　　　　　　　　　　　　　　　　　Burns.

THE autumn came on with its yellow sunlight and temperate warmth, like pleasant middle-age; bringing more simple pleasures to our two little peasants. The wheat grew tawny gold, and the oats yellow; and at shearing-time all the farm-children followed in the track of the sickles closely; some to glean; some to play in the stooks. But Tom alone was thought able enough to bind the sheaves for the reapers, being so much the eldest; and held his head high on being told by Keag that he worked like a man. The hedgerows that year, along the fields, were thick with blackberry clusters; as big as the grapes in the greenhouses at the Castle, very nearly, said little Lily, who had once paid a visit to the Castle gardens by the favor of the gardener, and was fond of recalling the notable event to less happy mortals.

Then, later, the black bean-stooks dotted the country, and the sunsets were orange bands under gray skies; and the turkey flocks pecked and cried "p-ya!" through the stubble. There was a smell of frost in the air, thought Lily, sniffing the damp leaves stamped in the hedgerows. The children never liked the winter well, they agreed; yet still they had fine games in the stack-yard, hiding round the ricks; and—the good God be thanked who cares for little ones!—Tom was warmer clothed and better fed that cold weather than ever he remembered before, in the death-times of the year.

And thus four or five years passed, with their circling seasons; and yearly Lily Keag and Tom Coulter grew heartier and lustier, and fonder of each other. But few changes, and these trifling and gradual, occurred, meanwhile, in their pleasant lives. Up at the Castle, the Misses Alexander still led their gray, blameless existences; still strove to do good; and gradually found that the habit of benevolence, by strengthening, became less irksome—even pleasant, as, here and there, they gathered some first fruits of their labor. Gradually, as they read the grand old lessons of faith and love to sick or dying, these last seemed begotten in themselves. If not full sunshine, yet the delicate light of a summer's eve came, and rested on their face.

One year the sisters had a new idea—a rare thing. They did not lay it aside, as people do who have a choice of such articles; but examined and talked it over with long hesitation. Then, one fine day, they went up to town, and, to their own surprise, put it into execution in a hurry by buying a large number of children's books. Their plan was to establish at their own expense a small lending-library for the Ballyboly school children; and the good ladies felt nervously pleased with themselves.

At first it did very well. Every Saturday saw a troop of children going up the drive to the Castle, for some volume to be read on that half-holiday and on the Sabbath afternoon. Unfortunately, the sisters chose too many tales of that kind which, as nurses say of priggish children, are "too good to live!" Some exciting ones of fine, old reputation had, however, crept in as a flavoring— gallant and stirring stories, which Tom's soul hankered to read when he got a peep at them in the hands of bigger boys who had first choice. And Lily again knew of certain more modern ones of American origin that the elder girls eagerly competed for; since their piety was sugared with love-making, and always finally rewarded by marriage. But, alas! on account of their more tender years, Tom and she could not hope for such delights for many a day.

At last the pair plotted to make mere age yield to deserving youth; and one Saturday found them at the Castle door long before their school-mates. By good luck the Misses Alexander were just coming in from the Castle gardens with their half-brother, the young Captain, who was owner of the estate.

"Dear me! Lily Keag, we are very glad to see you. And Tom Coulter, too!" said Miss Edith, in her gracious, abstracted manner.

"But you are far too early," said Miss Alice, in a less vague voice; feeling that exact punctuality was a virtue that saved herself the trouble of going several times for books, so she could not now commend the children; which she liked to do on the smallest provocation. In general, both sisters showed a good deal of favor to Orange Lily, as the tidy child of one of their brother's worthiest tenants; and to Tom for his sturdy self-reliance and honesty, which gave their shy minds less difficulty in understanding him.

The little lad touched his cap, the little lass dropped a courtesy; tokens of good-breeding somewhat rare in Ballyboly.

Said Tom, studying the nature of the carpet intently—

"The big ones always gets the nicest books; and I offered to swap a moss-cheeper's nest[12] and three eggs against another boy's book last Saturday—but he wouldn't; so I thought to be beforehand with him *this* day."

"Please, Miss Edith, there are some terribly nice books!" said the Orange Lily in a very small voice. "And—and—we don't think any of the big ones want them half as much as we do."

"O, don't let 'age go before honesty!'" cried young Captain Alexander, laughing, whom all the people of Ballyboly praised

---

[12] moss-cheeper = meadow-pipit

for his "free," pleasant ways. What do you call terribly nice books now, eh, my man?"

"Sharks and sailors; or red Injins," quoth Tom deliberately, though with some effort, and now gazing at the ceiling. "Not *foothering* stories about little lassies. There was one of Dr. Cumming's a boy had that I liked well; and a history of the Reformation—yon was nice too."

"And you read them?" asked his landlord, staring at this Ballyboly specimen.

"*Ay*," said Tom.

"Do you like them as well as the red Indians?"

"They're different," replied Tom, still more slowly, striving to explain that he hated his milk of instruction to be mixed with water, "but I like rightly what is good, and not *non*-sense."

"And you?" asked the young man of Lily, with a quizzical smile, as he glanced round at his sisters' faces, on which some consternation began to dawn.

The poor child's tongue clove to the roof of her mouth. She could answer the ladies with pretty propriety; but to be addressed by the Captain himself, who lived in London, and had often seen the Queen, and had killed dead no one knew how many Russians in the Crimea, as was thereabouts, commonly reported—this utterly crushed her courage. The very name of the craved-for book vanished clean from her mind, and she murmured, looking helplessly at Tom—

"I—forget."

"She disremembers the name," explained Tom, with a pitying air; adding confidentially to the others, "She's something shy."

"Can you not remember what it was about, my dear?" asked Miss Edith, smiling on the model child of the school; still as orange of hair and with as white a pinafore as when first they saw her, though both pinafore and hair were twice as long now as in those days.

Lily's voice gently murmured, while her eyelashes swept her cheek—

"*It was—religious coortship for Sunday reading!*"

At that came such a great laugh from the Captain that both the little peasants grew redder than usual; even Miss Alice could not control herself, and tittered. But Miss Edith cried kindly—

"And a very good description too. Come with me, my child, and you shall find it out for yourself."

Her brother followed her, wishing to make amends.

"Look here, I have taken a fancy to this lad," he said to his sister, "and if you have got my own old boys' books still, you must lend them to him whenever he likes. Poor little chap! fancy him craving for reading!"

"Here they are," said Miss Edith, leading the way to a closet stuffed full of childhood's reminiscences, like an old memory. With glad, greedy eyes, Tom stared and beheld shelves above shelves of books with delightful covers, promising contents about lion slayers, prairie hunters, and North Pole seekers; besides histories and school-books he would certainly try his mind on too.

"Man!" said he, with a deep breath. "It's grand!" Then, eying his benefactor, he added, in an outburst of gratitude, "I'll raise you a hare, sir, any day you bring the hounds down to Mr. Keag's; or near our own land." (That was one small field.)

"Oh, Tom!" uttered Lily, with a sort of reproachful alarm.

"What is the matter? Have you got a pet hare, perhaps?" asked the Captain, kindly, smiling on the trim little maid, whose blue eyes he could see were widened with some kind of fear. Lily's rosy-white cheeks became blush-roses.

"No, please, Captain Alexander. But his father beats him so dreadfully when he runs after the hounds—and I—" Her eyes suddenly looked as if they had been caught in the rain, and got a wetting. Every one around felt sympathy with and compassion for her, excepting Tom.

"Well! who minds a licking?" muttered that young scapegrace; his mouth firm set, his bright brown eyes fixed on the Captain's face, as if sure of sympathy. The latter looked with favor on the strong, black-haired, ruddy youngster, but asked—"Is running after the hounds worth a beating?"

"Ay! a couple," says Tom, "for my father asked Mr. Keag, as a favor, till box my ears for me too—and he does it well."

"Upon my word, I can't help agreeing with the boy," exclaimed the Captain, and that cheery declaration in his manful voice hushed like a spell the beginnings of a gently excited duet on the theme, Be good, from his lady sisters. For his word was their self-elected law.

From this it will be inferred that, pleasant as Tom considered his life, it was not made unwholesomely soft to him. And, good lad though he was held to be in farm and cottage, no one, excepting perhaps Lily, considered him anything near perfection. Indeed, though his father was really fond of him, Tom was never likely to get "blue-mouldy for want of a bating."

As the boy and girl went down the drive again, hugging their books, but every now and then opening the pages to gloat over their contents, little Coulter fervently exclaimed—

"I never thought such a heap of any gentleman in my life as of the Captain! I'd like bravely to be a soldier under him—I would that!"

"O, but—you'd have to go away! Don't do that, Tom."

"Still, mind you, when I see books like these, I think whiles I'd like to be a school-master," meditated Tom feeling literary ardor, fed purely on a red Injin story he carried, flaming no less warmly than that for military glory within his bosom a moment before.

"But I thought you were so fond of the farming. Would you not like better to have a house like the Majempsys'?" said the gentle, wee voice beside him.

"Troth! and that would beat them all!" exclaimed Tom, veering round finally, at last, to his strongest point of attraction, like a magnetic needle which abnormal influences may have caused to sheer about wildly for a time. "I could have the land then; and take out the gun whiles; ay! and ride to the hounds now and again. Then in the evenings I'd read to you, Lily." (The latter looked supremely happy at this arrangement.) "Only I'll have to go gold-digging first to get the money; or else—join some pirates," he ended, with a gloomy determination that he himself seemed rather to relish.

And Lily looked at him with admiration, yet fear for him struggling therewith in her little breast; but uttered no dissent. After many consultations about their common future, they had come to this wise decision some time ago; helped thereto by all the story-books Tom had begged or borrowed round the county. Their minds, like their bodies, had plainly grown since that evening when both agreed to share the pleasant farm-house by the sea, and all its store of goods and cattle, and foresaw nothing but a little time (itself an enjoyable abstract!) between their wish and its fulfilment. It may also be perceived that the schoolmaster's denunciations of the Ballyboly dialect had taken effect upon the speech of both. Lily's anxiety for self-improvement made her keep the door of her lips with constant care, so that she even spoke quite pretty to the baby, said her doting father. But Tom used English, it is to be feared, rather as the English once talked French, because it was considered modish so to do, and relapsed into broad northern pronunciation in all his moments of thoroughly vulgar enjoyment.

After that day, many a winter evening when Coulter would "daunder" up to the Keag's farmhouse as was his frequent custom, to chat with his richer friend, James Keag, and when Tom's bright face would appear behind him as they came out of darkness in to the glow of the farm kitchen, the latter would never fail to be greeted with an eager inquiry from Lily, "Have you brought your book?" Hans and Henry-Thomas would chime in noisily;

and, when Tom, of course, produced whatever volume he had last borrowed from the Castle, he was given a stool near the new paraffin-lamp, and not far from the hearth, while the children gathered round him. Lily had first begun this custom; since the dutiful bent of her mind made her take interest in all the likings of those she loved, and laughably try to believe her tastes were the same. And her friendship for Tom was no longer singular, since her little brothers had now grown up to believe they felt fully as much love for him—indeed, worshipping him as such small boys would any elder one who taught them marbles and ball-play against the byre-wall, protected them at school, and would fight for them on any provocation. On the whole, although young Tom was still on no real footing of equality with the Keag children from a social point of view, yet his was felt to be an exceptional case; and neighborliness—perhaps superinduced by common isolation behind the bog—gratitude, and true liking caused his lower station to be at present kindly overlooked by the Keag elders, though not forgotten.

So—when the boys came and leant close against him to hear him read more about grizzly hears, and Lily, knitting her father's coarse socks, stopped occasionally spell-bound to toss back her thick hair and fix clear eyes on his face, and little Osilla, who always clambered on Tom's knee, shivered with fearful delight—then Mistress Keag herself, sonsy soul, would draw near, pausing awhile in her ceaseless duties of preparing supper, or clearing it away, or hanging the big boiler with the pigs' food over the fire. And, at any pathetic passage, she would clack her tongue and cry, "My! but he has a fine voice. He reminds me of a boy I used to know in my young days, who would read out a murder in the newspaper so beautiful it would nearly bring the tears to your eyes. He took afterwards to crying 'red herrings!' through the country." (Tom and Lily disliked the man who once sold red herrings.) Then she would disappear again into the gloom and cold of the back kitchen, where she loved groping amongst pots, barrels, and potatoes, under the impression that a good housewife must take part in the dirty work herself; albeit she kept a servant-girl to do it.

On this subject Lily had already a different opinion, young though she was; and her orderly ways, which saved her much time, and certain little analogical ideas—such as that her father, for instance, would never get the crops in if, while he was ploughing the back side of their hill, he could not trust the farm-servant to work alone in the front fields—though yet unspoken, might later cause some dissatisfaction in her good step-mother's mind; who had come to "that time of life" when habits are crystallized, not to be easily melted again, nor admitting foreign elements of opinion. But, as yet, Lill had naturally no voice in the household management. So Tom read on; and by and by even the men would stop and listen awhile, the one nodding slow approval, the other ejaculating, "Remarkable! Verily most remarkable!" at all striking incidents of the story.

When, too, spring again lightened over the land, the farm children would beg Tom to read to them outside, in the long clear twilights. Chill though the air might seem to more delicately nurtured frames on those April evenings, they enjoyed themselves keenly, sheltered under the lee of some hedge dotted with faint green; while, maybe, a larch overhead was showing its pink cone-flowers, and the wee brown birds were hunting one another with gay twitters in and out bush and brake. O! the children loved well to be out, for those white twilights reminded them that dread winter, enemy of the poor and the birds, the shy hares, and most wild living things, was past, and summer, the blessed, beloved, the song-time and flower-time even of their harsh northern land, was coming; was still to be all enjoyed.

CHAPTER VIII

"Herbs too she knew, and well of each could speak.
That in her garden sipp'd the silvery dew;
Where no vain flower disclos'd a gawdy streak,
But herbs for use, and physic, not a few,
Of grey renown, within those borders grew;
The tufted basil, pun-provoking thyme.
Fresh baum, and marigold of chearful hue;
....
And plantain ribb'd, that heals the reaper's wound;
And marjoram sweet, in shepherd's posie found;
And lavender, whose spikes of azure bloom
Shall be, erewhile, in arid bundles bound,
To lurk amidst the labors of her loom,
And crown her kerchiefs clean with mickle rare perfume."

SHENSTONE.

A NORTHERN expression for any news, or unusual behavior, is "newuns!" This may be used with regard to Tom Coulter, on that day when he resolved within himself to go to Sunday school. Long had Lily tried thereunto to induce him; but the old Adam was still too strong in him, and he averred that week-day schooling was sufficient. Sunday, after service, was his one holiday.

First, the little maid, who in some few matters loved influencing him (woman-like, those pertaining specially to his mental and spiritual improvement), persuaded him to come to church with herself, instead of attending meeting, as he was wont. This at first occurred but fitfully, and was not made a regular practice by Tom for "nearhand" two years. The more honor to him! as the church service was, secretly, more enticing to his nature.

Then came a new clergyman, whom Tom met but once or twice in school and at the cottage, received a few words from, and felt ready to worship. He was a spare, tall gentleman, ill-dressed and angular; but with a loud, cheery voice that warmed the hearts of those he spoke to, and gray, quick eyes that loved all those he looked at—and that most who looked at him loved. A parson who had led a stirring life half his years as an officer in the Cape Rifles, as a gold-digger, lastly in the diamond-fields, and had finally enlisted with all his heart in Christ's army, to light therein upon earth till death.

"Yon's a man," cried James Keag, after first he heard him—"a man in a hunnered."

"A man in a thousand!" answered young Tom Coulter, to everybody's surprise; for "what call" had a boy of his age to venture on an opinion so freely?

Anyway, the clergyman came one day to the marsh; and, after delighting Tom's heart by stories of Africa, suddenly asked him to come to Sunday school.

"I will," said Tom.

"When?" said the parson.

"The morrow," said Tom. And forthwith he walked out of his cottage, and up the back fields to the farm on the hill, to borrow a prayer-book from Orange Lily, and have a shy at his catechism. Notwithstanding worthy efforts, however, he had only about three quarters of it learnt by Sunday.

"Keep near me, Lily, to encourage me, like," he said, on starting for the Sunday school with his favorite companion.

All went excellently well at first. Tom was most attentive whenever the clergyman was near, and began the catechism in grand style, especially at the first question of "What is your name?" giving a manful "Tom Coulter," with great heartiness. The next answers were naturally not so good; and though he brightened up over his Commandments, he went boggling through all the rest, more or less, till at last, on being asked the outward sign or form of baptism, he fairly came to a most unhesitating stop.

"Think over it, Tom," said his friend the parson encouragingly.

"You have seen Mrs. Keag's youngest boy baptized lately."

"Ay," quoth Tom, his earnest dark eyes and firm-set, rosy face showing that much working was going on behind that broad forehead of his; for within his brain he was ransacking memories of all the fuss made over the babe by mother, Lily, and *wee-men*-neighbors, to deduce therefrom his answer. Then his brow cleared, and his eyes lightened. Every gaze was turned upon him.

"You have it?" asked the clergyman.

"I have so," said Tom.

"And what is it?"

"It's the baby's pelisse!"

One sunny Sunday afternoon, a few days later, the young owner of the Castle strolled up to the Keags' farmhouse with his good, elderly step-sisters, to gratify his tenants with a visit. Surely enough, as they approached the door, all three heard a sudden little inward stir, and next minute Mrs. Keag rushed to the doorway, smiling like a summer sun.

"Och, and och! is it the Captain himself? You're welcome home! Dear! but we're proud to see ye," she cried, courtesying oddly, so that her black stuff quilted petticoat kept covering her feet. She appeared very slow to rise again, and held the door by one hand, while the other seemed pulling at something behind her.

"Well, shake hands!" cried her merry landlord, pulling that tanned fist of hers from the door-post gayly; for they two were old friends.

Next instant, Mrs. Keag's stout body tottered—and she fell forward on the young Guardsman's neck, with her arms thrown wildly about him, in an apparently ecstatic clasp. The gray-silken clad sisters looked galvanized, so suddenly did amazement convulse their unaccustomed features with mirth. The Captain staggered back under the shock of that loving but unexpected embrace— and a roll together on the farmyard seemed imminent—when, with one mighty heave, he restored their equilibrium. The good woman stood again on her feet—but one was bare!

"Ochoné—oné!" she burst out, hardly knowing whether to cry or laugh. "It was my dishabilities done it, Captain dear! Oh, ladies, but I'm the ashamed woman this day! … for my boots were tight at church, and I just took them off, to cool my feet upon the floor, when there ye come! … so I thought to slip them on unbeknownst, and was holding by the door to steady myself on the one foot, while—"

She stopped; for her visitors were laughing so much that, feeling more apologies superfluous, she joined loudly in the mirth herself, shaking as if she was a fine human jelly. Behind, James Keag was giving vent to a hoarse roar of great merriment; whilst the children's voices chimed in with cackling trebles. Then the visitors, declining the honor of the parlor, sat down in the pleasant kitchen, and the Captain, knowing how to please the parents' hearts, good-humoredly "took notice to" the children.

"And this is the eldest?" said he.

"Ay, Orange Lily, as the ladies once called her," smiled the rough-featured father, with but half-concealed pride. "'Deed, I took a terrible fancy to the name, and so it sticks to her; it's just a queer and nice one."

"Yes, for *your* first-born," laughed the landlord; then, looking with interest on the fresh-faced child, he liked her thick hair turned off her face in a reddish wave that her round comb could hardly bind—liked her dark stuff gown and long white pinafore, a contrast to the well-to-do untidiness of the rest—liked her douce, sonsy expression; so he said, "Your mother was maid to my mother, do you know, Orange Lily, so we ought to be friends. And I hear you can write and read like anything! What more can you do, eh?"

"Sew," said the rosy lips, whilst the big grayish-blue eyes looked coyly up at him, full of smiling light, from under her long lashes.

"'Deed and 'deed she does that, I will allow," chimed in Mistress Keag, eager to be talking again, and ready to praise all that belonged to her, "though where she gets the time beats me; for *I* do be always slatterin' through the dirt!"

This last remark as to her "through-other" self was so true that her young landlord took out his handkerchief to hide a smile.

"Dear me, now—do you use a thing as small as the like of that?" ejaculated the good woman, with a pitying air. "Hoot! ye should see the two pocket-naipkins I bought at the fair, for my James there!"

And, on the Captain's solicitation, she dived into a big chest, flinging out clothes behind her, much, one must own, as a dog flings back earth from a burrow, unheeding some murmured remonstrances from husband and daughter.

"Och! hould yer whisht, now. Sure the Captain asked to see them, and I'm not the woman to disappoint him!" cried she; then in triumph unrolled an (apparently) fine young table-cloth.

"Come! that is a pocket-napkin and a half!" heartily assented the Captain; and she clapped him on the back.

"Ay, I'll hould ye, one would make a dozen of your flimsy touch-me-nots!"

Miss Edith and Miss Alice sank on their chairs, feeling weak. For they had for once in their lives a positive desire to laugh, yet a fear of being unkind restrained them. To change the subject, Captain Alexander said—

"Can your Orange Lily sing, Keag? For here are my sisters, who are getting up a choir for the old church, and mean to play the harmonium at last; instead of hearing old McWhirter lifting the tune of the psalms[13] without any instrument except his nose—eh?"

Thus he dashed into the thick of a matter which the sisters would have approached with cautious hesitations. Verily men

---

[13] Lifting the psalms. The singing of unaccompanied psalms 'led' by a Precentor who sang the tune of the first line to 'lift' the tune was the norm for Presbyterian churches in mid-19th century Ulster.

are impetuous, thought both spinsters, yet looked with smiles of forgiving admiration at their fair, fine young brother. Then they uttered a mutual vague—

"We were only thinking—thinking, you know, about it."

Lily blushed with delight. Her step-mother cried out readily—

"Och! *she* can sing, and so can wee Osilla; and Hans and Henery-Thomas are always bumming round the house. We'll be glad to send them *all* to sing; if your honor and the ladies wish it."

"Even that fellow in your arms. He'd make noise enough." And the Captain smiled at an eight-month-old infant. "Come, Keag; what do you think of it?"

James Keag rubbed one hard hand slowly over his weather-tanned brow.

"Well," began he, smiling apologetically, as folk do who have but a poor other excuse to offer for themselves, "verily, no doubt the quality knows best; and maybe I am making too free to differ. Still I'm thinking that them new-fangled hymns is no part o' Scripture, so we ought to stick to David's Psalms[14]. And as to the tunes that they play at Maghrenagh yonder, I'd as soon listen to a jig."

"Well; but in our church none sing together. It is the most hideous noise! … all squalling just as they like; and even if old McWhirter does know the air, nobody seems to believe him. Would you not like some trained to sing properly and in tune?"

James Keag's eyes shrewdly twinkled, as much as to say, He may be right—but I doubt it." Aloud, he slowly replied—

"Weel, sir, I can *not* think the Lord cares what tunes we're at, so long as each one sings out as loud as they're able. Sure he

---

[14] Psalms of David. (Exclusive Psalmody) A prohibition on hymns and the singing of only unaccompanied psalms had been the norm for Presbyterian churches in Ulster since the 17th century. The contentious introduction of hymns, instrumental music (organs) and choirs was the beginning of a major controversy by the 1880s.

knows we're doing our best; and likes to hear us, every yun. And in heaven won't we all be singing different tunes, one Mistley, and one Stillorgan, and one the Ould Hundredth; but the Scripture says it'll just be bee-utiful harmony! … Och! David bids us 'make a cheerful noise'—that's the thing!"

He spoke most familiarly, but by no means irreverently. To him God was his father, heaven his home; he felt warranted to talk about both with an ease which some folk might consider freedom. But their reverence goes so far, often, as to keep them from ever mentioning their Master's name save at stated seasons. James Keag would have said that respect went "ratherly *too* far." For himself he would have added he meant no harm; and no harm, therefore, he was certain sure, would be put down to his account.

Which service pleases God best? thought the young squire; then, smiling, said—

"Very likely singing, and many another thing, will come natural to us there, Keag; but meanwhile we shall all be the better for some schooling in it here, I think, as your children are in reading and writing. So I am sure my sisters will like to see Orange Lily up at the Castle next Wednesday evening."

We shall be very pleased," said the gentle sisters.

"We'll be very proud," said the parents.

Only Lily herself hesitated, rolled her apron, and, eying the earthen kitchen-floor, murmured something to her father.

"She says Tom Cowltert sings better nor herself," laughed he, caressing her.

"O! Tom Coulter—my particular friend. Of course we must have him too," cried the squire. "And now, Mrs. Keag, we must be going."

But first, the good-wife declared, he must see their "garden;" a flower-plot, along the house-wall, of marigolds, wall-flowers, and orange-lilies—only weeded indeed by the human namesake of the latter.

"For I know you are terrible fond of a wee posy in your coat," quoth the farm-mistress.

"Very," said the Captain, and his sisters rather gravely smiled; for he was indeed a Sybarite in this respect, and what he spent on flowers alone was a small fortune, they feared.

"Aw, well now; I can give you some with a darling smell," cried Mrs. Keag, generously, plucking handfuls of peppermint, mint, and thyme for him; then stopped at one bush, and smiled.

"Captain dear—a word with you!" said she, enticing him nearer with one forefinger, a knowing look of sympathy playing on her merry, broad face. Then, raising her voice to a loud and audible whisper, "Ach, now, maybe there is some beautiful young lady in London you'll be courting?"

"Maybe," laughed the Guardsman, and felt a moment almost discomposed, since there was a certain hard-hearted angel … and he felt his sisters' eyes instantly upon him. Though too delicate-minded to breathe a question, they felt and looked curiosity often, as he was aware; and at such times he felt their worship of himself inconvenient.

"Maybe; there is no knowing."

Mistress Keag pulled a branch off the bush.

"Then I'll bestow *that* upon ye; and if ye'll just eat a leaf before you go to see her, it is known to be the beautifullest smell—at all, at all! Not a boy or girl coorting through the country but comes begging for a bit, for it makes their breath sweeter—O!—nor peppermint lozenges. Bless ye!" with a clap on his arm, "I wonder you have not got that in your own Castle gardens. There is some sense in that bush."

CHAPTER IX

"Now let the sacred organ blow,
With solemn pause and sounding slow;
Now let the voice due measure keep,
In strains that sigh and words that weep,
Till all the vocal current blended roll,
Not to depress, but lift the soaring soul."

MALLET.

"The muffled goodwives making haste to leave
The gusty minster porch, whose windows shone
With the first-litten candles, while the drone
Of the great organ shook the leaded panes."

MORRIS.

ON the first night of the choir-practice at the Castle, Tom dressed himself in his best; then sallied up to the farm on the hill above, to meet Orange Lily. He felt manly in doing so. All the young men of the country above his age of fourteen years who were bidden also, would be escorting their sweet-hearts: so would he.

It was dark enough on the earth below; but overhead the stars were such a glory that his heart felt quite full, and he stumbled now and again up the lane, not being able to take his eyes off that thousandfold silver glitter in the blackness. He thought of all the expressions he had read about them in the books lent him from the Castle, of spangled skies, studded vaults, of Lily's notion, when a wee child, that they were the nails in heaven's flooring; and he wished that he, too, could just invent something new and grand to say of them. But, after thinking in vain, he only said to himself, looking up at the Plough in the north-east, "It must be a grand angel that drives yon through the furrows." For he had lately been promoted to hold a plough, so had a hearty fellow-feeling with that angel; liking the work hugely, and thoroughly believing there was no wholesomer or sweeter smell than that of the fresh-turned brown earth.

Tom's soul felt opened to all good, sweet, and holy influences, and he was just meditating whether he could not make some poetry upon the stars, when three shadowy figures came round the corner. Lily!—Orange Lily herself, in company with another girl and a young fellow, the latter apparently about Tom's own age. They stopped short.

"Well, Tom Coulter, and how are *you?*" said the new comer, patronizingly. "We've not met these several years, so most likely you don't remember me."

"O, I remember ye—finely," retorted Tom, though taken aback for one brief moment. Though town-varnished, more mincing than of old, how could he forget the voice of "the fallow" that had left Lily to drown—his enemy as a child—Daniel Gilhorn? "I never heard tell ye were come back. You'll be staying with your grand-father again?"

"Just came yesterday on a visit … Met the *Cassel* ladies this very day; and charmed them by showing you country folks how we sing in town … Got a little vacation from our place in Belfa*ss*t," fluently replied young Gilhorn, speaking more would-be finely than ever, and dodging to get beside Lily as she moved on.

"I did hear word ye were selling ribbons in a shop there," grunted Tom, surlily enough, dodging him in turn by getting on Lily's other side, the path being only wide enough for two; and so they went stumbling up against the hedges.

A moment or so this continued, then our hero stopped abruptly and said—

"Daniel Gilhorn, Lily Keag trysted herself to walk to the Castle with me; so I'll trouble you either to go behind or in front of us. Please yourself.

"Well, and she has promised since to go with me; ladies can change their minds. You were late at the meeting place, my dear friend, I apprehend," simpered the city youth.

"There are no ladies here," said Tom, in a tone that boded evil; his suppressed anger being likely to explode with all the worse after-bang. "Is this true, Lily?"

"Oh, Tom dear," murmured that most forgiving little maiden, "I thought it would not seem neighborly else, because you can always have me; and he might have thought I hadn't forgotten the—the bog—otherwise."

Tom fell back without a word.

"I could not well walk with my own sister—he, he, he!" complacently observed Danny, with a smirk; and then looking back over his shoulder, "Coulter, you don't seem to remember my sister Susan. Let me (ahem) introdjuice you."

A smartly-dressed girl, or who seemed such in the darkness, bowed. Tom, who had never been "introduced" in his life before, simply stared with blazing eyes, keeping his hands in his pockets; recognizing with some difficulty in the mincing damsel a little school-mate of long ago, who had seemed to him then as ill-featured and crooked-minded as her brother himself. Then he gruffly said,

"So you are *Shusy*—are you?"

"Well, upon my word, Mr. Coulter, time hasn't mended your manners!" replied his companion, in a sharp voice of anger and contempt, and she stepped on briskly after the others. I'll trouble you to call me Miss Gilhorn; and not to bring up whatever low, vulgar name the ignorant set in the country here used to call me by."

They came to a stile just then.

"I beg your pardon," said Tom, most deliberately; "it was ill-mannered of me." And he helped her over.

"So you're not ashamed of owning to having been in the wrong?" cried Miss Gilhorn, in a sprightly manner, believing she had made a sudden conquest.

"No," said Tom, but without a spark of answering vivacity; almost sullenly. "It's easy enough to do things wrong—there's nothing easier in life; so what for need I be ashamed of owning till it? It's *sticking* knowingly in the wrong that would shame me—nought else."

Miss Gilhorn found the conversation taking too moral a turn for her taste, and changed it by giving him unasked a lively description of the delightfulness of living in town … and seeing life, and the fashions, and the bustle of the streets and their shops … instead of being stuck down like a turnip among miles of dirty fields, with only a few old-fashioned country folk in some farmhouses to talk to. She would have added, "and ill-dressed farmers' sons to keep company with," but refrained for the moment—half a loaf being better than no bread.

"And are you in the same shop as Dan—as your brother?" asked Tom, at last.

"Not I, indeed; goodness be thanked! He'd know too much of my fun, and spoil sport, maybe," answered Miss Gilhorn, with affected giggles that made Tom long to take and shake her soundly; but he also refrained, and quietly remarked—

"Well, if I *had* a sister, I'd like to look after her."

Then they arrived at the side-door of the Castle, and his ordeal was over. She was like nasty physic to Tom's mind, and the worst was that he could not feel the better for her; she altogether disagreed mentally with him, he concluded. There was an organ in the Castle, kept in the cold, lofty hall that was all floored in black and white stone, diamond-patterned. Miss Alice was seated at the instrument, like a gray nun, as the choir shuffled in. Miss Edith nervously fingered a pile of worn music in the shadows. A big iron-ribbed lamp swung from the domed ceiling, throwing bands of light above, but leaving shadows below. Cold airs whistled from the chinks of the great hall-door; from the passages to the servant's regions. The steps of the incomers, who now mustered some dozen and a half, echoed dismally on the stone; and they traversed the empty space with chilled, discomforted minds, for the most part.

"Oh, Tom, it looks so cheerless! I'd rather be at home," whispered Lily, almost frightened.

"I like to see it. It's like a picture," he replied; but could not have told why like a picture to his mind; or why the ill-lit vaulted apartment pleased him, as did also the severe lines of the organ pipes, rising from the shadowed end of the hall, giving him a vague idea of an instrument made for heavenward aspirations.

Two tall wax candles in silver sconces showed two patches of light against the gilded pipes, and faintly shed rays on Miss Alice's meek head, and on her thin fingers, touching idly the keyboard. Her silver-gray silk gown just caught the sheen here and there, its severe folds sweeping far behind on the floor. Beside stood her sister, as like her as could be, pale, thin, angular, but gentlewomanly, even gracious, from head to feet. In the background some suits of armor were ranged against the wall. Lily fearfully believed she saw eyes gazing at her from the hollow casques, and crept nearer Susan Gilhorn, all the girls clustering together. Tom half imagined the same; but felt a thrill of pleasure in his fancy. The gloom, emptiness, and loftiness of the hall were in keeping with its furnishing, he thought, and caused a curious severe pleasure in his simple northern mind. Now he could picture to himself the surroundings to many a group of high-born cavaliers and dames of whom he had read in his borrowed romances.

The younger lads were ranged together, and Dan Gilhorn, whose eyes were roving too, now whispered to Tom, next whom he stood—

"What a place for rats and mice! Ugh! I feel quite uncomfortable."

"Glad to hear it," growled Tom, but too low to be distinctly heard.

"What's that you say?" went on his neighbor; then, with a superior air, "Now, if I were Captain Alexander, I'd smarten up this old barn a bit, I can tell you."

"If you were *who?*" said Tom, ironically; having heard well enough.

Gilhorn raised his nose, and continued, with a smile of disgusting conceit, in Tom's opinion; and with a fluency of speech which marked him also in our hero's mind as a "talking fool"—

"You'd see! There is a Kidderminster going cheap at our place now, I'd cover the floor with; and paper the walls with roses to match. Looking-glasses everywhere for the girls to see themselves—he! he! he!—and gilding. Gilding is the thing! Up in town, Coulter, we learn taste, you see; we learn the fashion; we learn—"

"*Blathers!*" said Tom; no more. But that single expression of his sentiment was enough. Young Gilhorn looked at him with furious, piggish eyes; small blue ones they were, white-lashed, and weak of gaze. Neither dared use his voice in more speech to the other, however, for the hymn singing began; and peace and good will alone came from the lads' lips in vocal harmony, though each just longed to shy his hymn-book at the other's head.

"I fear it is very dark here," said Miss Edith, nervously, coming up as the hymn ended. "I heard that you were obliged to miss many of your words, Tom. Perhaps you and your friend will hold this candlestick between you?"

And she handed them a tall silver one.

Tom, who knew well he had omitted of set purpose all the Christian sentiments to which his heart was not then attuned (for he hated hypocrisy), groaned within himself as they began again.

You be—" (treated like Haman), muttered Daniel Gilhorn, after a minute.

"You're dropping all the grease on my coat. D'ye think it's a shoddy-bag stitched up in the village here, like your own?"

"Mind what your tongue is wanted here *for;* and keep your

bad language till I can answer it," sternly retorted Tom.

"You're blowing the light out," went on Danny, maliciously raising his voice.

"You're sticking the can'le down my mouth!—so how would I be able to help it?" burst out angry Tom, with truthfulness, but also incautious loudness.

There was a horrible pause; and every one looked round at them. Then Miss Edith spoke, with a gentleness that reduced Tom to utter quiet at once, and made even Gilhorn feel reproved, though in a slighter degree.

"I am afraid you two cannot sing well—together."

"Really, Madam," interrupted young Gilhorn—and his quick reply made all present, to whom slowness of speech to superiors seemed a due courtesy, gaze up amazed—while he waved one hand gracefully, as if inviting a customer to a seat on the other side of the counter, till he, with reluctant truthfulness, should depreciate the goods of the shop over the way. "Really, Madam, I regret to say it, but Mr. Keag sings so flat it is puffed agony to be beside him; while as to time or tune—"

The gentle youth's voice died mildly away, as if he would say no more—albeit his nerves had been excruciated.

"Flat! Let me once get a grip, and *I'll* flatten you!" thought Tom; all the more bitterly that he did not understand the accusation. Aloud he said doggedly, and very slowly—

"I'll acknowledge till this, Miss Alexander ... that I can *not* lift the tune beside—him. But if you'll kindly try me myself a minute, I'll engage I'll raise her."

The ladies gazed with unimpassioned yet discerning eyes on the two youths who stood singled out from the rest. The town shop-boy was tallest, with a slender waist he was proud of; the most color he had was in his reddish head, which drooped on one side of a long neck. He simpered would-be pleasantly, and expanded the palm of one hand, turning his fingers down, to illustrate thereby the emptiness of his rival's claims to any consideration in singing. The peasant lad stood with his shoulders a little raised, and his mouth doggedly closed. Stout, square-headed, with black hair and eyes, and rich coloring, due, perhaps, to a dash of true Irish blood in him—he was undoubtedly handsomer, like the few other dark men and boys, through the country, than the fairer-haired, purer Scotch race which King James had planted in the homes of the "meere natives."

It was but natural the ladies should eye with most favor the ruddy ploughboy. However gruff and awkward, he looked filled with respect for them; with sturdy self-reliance amongst his fellows. Yet Miss Edith corrected herself. It was human duty to think as kindly (nay, more so!) of the reddest-haired, piggiest-eyed specimen of our race that God made, as purposely as the handsome ones. Would not she herself be a deep-bosomed, grandly-wrought woman, of a fair countenance, if she could? Did not her spirit cry out still at times—though youth was past—that its clothing of flesh and blood was ugly and mean, and niggardly eked out?

"Still surely he *might have been* a gentleman, had he been born among us," she said within herself of Tom; with the vagueness peculiar to her uttered speech in general.

"Surely he *has* some of the feelings of a gentleman," thought Miss Alice, who was slightly bolder-minded.

If neither went further, and said, as they ought, that a ploughboy not only might have, but in many an instance has, all the feelings, though not habits, of a gentleman—courage, gentleness, and hatred of all things mean—forgive them! since the mind-shackles of their breeding, traditions, and habits of speech were weighty upon them; and women in their days were not expected to let the flame of their own thinking burn up much under the heaped slaked-coal of their ancestors' opinions. Besides, Tom was still undeveloped; they knew him little; and it would cost him tough struggles yet before he should cast out the dross of his nature.

Maybe it would need to be burnt out by fire.

The choir-singing had ended. Then Miss Alice said, gently, "Now, Coulter, will you try that hymn once by yourself; to be sure of it by Sunday?" and Tom stepped forward alone to fulfil his offer, and stand a fair trial. He was in no humor for half-measures, for gentleness, or any expression save that of defiance to his rival. The consequence was that he bellowed like a young bull of Bashan, though he did stick to the air well enough.

"And now, Gilhorn," said Miss Edith; her quiet face inexpressive of opinion as ever.

The last-named youth, with an elegant bow to the company, began in his turn; his head more sideways than before; his very nose trying to keep up the simper his mouth was forced temporarily to drop. A shadow of vexation passed through the ladies' minds. In all fairness, his was the sweeter voice—the somewhat trained one.

"Thank you, Gilhorn. You would be of use to us, but I understand that you live in town now. Had we known that sooner, we need hardly have troubled you to come; although we are much obliged to you for doing so," said Miss Alice, with her grave politeness.

"Pray don't mention it, ladies. Anything I can do to assist any of"—("your sex," he was nearly saying, but some grain of sense in his windbag of a brain rattled very likely, and he substituted)—"your family, I am only too happy, I am sure … I'll be taking a run into the country, occasionally, for my health, and to visit our people here, from the Saturdays till Mondays, and will be glad to give you what help I can, at such times."

His air implied that they might use him as a model if they particularly wished it; though by nature he was modest.

The ladies now gravely rose. Then, turning to the whole choir-group, Miss Edith, as nominally the eldest, nervously said in dismissal—

"We are very much obliged, indeed, to you all for coming to sing for us … though, of course, we know that it is not for us at all, but—but solely to help in the service in church …"

"Ach, sure! we'd come for your own sakes, too, if ye wanted us," came in a murmured interruption; and poor Miss Edith, who was not prepared to have the ground cut away from under her, felt quite discomposed.

"It is very right of you … especially on such a cold night, too—that is, I mean—"

"Och, never mind, miss," in another many-voiced murmur.

"We are very anxious that you should not take cold," burst out Miss Edith, now desperate, "and will feel really—obliged—if you will all muffle well; especially at the throat; and we thought a little hot drink now before going—"

She stopped short, and an agreeable thrill ran through the choir.

"Would be good," took up Miss Alice. "Though, of course, we do not approve of anything strong; and tea or coffee is bad for the nerves and voice—"

"And always prevents *us* from sleeping at night," went on Miss Edith. "So we can but hope you will like what we—ah—have provided."

"Ah! no fears," encouragingly grumbled the three oldest of the singing men; the singing women smiled and giggled.

And so—good evening," said the poor ladies, with a last effort.

"Good evening, and thank you kindly," said all the choir-group, and shuffled out whispering, "Man! is it whiskey and water, hot?" "Woman dear! it'll be wine." "Boys, O! but this is a spree."

Ranged on a table in the back hall were noble sized cups apiece of hot—whey.

CHAPTER X

"'Twas when the stacks get on their winter-hap,
  And thack and rape secure the toil-worn crap;
  Potato bings are snugged up frae skaith
  Of coming winter's biting, frosty breath."

"Ae dreary, windy, winter night,
  The stars shot down wi' sklentin light,
  Wi' you, mysel', I gat a fright.
  ……………………………
  Each bristl'd hair stood like a stake,
  When wi' an eldritch stoor, quaick, quaick,
              Amang the springs,
  Awa ye squatter'd like a drake,
              On whistling wings."
                                    BURNS.

THE girls had all passed through the side door first, therefore the
young men and lads were a few steps behind. Two cousins of
Gilhorn's now turned to Tom jokingly—

"Well, boy! Danny took the conceit queerly out of you in that
last trial. Ye'll hardly sing before him again."

"Ah! you want me to teach you a thing or two," responded
Danny, sticking his thumb with playful familiarity into Tom's side.
To do him justice, however young Gilhorn might be offensive
to others, it was very hard to offend himself; which knowledge
perhaps made the offended ones all the angrier.

"Keep your thumbs to yourself, please," growled Tom; con-
trolling himself enough not to answer with a blow, and only
giving a quiet but decided shove of his elbow to ward off further
playfulnesses.

"Give him a hit, Danny. Don't let him hold his head over
you, man!" cried his eldest cousin of nineteen or so, with glee,
thinking a quarrel between the boys would be vastly amusing. The

76

other lads closed round, idly sharing his opinion. No unkindliness stirred them; quarrels, indeed, even among men, were rarely attended with bad consequences thereabouts. But their lives were very dull. All day they worked in the fields apart; in the evenings there were next to no games in common; nought but a little ball play (if an unwindowed wall could be found), and little of that. Nothing but courting the girls for amusements; and when that palled, lounging round the public-houses, of which there were just as many as there were wells in the village district, namely, three— (and the latter ran dry in summer time, unless rain refilled them). So some angry words and a few blows between any two would stir the monotony of their fellows; give rise to some coarse mirth. Surely some praise is due that this did not happen far more often, and that so little mischief came of it. Young Gilhorn felt unusually brave with his cousins to back him; and also because—since they were still close to the Castle here in the shrubbery—his friends durst not let him do more than indulge in valiant demonstrations.

"'Will you fight?" cried he, squaring up in front of Tom and attitudinizing like an impertinent spider; and the girls in front heard that, stopped, and ran back.

"Fight!" said Tom. And, at the word, a big fight began within him. Then—with a great gulp, and gazing at the Castle walls rising above them, lit by a single light high up—"Not here."

A jeering, coarse laugh passed round the circle, which, though he had not the finer nerves of an aristocrat, made Tom long to knock them all down.

"Oh, Tom! Danny!—don't quarrel," prayed a frightened little voice from the outside of the group, and Lily Keag tried to slip in nearer them.

"I wonder, Danny, you would demean yourself to touch him with a pair of tongs," shrilly exclaimed Susan Gilhorn, in contempt.

"Don't fight to-night, after singing the hymns for next Sabbath together—don't, Danny!" wept poor Lily, afraid of being forward; yet resolute to do her childish best to stop them, her face turned to Gilhorn pleadingly, but her hand laid on Tom's coat-sleeve.

"I'll thank you not to meddle," retorted the former, rudely.

"Ay, ay! Lass—I mind—let me be," muttered the other boy, doggedly, and did not shake off her hand, but removed it.

"Coward!" uttered young Gilhorn.

Tom turned upon him.

"I'll not fight *here!*—because I think too much respect for Captain Alexander; nor yet this night. But meet me at the cross-road the morrow morn, before I go to the ploughing at six, Danny Gilhorn; and you'll see which of us is the coward. Or at twelve, when I quit work; or in the evening, when it's done."

"Ay! ay! a fair offer," cried the elder Gilhorn, perceiving with glee that his brother was bent on urging their young kinsman to a pitched battle; and entering into the plan with zest. "I'll be by there, on my way to our fields, and see fair play for ye, Tom Coulter. You're the boy for me! You'll stop your work for no man."

"Will you come?" reiterated Tom thunderingly to his rival.

"I'll—I'll—just murder you if I catch you, so you'd better keep out of my way," stuttered Gilhorn, passionately.

"O! ye must go!" "Ay! ay! he'll be there," cried all the rest, laughing.

And, just then, the Reverend Robert Redhead, who had been visiting a sick man at the far lodge, came down the drive behind them with long, swinging strides, and passed, bidding them a cheery good-evening. All voices hushed as the clergyman neared, and the group reached the lodge in comparative silence, Tom walking quietly last. Then, when Mr. Redhead was out of sight, a babble of gibes and rough mirth broke out again, as the group stopped before separation. Tom, however, was not to be seen. He had likely struck homewards, by a short cut through the marsh.

"Let me convoy you back, Miss Keag," simpered Danny, with

a sudden return of his blandest suavity.

"Thank you kindly, but I'll go my lone," answered our little maiden, speaking for the first time since the quarrel; and now absolutely forgetting her good English. Therewith she turned up the narrow lane leading to her father's farm.

The neighbors had passed on down the dark road, and Lily was all alone. Then, and then only, she took out her handkerchief slowly and prepared to indulge in the luxury of a cry, like any older person of her sex. First she rubbed her eyes a little, feeling them water; her lips twitched; her heart swelled. Then, being sure that she was for once in her life very miserable indeed, she let a small, stifled sob come, followed cautiously by others. Danny Gilhorn had insulted her—worse, Tom had gone without saying good night to her, for the first time in his life; meant to fight in the morning; would be all bloody and blackened and bruised. Her heart turned sick at the thought. If not so late and so dark, she would almost dare to pick her way through the marsh to his cottage and once more beg him to desist. Dare she—could she—? It *was* very dark, but for the cold, far stars, as she stopped and looked around. The glimpse of the marsh she caught through the hedge looked a gruesome, mysterious waste; the thin hedges, too, on either side shivered fearsomely in the night wind. Fancying a bogie behind every tree and horrors ready to spring out on her from the blackness of the banks on either side, she crept on doubting, fearing, crying—poor, little, honest heart, when … ! Something ghastly did rise from the ditch close to her, with an awful groan. A whitish ghost like a naked being, but going on all fours.

Lily gave one great scream; but next moment, as the horror began to crawl towards her, shaking a big head that seemed ready to eat her up, the poor child's tongue clove to the roof of her mouth—and with an awful longing to run away, to her intense fear she found she could not stir an inch. She thought she must surely die, when a friendly shout came from the hedge overhead.

A dark form jumped through the branches, and she felt Tom Coulter catch hold of her.

"What ails ye? What frighted ye?" he cried.

Lily could but gasp and point at the—*thing!* Tom burst into a great roar of laughter.

"What! ye don't yet know your father's own old sow? Sure, she's got a trick of undoing her stye-door, and goes squandering away through the country. Ho, ho, ho! And you startled me, too, queerly."

"But how came you there, Tom? Why did you not come back with me?" asked Lily, now recovered, but still gladly clinging to him.

"I thought—Gilhorn—would be seeing you home," said Tom, slowly. "So I kept away, not to be in the road of you both; but still I was nearhand if you did want me."

"Did ye think I'd have him, after what happened? Sure, I forbid him to come!"

"No! Did ye?"

"I did so."

A short silence of utter ecstasy on Tom's part.

Then, as if thinking he had had enough of a good time, the little maid took up her speech again, and severely reproached him. She neither scolded nor complained like one on his own level on these rare occasions, but took such high moral ground that Tom was utterly impressed with a sense of his own degraded mind. And she said shortly and honestly what she had to say, and had done with it. (A rare virtue, that last, in his eyes.) Still he turned upon her solemnly now, an unconvinced young heathen.

"Do you think any man could refuse to fight, if he was called a coward?"

Lily was absolutely silent; she could hardly go to such lengths as that.

"I did allow you were right, about not fighting this night," went on Tom; apparently ready to agree with her so far as his conscience would permit. "I do allow it's wrong to bear ill-will; and what's more, I won't, as sure as my name's Tom Coulter. But I am confident that I'll feel the better, and so will he, if I give him a few clouts on the head, just to teach him to be mannerly. Then we'll shake hands and be friends."

His frank, healthy voice reassured and convinced Lily wonderfully. His way of looking at things might not be quite right, but surely was not very far wrong.

"And you're sure he'll not hurt you much," she ended, with a last touch of loving anxiety.

Certain sure," said Tom.

"Nor you hurt him?"

"No more than I can help."

They had reached the stackyard now; and stopped at these last words under the shelter of the great hayrick. Somehow, in stackyard or farmyard, amongst hay and straw and farm odors, Tom would lose sight utterly of the fancies of foreign lands that filled his mind at other hours, and the material-loving, simple, sensuous body and soul of him, nourished amongst wholesome-smelling, fresh-turned furrows, clave to the ideals of earthly happiness of those with whom he had been bred, and no blame to him. And then he would feel a longing to have, he too, his good farm and warm hearth in the time to come—and bonny wife. Just as these vain hopes revived with the old smells, the old associations— but troubling the poor servant-boy newly, wanting to be spoken while his speech was shamed—Lily uttered softly the old loving admonition since childhood,—

"Tom, you'll remember your prayers to-night?"

"I will so," said Tom; then, suddenly, "And you'll promise to be my sweetheart; now and for always?"

There was a moment's silence; then Lily answered,—"I will so."

Tom put his arm round her neck, and gave her a hug like a

bear or a brother; not having yet changed his boyish opinion that kissing, as a sign of affection, was a truly ridiculous custom. Thus, their second betrothal took place in the stackyard, while the chill autumn winds blew, and the darkness brooded over the ploughed fields of Ulster, but the bright little stars twinkled bravely overhead.

As young Tom walked home, and looked at his friendly Plough again, he felt joy reinstated in his heart and good will to all men, Dan Gilhorn—poor creature!—included. On reaching home, he found its inmates already retired to rest.

"Father," said Tom, sitting down on his parent's bed, as the latter roused up hearing his step in the kitchen, wherein father and son slept, "you waken earlier than I do. Could ye call me the morn', well before six?"

"What for, my son?"

"I promised to fight a boy before working-time," said Tom, coolly; "and it would look ill to be late."

"I aye advise you to keep from the fighting," remonstrated the quiet father.

"And so I mostly do," said Tom, "but this time I *be'd* to fight." And he curtly told the cause of quarrel.

Fully satisfied, his father turned on his other side to sleep again.

"O! I'll call ye in time; never fear."

So Tom said his prayer, trying to put all malice against Dan Gilhorn far from him. And—in the full belief that he might be doing rather a good turn than otherwise to Danny by whacking him—and was undoubtedly taking the only means to make himself feel friendly unto the said young man—he fell asleep.

CHAPTER XI

"He was a shepherd, and no mercenary,
And though he holy was and virtuous,
He was to sinful men full piteous.
....
But Jesus' love which owns no pride or pelf,
He taught—but first he followed it himself."

CHAUCER.

LILY slept but brokenly the night after the choir practice; and next morning slipped out as early as she dared to the field, where Tom was calmly holding the plough behind gray Jessie and the Tory. Not a scratch seemed upon him.

"Well?" she cried.

"Well!" said Tom. "I was at the tryst—but he was not. Hup! Wynd! Wynd!"

And he unconcernedly turned his horses at the head-rig. During the last half year, Tom had become a regular farm-laborer under James Keag, and had consequently been obliged to give up his schooling; but he attended night-classes, and read all the more hungrily than ever, therefore.

That noon little Hans and Henry-Thomas Keag appeared, as messengers of war, at the Gilhorns farm.

"Is Danny within?" they asked; and, on seeing the object of their desires, said significantly unto him, "Tom Coulter is waiting on ye, at the cross-roads."

"Let him wait," responded the sought one, flaring out at them.

"He was ready for ye at six this morning," piped the smallest boy.

"D'ye think I'd rise from my bed at that hour for—for the like of him?" blustered Gilhorn, in weak passion.

"We'll go back, and tell him ye're feared," cried the other boy, with delight, in a tone of mock pity; and both retreated.

Dan dashed out upon them in a fury; whereupon they took to their heels down the lane. He might have run after, to "box their little, imperent ears," as he thought to himself, and, being so much bigger, must have caught them, when at that moment he spied a black clerical hat moving rapidly behind the high-road hedge that ran below the farm. Daniel stood still a moment; then, turning hastily into the kitchen again, took a sudden resolution—and therewith his hat from the peg. He was soon striding down the lane as fast as possible; not running after the parson—that would have attracted attention, as remarkable—but stretching his legs till they resembled extended compasses.

"Please, sir, might I speak with you?" he meekly called, when his last great effort had brought him just behind Mr. Redhead. The latter started, and no wonder, for Danny had come up almost noiselessly.

"I am in a great hurry, Gilhorn. I have to visit a sick woman in that cottage, and christen her infant; so—"

"There is something heavy on my mind, and, if I might consult your reverence as a clergyman, I'd be happy to walk that far beside you, if not presuming," Gilhorn entreated, with deep humility; keeping step for step with Mr. Redhead's quick strides.

"Very well, my lad; say it out," said the latter, with hurried kindliness.

"Is it—is it right for Christians to fight, please, sir?"

"Eh? Why, yes; fighting for your country is a fine thing. Remember the centurion whom St. Peter visited, a good man and a good soldier, which brought him far on the road to being a good Christian. But you are not thinking of enlisting—eh?"

"Oh, no, indeed—indeed not, sir, I wouldn't be so foolish for worlds, Mr. Redhead. It is *quite* different," gabbled his hearer, very anxiously. "It is, if a person wants to set on one to give one a beating for—for nothing at all. What ought a Christian to do then, sir?"

"Don't let him. Knock him down, of course, in self-defence; but keep your temper."

"I thought you would have said it was our duty to forgive our enemies, and I'm sure I'm *quite* ready to forgive Tom Coulter," murmured Daniel, in a most unhappy voice, feeling ready to cry.

At the mention of Tom, a favorite of his, Mr. Redhead pricked his ears more attentively and demanded an explanation. A little heartened, Danny fluently, almost breathlessly, since they were fast nearing the cross-roads, began his tale; grieving to say that jealousy of his (Daniel's) singing had so demoralized Thomas Coulter that the latter had been challenging him to fight ever since, and even now awaited him yonder—as his reverence could see.

"Go and tell him you won't. That would be more courageous than fighting," said Mr. Redhead, decidedly.

"So it would, sir—yes, indeed; but I fear I have not the moral courage. They would laugh at me, sir, and I'd be sure to fight *then*. It's only ten yards out of your way," said the unhappy youth.

Immediately afterwards, Tom Coulter, the two elder Gilhorns, and some small boys, were startled by seeing Mr. Redhead bearing down upon them in hot haste, and Danny Gilhorn, with an air of conscious virtue, keeping close by his side.

"I have come to put a stop to this, my lads," said the clergyman, with bent brows and stern voice. "Tom Coulter, I did not expect such ill-feeling from you. Were I not going to christen a dying infant, I would stop and say more to you all; but, as it is, I can only ask you, as your clergyman, to have no fighting … You'll all do that much to please me, I believe."

"Ay, and more," hoarsely murmured every one.

Said the elder Gilhorn lad, in a shame-faced fashion—

"It was but some nonsense at the most, sir. We were carrying on for fun, like; but ye may depend upon us now till have done with it, Mr. Redhead. None would annoy you."

"Thank ye—thank ye. And I hope you'll make it up and shake

hands, boys," and Richard Redhead turned to go.

"I'm ready to do that now, sir," ejaculated Daniel Gilhorn, in a hurry. "Thomas Coulter, I quite forgive you," and he extended a limp hand.

As it touched Tom's brown fist and withdrew itself, Tom—whose fingers had opened reluctantly, but perforce, as it were, to receive that precipitate token of reconciliation—could not suppress a rude stare, nor a slow grin that illumined his countenance. But Danny had already left the group, and was hurrying closely after the parson; evidently afraid that his good resolutions would melt, if he tarried one moment in the evil company behind.

An hour later, Mr. Redhead, emerging from the cottage with a quieter and cheerful air—for child and mother seemed likely to live; and, at least, he had thoroughly performed his duty and left comforted hearts behind—came upon Tom Coulter sitting moodily under the damp hedge, chewing a lump of tobacco, and (with consequent difficulty) attempting to hum,

> "Holy water, holy water,
>   Sprinkle the Catholics, every one;
>   We'll cut them asunder, and make them lie under,
>   The Protestant boys shall carry the drum."

Now, as it happened, Mr. Redhead had a strong dislike to all party-feeling, orange or green. He also still more forcibly objected to the cutting of sound Roman Catholics asunder, as a notion chiefly held by sorry Protestants. He even would have preferred that his Ballyboly boys should not carry the drum; but as to *that*—common sense told him he might as well hold his tongue.

"I am sorry you can find nothing else to sing, Tom," he said.

"So am I, sir," said Tom, slowly rising to his feet. "But I know no other tune but hymn ones … I've little variety."

"And, by the way, chewing tobacco is an idle habit, and sometimes an unpleasant one; especially in church," said his pastor.

"Maybe, sir, but it keeps a body from feeling *hung-ery;* and I had to want my denner because I waited to speak to you," replied Tom, unabashed.

"Did you? And it's past one o'clock now, so I'm afraid you'll get none," said his friend, more kindly, knowing work began again at half past one. "What had you to say that you waited so long?"

"I was sore vexed that ye thought ill of me about the matter of Daniel Gilhorn," quoth Tom, wrinkling his forehead like any old man, as he trudged on beside Mr. Redhead. "Ye've heard his half of the story, sir; now will ye hear mine?" And he quickly related his unvarnished version, compelling belief by his honest voice and manner.

"So he wanted to fight at the Castle, and called you a coward?" said Mr. Redhead, with a queer smile.

"Ay, he *darred* me there, on the top of" (after) "we'r hymn-practice; then to-day he—forgave me," quoth Tom dryly.

The Reverend Richard Redhead stopped on the road and looked Tom in the face. Tom did so likewise to him. Then both burst into such a great laugh of hearty mirth that they vastly astonished a flock of rooks which were banqueting over a ploughed field hard by.

CHAPTER XII

"For roads were clad, frae side to side,
Wi' monie a weary body,
In droves that day.
Here, farmers gash, in ridin graith,
Gaed hoddin by their cotters;
There, swankies young, in braw braid-claith.
Are springing owre the gutters.
The lasses, skelpin barefit, thrang,
In silks an' scarlets glitter;
Wi' sweetmilk cheese, in monie a whang,
An' farls bak'd wi' butter
Fu crump that day."—BURNS.

SEVERAL seasons of Lily Keag's and Tom's pleasant lives had slipped away among the well-cultivated, if treeless, windy fields of Ballyboly.

During that time both had left childhood behind them, with its easy joys and quick griefs. Sleeping and rising, working and resting, they had grown, almost without knowing it, into the youth of manhood and maidenhood; with its more serious troubles and duties, but also its stronger, fuller-filling joys. Their souls were ripening to gladness like grapes i' the sun, that should yield good wine—ripening both to give and feel it, as at that age all human souls should. But some fruit remains sour on earth; and, at best, the capabilities of us all to feel keenly must be shrivelled, sooner or later, with the heat of life's long day.

The friendship betwixt the farm maiden and the lad from the cottage was often made somewhat difficult to them nowadays. It had also become instinctively more hidden even from each other, but not lessened—strengthened, rather, iron-like, by blows, being hot with youth. Both, more especially Tom, began to undergo the sharp discipline of circumstance, and first felt it thus. During the winter and spring Lily had been allowed to go to one or two harvest-home barn-dances; besides the more frequent entertainments of school house concerts, meeting-house "swarrees" to enjoy tea and cake and hear moral addresses, much spiced with amusing anecdotes (like currants in a common loaf, "to make it more tasty-like")—also lectures and prayer-meetings. To most of these her parents took her; but, whether or not, Tom Coulter was also often her companion, save where, owing to his position, he was naturally uninvited. To his mind (secretly also to hers) Tom was squiring her. To the parents he was merely their farm-servant, kindly allowed to accompany them, or sent to escort their daughter home. None else lived near enough to do so. And they liked him well—in his humble position.

So people see the same thing from opposite sides, and wonder angrily at each other's different views thereof. What, indeed, could show us the whole of any matter, up and down its linked lines of causes and consequences, without end on this earth? No human eyes—not even, perhaps, the sight of purified spirits.

At some of these gatherings Daniel Gilhorn also appeared, since once a fortnight he came down to see his grandparents. He had quite a petty knack in timing his visits with any small merry-makings that could make the country less of an unprofitable yet still rude wilderness. And, at such times, he always paid particular attention to our Orange Lily. Tom believed in his angry heart that this was out of malice to himself. Lily naturally thought it was from admiration of her own douce self (and also, maybe, jealousy); and being but a simple lassie, thinking men's liking harmless, did not see why she should be very unkind to the poor fellow, who had not much amiss in him.

Both were right, after all.

Matters grew worse between the twain in summer. It was the first Twelfth of July on which Lily Keag was old enough to go to the great meeting with her father and step-mother; and therefore a day of days to which she and Tom Coulter had looked forward since both were very small "weans." For, though Tom had already gone thither several years, the delights of the Twelfth were still but gross material without what was life and soul in all things to him—Orange Lily's presence.

Long ago—so long they could not remember when—both had solemnly agreed to "keep company" on this day. Lily had a new blue and white gown to wear, and a straw bonnet, trimmed with blue ribbons. It was not so gay as the flowery and feathered hats of many of her companions, whose imitations of the fashion were grievously vulgar—if vulgar means a striving to appear that which one is not; but it was very becoming.

As she made her father's breakfast that sunny July morning, at six o'clock, he thought his girl's voice as gay as the larks singing outside on the big hill; while her skin was as white as milk, and her cheeks ruddy as roses. She was pinning a fine orange lily in her bosom, when he said, smiling,

"Dan Gilhorn was telling me last night he'd look after you and your mother; for what with being Master, and one thing and another, I'll maybe hardly can see you the day."

Lily's fresh face suddenly fell; the light of the summer morn seemed changed to her.

"Oh! father, I don't—much—like him," she slowly said.

Danny Gilhorn had dug a pitfall for her in going behind her back to her father; worse! he was no doubt rejoicing in having got the better of Tom. She saw that much in a minute. And although she could not think altogether badly of any well-behaved admirer—attachment to herself being of course, in her girlish mind, a proof of latent good in him, and some excuse for his ill-conduct to Tom—still she felt bitterly aggrieved that his admiration should spoil her day's pleasure. She liked him well enough—when Tom was not by. But to claim her on this Twelfth was—was—too bad.

"Hoot! Not like him!" uttered her father, between the

difficulties of first swallowing an oatmeal farl almost wholesale, then a saucerful of boiling tea in a succeeding gulp.

"Don't be silly, my lassie. Isn't he the grandson of my ouldest friend, nearly. What for do ye not like him?"

"He was very unfriendly and overbearing to Tom Coulter there, the other day too," came evasively from the girl's rosy, reluctant lips.

"Come! if that's all ye can find to cast up against him! ... Tom is a good boy, ay, verily! for his position in life—but a wee thing over-inclined to think himself as good as his betters," said her careless father, slipping his gay, embroidered orange sash across his breast, and wrapping the red cloak of mastership about him as he rose. "Ye must mind he's only our servant-boy ... Young Gilhorn will have his grandfather's farm, most likely, left him, as he was telling me, so Tom would not be so impudent as to even himself with *him*.'

"Let the boys mind their own quarrels; the girls have no call with them," added Mistress Keag, with some significance of tone, as she poured fresh water into the teapot and then shook it soundly, as if hoping thereby to extract more strength from the tea-leaves.

The drums began to beat in the village; the children clamored; all went out in haste to join the neighbors and follow the procession of flags, drummers, fifers, and gay-scarfed Orangemen. Poor Lily felt all bewildered—it was so unlike the day she had dreamed of beforehand. There was Tom Coulter, handsome and strong and straight, marching with the rest, but glancing darkly towards herself with Daniel Gilhorn simpering by her side. At the start he had come near her, and whispered—

"What's wrong—why won't you look at me—what is Gilhorn up to now?"

But she could only answer, without being overheard—

"It's all wrong! Go away for a bit, Tom; but come again."

She saw he was amazed, proud, and deeply mortified. Little wonder!—as, on the very evening before, they had smiled rather meaningly in each other's eyes when Tom had asked, but with quiet assurance of favor and significant emphasis, "I may walk with you the morn'?" in a tone reminding her of bygone promises to that effect; and she had answered, "Surely."

Now all was changed.

She was quick-witted enough to guess that her step-mother had lately been giving her father some hints that, since she was "already a lump of a lass," it was time to see that she kept company with her social equals; for honest Mistress Keag was an inveterate match-maker. It was not that they were angry with Tom.

"No! worse luck—they never even *thought* of him in such a way," reflected the poor child. Unpleasant self-suggestions, care-less words of others since a year or so back, had in some degree awakened her mind to the plain truth that socially Tom was, of course, much her inferior. But, until this morning, the thought had never been called on to fully confront her—or rather its con-sequences. *Or rather its consequences!* She had never truly thought about them, not being given to thinking, honest and sweet young soul, but only to feeling; and she could not think now. But she shivered slightly; and Daniel Gilhorn beside her laughed.

"One would think you were cold, Miss Keag," said he. "And this such a sultry day! What a warm heart you must have, he! he! when this weather is too chilly for you! I'd like to have such a heart," with an affected sigh.

"I'm not cold, thank you," retorted Lily; looking now, in-deed, hot with vexation. She felt utterly incapacitated by young Gilhorn's fine speeches, which made her feel foolish; quoth Tom once bitterly, "the foolishness was in themselves."

As the stream of people passed down the dusty roads, and the drums beat noisily, and the sun grew hotter, the fun and jesting somewhat slackened. Mistress Keag, who had been very merry at first with the neighbors, began to complain of her corns. Danny, who was in dudgeon because the Orange Lily did not properly appreciate the honor he was paying her, became snappish. Lily thought she alone really had something to be cross about; the day was so disappointing. But the sight of Tom's cap ahead a little comforted her. She would manage to get near him soon.

"How much further have we to go? These roads are very different walking from the streets," asked Dan by and by, limping, as Lily thought, with contempt, effeminately.

"Three miles more—five in all," she said briefly.

"What a pity we didn't take the cart to bring us all, and Tom Coulter would have driven us!" cried Mrs. Keag.

"It's not a vehicle I am partial to," said young Dan, mincingly, to Lily; but under his breath, so that her step-mother should not hear. "A jaunting-car is more in my style. And Mr. Thomas Coulter's clothes is not a handsome coachman's livery—he, he!"

"He doesn't spend all he has upon them, certainly," retorted Lily, looking sideways at her companion's round hat and the gloves he absolutely wore with such a conscious smirk.

"His all would not be very much, anyway, I should think," replied Tom's rival angrily.

And Lily said nothing, being too slow of speech; but thought with some exasperation that Dan always seemed to hold her father and mother and Tom as vulgar, dull folk, of no account. "His town ways just make me uncomfortable," she thought. But then, without doubt, many of the other girls were envying her such a fine admirer.

Other lodges now joined them, swelling the procession; the din of drums became deafening. When they reached their meeting-ground—a green hill, with a platform erected half-way up it—there were several thousands of people already assembled round the latter central point, where some clergymen were conducting prayer.

Suddenly Lily missed her step-mother, and, a few moments later, saw that "tearing, fine" Orangewoman fighting her way to the platform through the thickest of the throng. Left to Danny's sole care, the girl could only remain disconsolately on the outskirts of the crowd; but tried to compose her disappointed mind by reverently standing still, and seeking to catch what words of devotion came floating down the wind. Danny, meanwhile, sniggered, and jocularly asked her, from time to time, whether she wished him to go down on his knees in the open field. Lily grew much annoyed. The staid, honest little maiden felt she could better bear anything than ridicule.

When she had heard with difficulty part of a speech about the battle of the Boyne, that day thus gloriously celebrated, she grew weary—and yielded to young Gilhorn's urgings to walk about the outer limits of the large field with him, like some hundreds of other couples. But, as it was now some two hours past noon, and that both were hungry and tired, they spent the time in bickering on Danny's part, in disconsolate forbearance, unlit by a spark of gayety, on poor Lily's.

She could not quarrel, nowadays, any more than as a child; but she could look thoroughly, silently wretched, which offended her young man much more.

"I see my company is *dee tropp*, Miss Keag," he said stiffly at last; adding, with a curl of his nose and lip, as if there were bad smells about, "if you know what that means. Indeed, I would have gone to escort some other very handsome young ladies two hours ago; but thought it a pity to see you deserted by your friends."

"I'm sure I wish *over anything*[15] that you hadn't inconvenienced yourself for me!" cried Lily, with reviving spirit; then, seeing a

---

[15] over anything. A literal back-translation of the Ulster-Scots *ower och* (meaning 'best of all') used elsewhere by the author ("*It's ower och —it's beyant the beyants!*")

neighbor at some distance, she hurried towards her, and asked protection for the remainder of the day. The neighbor, who was known as a deaf and particularly querulous old woman, accepted a victim grudgingly enough; although secretly rejoicing.

"I hope you'll enjoy yourself, miss." said Dan, turning away with a malicious grin.

Another miserable long time was spent by poor Lily in turning her neat head anxiously from side to side, watching for deliverance, yet endeavoring to be agreeable to her caretaker, who insisted on being told all the gossip of Ballyboly.

"O! here is Tom Coulter!" she cried at last, with sudden joyousness, beckoning to him eagerly.

"Well, ye're the terriblest wee girl of your age in looking after the boys ever I seen," said the old neighbor vindictively. "It's 'stay with me' while ye want me, but if a lad comes within a mile, hi! ye're up and after him. O—! that's the lasses, all over the world."

"Don't heed her talk. Come away," muttered Tom imperatively; and, as usual, Lily meekly obeyed him. Then, when they had got safely off, he turned to her. "What on this earth took ye to thon ould witch? Ye looked like a poor wee pigeon beside a gray crow!"

Half laughing, half crying, the child told him how matters had gone. But now she felt thoroughly happy; the day was glorified on a sudden; with Tom she had a thorough trust of being cared for, as with no one else she then knew on earth.

"You look as starved as a little crowl. Have you had nothing to eat?" went on Tom.

"Mother had all in her pocket; and so when I lost her I lost my dinner," laughed Lily, as cheery again as a bird. Tom had noted her disconsolate face all morning, from afar. He saw the change now, so no wonder he spoke tenderly to her. Lad though he still was, their disappointment on separation that morning had worked in him to thought already.

He took her away to one of the little temperance booths, and treated her to a cake or two, and some sarsaparilla-water[16], the favorite beverage of teetotalers through the country. Then said Tom, with sparkling eyes—"Have ye heard the news about the Catholics? Boys! but we'll have a spree this evening."

"No. What are they after?" asked Lily, looking up from her tumbler with parted lips.

"Sure, our ones are not going home the same road, but away round by Maghrenagh; and the Catholics say they are coming out to meet us there. And if they do! … Hurroo! there'll be the biggest shindy *ever* was!"

And Tom threw up his cap with a gesture of ecstatic delight. Lily clutched his arm, to his astonishment, she that was, in general, so far from easily frightened.

"But, Tom, they'll kill some of us—they'll maybe hurt *you*."

"Not they. We'll kill them," returned Tom confidently. "Don't be feared. All you women and children will go back the same road as this morning. Do ye really imagine we'd let one of you be hurt?"

"But, Tom, you'll come back with me? Oh! do—Tom! You asked me yesterday to walk with you, and I'll walk home with you," poor Lily still pleaded, with tears in her eyes, her voice trembling.

"What! and miss the fight!" and Tom's face fell as much almost as her own. "Lill, dear, you know well I'd do a heap more for you than for any other one on earth, let alone my own father. But don't ask me to give up this fight—don't now."

So Lily swallowed a sob, and of course did not ask him. They turned away, and almost immediately met Mistress Keag.

"The dear bless us and save us! if I haven't searched for you, child, till I'm heart-sore and sorry," vociferated that false, merry

---

[16] sarsaparilla. Originally a non-alcoholic 'root beer' drink in America produced in the 1800s in Belfast, Maine, USA, and made popular in Ulster during the Temperance Movements of the 1880s.

soul from afar. "Come away home, woman dear. There will be queer work the night—and we've got a lift in a cart. Ochone—O, my corns!—but they'll all be kilt. (It's the boys, I mean; but shure I'm just daundhered in the head!) And Dan'l Gilhorn, quiet lad! will take the seat with us; for his old grandfather would take on the worst *ever* ye heard if he was no' back early. A good grandson! … Take ye that to heart now, Tom Coulter, and stop yer grinning. Danny will be a decent well-to-do man, when ye, maybe—"

"Won't own as much ground as would sod a lark; except, maybe, what might be on my grave, Mistress Keag," answered Tom, with a bitter laugh, for a young lad of his age, when she paused for want of an idea; his allusion being to the fresh scrawls or sods that are daily placed in the cages of caught larks to encourage them to sing. The good woman looked at him surprised; but hurried away to the waiting neighbors. Then Lily was packed into the hinder end of the cart, on a board placed across it; and squeezed between her step-mother and another stout body, shaken to a jelly with jolting over the rough roads, but minding nothing but her fears, was taken homewards at a crawling pace.

"Dear, oh! … The Lord grant there may be no ill fighting," ejaculated the women beside her, at various times. She alone did not thus pray aloud; but only because she was praying all the while in her heart as strong and long as she could, that not a black hair of Tom Coulter's head, nor a gray one of her father's, might be hurt.

All day it had been sultry; but, for an hour back, the sky had been redly copper-colored and lowering. Then—just as the Keag women reached the farm, and just as it was calculated that Orangemen and Roman Catholics would be then about meeting—broke out the most furious thunderstorm ever remembered thereabouts for years. Both bodies of intending combatants scattered away for shelter, it was known afterwards. Had they stayed, it seemed almost as if they and every living thing on the earth's face would have been drowned. Even when the fury of the storm abated, the rain continued to pour in torrents long after the rattle of thunder and blaze of lightning had died away. All straggled homewards then in twos and threes; as James Keag related when, wet and weary, he too reached his door.

"Ochone! but the weather made a sore hand of this day's diversion. My! but it was a pity ye couldn't get at those black Papishes to give them a beating," now bewailed Mrs. Keag, being of such stuff that she herself would willingly have filled her apron with stones to clod therewith all religious opponents. Lily alone was sad and silent. She crept away to the bed she shared with her little sister Osilla, and wept. Wept the night after this great Twelfth of July to which she had so long looked forward; but its disappointments had been so many, and the thoughts it had created so bitter. Still there had been a few bright moments even therein; and Tom had called her "Lily—dear," which for months and months back he would not have ventured to do. Nevertheless, he had been despised, as to his humble birth, by those she held dearest; although praised for well-nigh all things else. Her simple little brain grew confused, till it felt sick, over this complication.

In the morning Osilla woke her up by pushing her and crying—

"Lill, Lill! the rain must have come through the roof last night—look, I see the marks of it on the pillow! That was sore rain, surely!"

And her sister, without seeming astonished, answered, with a sigh—"'Deed was it, Silla dear."

All her life after she remembered that Twelfth of July like an ugly dream.

CHAPTER XIII

"March was it, but a fortaste of the June
The earth had, and the budding linden-grove
About the homestead with the brown bird's tune
Was happy, and the faint blue sky above
The blackthorn blossoms made meet roof for love."

W. Morris.

"Soon as the gray-eyed morning streaks the skies,
And in the doubtful day the woodcock flies,
Her cleanly pail the pretty housewife bears,
And when the plains with ev'ning dews are spread,
The milky burthen smokes upon her head."

Gay.

ALL through the summer, autumn, and winter months after that Twelfth of July matters went on between the inmates of the Keags' and Gilhorns' farms, and with Tom Coulter, much as they had gone upon that unlucky day.

"Except worse," said James Keag's young daughter to herself. "Just the same, but worse!"

Then she, poor child!—for though seventeen now, that is over-young for trouble—would sigh and work the harder at her milking or churning or baking, for thinking did her no good; it only puzzled her honest little brain. Thoroughly obedient and simple as was her nature, she tried duly to please her father and step-mother by subduing ill-will to young Daniel Gilhorn. who began to pay her more and more attention during his regular visits to the country—tried, too, to please poor Tom, and thereby herself, in what small ways she could.

Slowly she had come to feel, rather than know, that she could no longer behave towards Tom, her father's servant, as she had towards her former little playmate. Quietly she acted thereupon—so quietly that even her parents saw no change in her manner, except the becoming reserve natural to her years. But what she and Tom silently felt at this slow sundering was another matter; and would have considerably astonished the elder good couple.

"But they don't mind how much we were together once: they've clean forgotten," thought poor Lily, fairly wondering at times that they never guessed what this anticipated obedience to their yet unaroused wishes cost her.

She did not avoid Tom's company: that was more than she had strength to do. She only avoided yielding to her own wishes to be more with him than was simply necessary—strove to make no occasions for so being; and a strong, continuous, daily temptation she had to struggle against. On the other hand, when the natural events of farm life did bring them together, her secret joy was all the more intense—was shared even more deeply by Tom. She guessed that, indeed; just from a mere look, at times a simple word, that all the rest of the world might, and mostly did, hear and see without noting—all saving herself! And Tom appeared curiously to understand and second her conduct. In silence (for no actual words of explanation crossed their lips) they seemed to agree that thus they must act; as silently resolved that outward necessity should make no difference to their inner feelings.

For their years, such self-control might have seemed to hotter natures impossible. But to them, steadfast, almost stolid, Northerners that they were, it was less difficult than may be imagined. Many a girl round the country had carried on a love affair, not like Lily repressed one, under the very eyes of her unseeing parents. It was but too common. And they were facilitated by a certain amount of free-and-easiness allowed them in behavior, which made a fair-sized cloak for phlegmatic courtship.

Tom indeed bore the oppression caused by this concealment of their feelings far less patiently than the girl. He was moody at his work, and seemed best pleased when alone for hours with his plough and horses; at last, Lily grew aware with secret pain that he frequently avoided her company. She did not know it was to spare himself the necessity of a studied behavior that, to his honest nature, seemed at times unendurable. She had never heard that

"Women can with pleasure feign,
    Men dissemble still with pain—"

what cynical truth therein lies being, perhaps, in its root-origin far more unflattering to men than to women. For are not concealment and subterfuge among all animals, human or otherwise, the resource of the weak oppressed by the strong, and their sad inheritance through generations? God speed the coming of that good time when there shall be no more fear, no more pain of concealment; when all timid, tender natures, often miscalled cunning, shall lose both that semblance and evil reality, and dare to show themselves true in his light—brighter than earthly sun!

And always Lily tried to cheer herself, thinking—"When the new year comes—when next year comes—there must be *some* change." But the new year came, and slipped on; and no change at all came with it, but the lengthening of daylight.

At last, one spring Sunday in church, as she worshipped in her father's pew, and when Tom Coulter had by chance got a seat, with other pewless young men like himself, near her, she grew aware of his eyes seeking her during the lesson. As their glances met, his sought his book again with hasty significance. In some confusion the girl, whose thoughts had been wandering, did likewise, believing that Tom had somehow detected her neglect and was reproaching her, his own attention during service being steadfast. Then, for the first time, she became aware of what words were being uttered by the clergyman. It was the beautiful old love-tale of Genesis; how, ages ago, Jacob served Laban fourteen years, holding them as nothing for the love he bore Rachel, his master's daughter.

At that, Lily bent her eyes downward, and never dared to raise them again during the whole of the service; quiet as she usually was, she became even stiller. But she prayed that day with a sudden frightened fervor, a desperate humility very unusual to her sober soul, feeling her heart strangely stirred, and its excitement thus overflowing.

One day in the following week there was some talk up at the farm about a wedding to be held on the morrow in the village of Blackabbey, about a mile away. The Keags were all bidden to it; but James Keag said, with a smile, that "verily, he had something else to do." And the mistress declared that she also was "too throng" with work to gad about to weddings, her youngest-born being ailing. Otherwise, no one would have gone more readily.

That evening, as Lily was feeding the calves, Tom Coulter, coming out from the byre close by, stopped a moment; and looking at her, and then away at the sweet pale spring sky, remarked quietly—"So you're going to this wedding the morn'?"

"Yes," said Lily very softly; she did not know why. Then aloud she reproached the calves who had started at Tom's approach, lifting their dripping, soft muzzles out of the milk-pail, to transfix him with a great dark-eyed stare. "Sukey, Sukey, … surely you needn't be scared at Tom."

"Would you—be afraid of coming back your lone?" asked Tom, in a voice still more curiously subdued.

"A—wee thing. At least—that is—I'm glad of company—sometimes," murmured Lily, stroking the youngest calf's red head; then, womanlike, found voice to add, "Why—?"

"There's a till-iron" (crowbar) "there needs sharpening. I'll maybe be taking it to the smiddy about the time you'd be coming back," he answered very low; not as if afraid of being overheard, but rather as if awed and quieted by his own words.

As he spoke, his eyes had been fixed upon the half-cut winter-worn ricks behind them, brightened by the dying sunbeams.

Now they came back, to rest a moment on her smooth auburn hair and meek young face, down-bent. Other folk, accustomed to more beauty than is mostly found in that mixed northern race, might hardly have called Lily Keag handsome. But in the eyes of that simple and steadfast-hearted young ploughman she was—from her neat head to the hem of her winsey gown—more bonny and sonsy and douce than any other lass he knew—or ever cared to know.

As he looked, there came a wild, twittering rush of brown sparrows, whirring out from the ricks and down from the eaves in a winged cloud past their heads. The old tortoise-shell cat was peering out of the hole in the hayrick, wherein she had deposited her kittens, with a stealthy air of half gravity, half contempt.

Tom turned away without another word, and left Lily still holding the pail for the calves, that still dallied playfully with their milk. Whish! whirr! … back rushed the sparrows with more noise, as if they had all been startled by a false alarm, or had only been indulging in frolics before roosting time.

The whole farmyard scene around those two would have made a pretty enough picture; but only the cat was there to see it.

CHAPTER XIV

"I told my nymph, I told her true,
  My fields were small, my flocks were few;
  While faltering accents spoke my fear,
  That Flavia might not prove sincere.

"Of crops destroyed by vernal cold,
  And vagrant sheep that left my fold;
  Of these she heard, yet bore to hear;
  And is not Flavia then sincere?

"How chang'd by fortune's fickle wind,
  The friends I lov'd became unkind,
  She heard, and shed a generous tear;
  And Is not Flavia then sincere?

"Go shear your flocks, ye jovial swains,
  Go reap the plenty of your plains;
  Despoil'd of all which you revere,
  I know my Flavia's love's sincere."
                                   SHENSTONE.

IN the following afternoon Orange Lily was sedately tripping homewards after the wedding. She was rather early, she thought, for—meeting any one; so took her time, and gazed about her with enjoyment.

It was late March, and the road was white with dust before her, to her gladness; thinking, like a sensible daughter, of her father's crops, and the farmer's proverb that "A bushel of March dust is worth a bushel of gold." Behind her the noise from the distant village had almost died away. Overhead the sky was brightly blue, swept clean of clouds by late roaring gales, and the sun was smiting in a broad white flash on the land locked salt waters of a lough running up among the low round hills by the south there, while away eastward she caught glimpses through the hedges of the true sea itself, a sapphire edging to the emerald isle.

The gorse hedges around were a golden blaze of yellow blossom, cleanly and sweetly smelling. And Lill felt glad, she did not know why, at sight of the bonny flowers set on their dark-green prickles; the gray slate-cuttings on either side the road; the very gray-green fields, with tufted herbage, where yet the hew grass had not sprung; the brown plough-lands; the low hills roundly rising, one after another, away to the dim blue peaks of the Morne mountains, and Slieve Donard—all broadly lying under that laughing spring sun.

"If Tom was here, but—he would liken it to something for me; and put, what I'm only thinking, into words. He has such beautiful language," the farm-maiden thought, and a tender smile came slowly over her face, making it almost lovely, like the bare land around her, under the influence of the sun-light.

The road ahead took a sharp turn, and round that corner she heard footsteps coming. A sweet blush quickly joined the glad smile on Lily's face, her eyes brightened lovingly, but still she tried to preserve perfect composure; and next moment met face to face—only Daniel Gilhorn!

"O—my! Is it you?" she ejaculated, giving a little jump back at sight of him; then, collecting herself, she more slowly added, "I never expected to see you here in the middle of a week, too."

"He! he!—a pleasant little surprise," said Dan. and smiled at her with his head on one side, fascinatingly. "Well, indeed, the fact of the matter is that me and the heads of our place yonder" (and he inclined his head in contrary direction, as indicating the shop he was employed in, in a certain street of Belfast), "we couldn't agree. So, as I *ree*lly wouldn't put up with them any longer, I just gave them a day's notice and left."

"Humph! Maybe you got '*the turn-out!*'" thought Lily, with sober doubt, but only said—"And so you came this way by accident.

You were, maybe, bound for the wedding?"

"Not I. I was up a bit ago to call upon ye-ou," replied her admirer, with a smile that was insinuating like a wriggle. "And I heard you'd be on the road; so I'm come to escort you, miss … if my company is not disagreeable."

What could poor Lily do? With an inward groan she looked down the straight road for nearly a mile before them. Not a living speck was to be seen on it—no Tom. She was obliged to accept the inevitable.

"And what has become of the weddingers—of the bride and groom?" asked her companion softly, twisting his long neck to fix a gaze of weak-eyed admiration upon her.

"They are gone with their friends on a drive round the country; themselves in an inside car, and two jaunting-cars full, besides. All very nicely done," said Lily, pursing up her lips, as she uttered her verdict of commendation, with quite an old-fashioned air.

"Happy pair!" sighed Danny, in yet more dulcet tones, passing his arm round her waist.

"Och, be off!" retorted Lily, vigorously repulsing him.

He had attempted such endearments before this day; and, like an unsentimental country girl that she was—where her own heart was not concerned—Lill had snubbed him soundly just as often. But now an unpleasant thought struck her from the fatuous expression of his face. He must have passed through the village after his visit to the farm. "And he's been at the drink," she thought. He had not taken much; but "some" he had had.

"You're always so prim and stand-off in your manners," answered Gilhorn, rather crossly. "All the country says it of you."

Which was true enough: but the greater propriety of our poor Orange Lily's behavior, over that of other country lassies, served her but little this day. Whilst they walked on for a mile or two all her wits were busied with trying to keep as much distance as possible betwixt herself and her companion, without attracting his suspicions. She talked, with incessant and demure nervousness, on the most unsentimental subjects; the crops and the weather; what a good price her father had got for his last pigs; and how the baby at home had taken the measles.

In vain! Again and again she was obliged to avoid or downrightly repulse Gilhorn's advances, as before; which only drew on the weak youth into greater eagerness, and tickled his peculiar sense of humor so much that between his jests and continued efforts at teasing, as he regarded them, he found his walk quite delightful—and her timidity emboldened him. Poor Lily's real refinement of mind made her exaggerate moment after moment fears which bolder-minded girls would never have entertained. So that between fretting as to what neighbors would say were they seen walking together, and naturally supposed to be courting, and visions of Tom's feelings thereupon—together with growing dislike to Gilhorn himself—she worked herself into such a state that at last she felt ready to burst out crying.

"So I'm off to Glasgow next week for a situation," said Dan, ending a fresh recital of his wrongs, and again drawing near her.

Lill gave one miserable glance up the road, for not one soul was to be seen on it; and yet *he* had *said* he would meet her—! On one side their highway skirted a belt of Scotch fir-trees, with an undergrowth of gorse, through which could be perceived the surrounding rocks and scree of a long disused slate quarry. On the other lay the open country, with its neat mapping of fields and scrubby hedges, and never a house near, save the smithy far down a lane which neared this one at right-angles. That lane had been the goal of her hope; but she could see no sign of Tom, or other living being, behind its banks topped with whin-bushes. "I'll be soon far from you, across the watter," sighed the young shop-assistant, his mincing town accent sounding odiously in Lily's ears.

Dan succeeded in gazing into her face with spirituous tenderness as he spoke, and noticed its nervous expression, and that her large gray eyes were swimming with frightened tears. With an offensive laugh of delight, believing she was crying at losing him, he rudely caught her again, and, despite struggles and outcries, she felt his lips touch her face with horrified disgust. At that she gave a loud scream of indignation. A shout answered it from the lane. Then, leaping the intervening bank, Tom Coulter himself, stalwart and active, made but a few bounds across the angle of field between, and jumped into the highroad beside them—flinging, as he did so, a crowbar, that he carried on his shoulder, into the ditch, with an impulse that was a strong contrast with Danny's corresponding first instinct, for, to avoid Tom's upraised arm, he sprang behind the girl.

"Coward!" uttered young Coulter between his teeth.

Next instant, however, he was faced by Gilhorn, who dodged successfully one sledge-hammer blow, then attacked him in turn. While the lads fought, Lily stood by, giving fresh little screams at each blow that seemed likely to hurt Tom; but very soon perceiving he could not only protect himself, but was giving his rival a terrible punishment, she calmed in a wonderful degree, yet still fluttered round them, crying, with pitiful entreaties—

"Quit now, Tom dear—ah! quit; don't hurt him more, he's had enough."

"Go, then," said Tom, releasing his victim with a parting kick, "and thank the girl you thought no shame to insult for being let off with a whole bone in your body."

So, recovering his breath with difficulty, slowly picking up his hat, and glaring at them both with dazed eyes the curses he feared to utter, down the road Danny crept.

"What did he to ye?" asked Tom, turning to the young girl, and still heaving with excitement and passion.

She told him.

"Ill-mannered brute!" was Tom's only comment.

Then he turned on his heel, and in a methodical manner began to pick up his crowbar and search for a bag of nails he had dropped somewhere in the lane. Slowly he came back, and found Lily sitting on the bank and still gazing disconsolately down the road at her late persecutor's retreating figure, which had now dwindled to a speck.

"Do you think he'll go to my father and tell on us?" she asked in a timorous voice, dreading that somehow the same view might not be taken by her parents of her defender's conduct as by herself.

"Let him," answered Tom, with a face still sullen with unvented anger; then added, more kindly, "Will ye come home now by the road, or the pad through the fields?"

"Och, through the fields—we'll meet no one," murmured the poor Orange Lily, as ashamed of encountering any neighbor then, as if all could see on her cheeks what had occurred.

"It is more lonesome, certainly; but ye've no need to be feared with *me*, said Tom, with a sarcastic touch in his voice; then again, "I was wondering a bit ago whether you and he would not take to it, and enjoy yourselves more than in the road."

"You saw us then; though I looked and looked and never could see you. When did you—? Oh! Tom, why did you not come sooner?"

"I saw you both a good while ago. Why should I have joined you sooner? For aught I knew, I might have been disturbing good company."

The young girl looked up quickly. She saw his face still dark, while his voice had the offended but truly virtuous "there's-nothing-to-forgive" ring, with which angry folk often aggravate those who love them. What had made Tom so hard and unlike himself? She did not know, and her eyes again silently filled.

They were going through the little wood now, amongst bluish slate-rock and brushwood and reddish-stemmed, dark-topped Scotch firs; and descending a hollow, came into a little opening towards the cultivated country. On either hand beside them rose a bed of rock, all ablaze with such a golden glory of gorse as one great man once dropped on his knees to thank God for giving him to see; and in and out of this whirred the wee brown birds and linties[17], and droned the early bumblebees. Behind and above them, on either side, was the wood, itself a pleasure in that mostly treeless country, and away in front sloped meadow and plough-land down to the broad band of sea, that "blue end of the world," dotted this day with many a sail of lately wind-bound vessels. It was a bonny nook.

Orange Lily's steps lingered as they entered it; soon she stood still.

"Are you not a wee bit tired with carrying that heavy till-iron, Tom?" she hesitatingly asked, glancing at the crowbar on his shoulder.

Tom looked sharply round with an inquiring glance in his dark eyes; then, despite himself, smiled.

"You're tired yourself, and won't own to it. Well—rest awhile," said he; and, merely dropping one end of his burden on the ground, he leant against the rock. As to his master's young daughter, she did as he bade her with a dutiful air, and, finding a resting-place close beside him, let her hands drop in her lap as if weary, and her eyelids droop patiently over her sweet meek eyes. It could not surely be real fatigue that ailed her, that was ridiculous; nor yet nervousness, even considering the scene she had lately gone through, for she would not allow herself to think she had such poor nerves as a fine lady. Still she did feel secretly weak, and, as her step-mother would have said, "all-in-a-tremmle," and was ashamed of her emotion.

But she had been so "put about," she thought, in self-excuse; and so sorely troubled to guess what ailed Tom. *That* was worst!

Once or twice she strove to command her voice and ask him

---

[17] linties = linnets

what was amiss; but could not speak. So they remained there silently in the sunlight. At last, good child that she was, Lill looked softly up at him and asked, with a gentleness that made the words creep softly into his heart—

"Tom, what is wrong with ye? Are you angry still about Daniel Gilhorn?"

He started, touched to emotion at her tone. The brooding look in his face changed swiftly to one of visible passion, to love and anger mingled, that shook his voice unrestrainedly, too, as he answered—

"He kissed ye; and I never even offered [attempted] to do it!"

The answer came low, but clear—

"*Well, Tom—and why didn't ye?*"

Tom looked at her, so staggered, he could not believe his astonished ears.

"Eh!—what?" he uttered, after a moment or two; then burst into a mighty roar of laughter, which, simply as she had taken the matter, made her shamefaced. Then putting his arm about her, for the first time since they had stood as boy and girl under the beanstacks together and sworn to be sweethearts one winter night, Tom took her at her word; although, now that she saw how much greater store he set by the matter than she had (who remembered their childish endearments), the Orange Lily would have drawn back.

A little time later, they were no longer glooming apart, but sitting side by side, and now and then smiling at each other. Any passer-by might have thought them a most soberly-behaved and silent young couple resting there in the sunshine; while in truth they felt giddy with foolish happiness, and did not speak because their bliss was so exquisite they dared not—also because they had known each other so long and so well. After a while Tom gently broke the stillness, in a voice so low and fond that, well as she had thought she knew him, the girl looked up surprised—feeling as if she never *had* known him.

"Did ye not guess, Lill, why I was so backward this good time past in speaking the word?"

Her lips framed a modest "No," bravely uttered.

"How could I name such a thing to you?" the lad asked, with deep feeling," when I had no right so much as to think you would even *look* at the like of me—and no more have I now."

Orange Lily's eyes widened, her lips parted; her whole round, comely face seemed to unclose itself, as it were, from its usual expression of modest reticence to one of open wonder. It was as if a heretofore folded flower had opened its petals wide and displayed its heart.

"But, oh!" she said, "I always looked to marrying you, Tom, and no one else. You surely knew I never *thought* of any other man!"

"I won't deny but I did think—something—of that sort, hesitatingly replied Tom; for, with true refinement and delicacy of feeling, he was loth to admit that he had known well her attachment to himself, the while he had struggled to keep aloof from her, and had never fairly asked it. "But there was so much to sunder us—and is still," he ended, with a sigh.

"What is there?" asked Lily simply. "Did we not agree, when we were wee things, that you were to work, and I was to wait for you?"

Again Tom looked round at her in pure surprise. So that one idea had so sunk into and colored all her simple mind that it seemed now the most natural one possible to her, the only thought of future she was capable of entertaining; whilst *he*—! For days and days, weeks, months back, had he not been on the rack under the pain of alternate plans, doubts, despairs; and yet again hopes that seemed midsummer madness to himself? These had in a perceptible degree sobered him, so that, by common consent, he was granted to be steady now beyond his years, although given to occasional outbreaks of wildness—to himself, when, in desponding moods, he seemed to bear a head grizzled and wrinkled with care already on his young shoulders.

So now, as he still looked at his sweetheart's placid face, and the gray clear eyes that looked back into his with so comfortable an assurance that all would go with them as they wished—because they wished it!—the contrast so vastly tickled his inner self, that seemed conscious of such a dreary store of worldly wisdom, unknown to her, that he surprised both himself and her, and the birds around, by exploding in a long-sustained fit of laughter.

"Don't, Tom—I don't like to be laughed at," said the young girl, with a new and rather pretty pettishness of tone, as being sure of him.

He put his arm about her again, laying his hand on her shoulder in a kindly, protecting manner, and said, with a sigh, and a touch of superior wisdom, rubbing his wrinkled forehead—

"Och! never mind me, dear. I was but laughing at myself … and by reason of being—just too happy."

"But what *should* sunder us now?" she persisted, more fretted by trifles than by greater trials, like many women.

"Let be, dear. No matter! Let us be happy the now," cried Tom, with a wild impatience of surging, quick-thronging warnings, that were even then trying to force themselves on his blissful mind—with eagerness to taste unalloyed joy, he, too, Tom Coulter, for that one most blessed afternoon.

Had he not foreseen all the obstacles between himself, the farm-servant, and his master's daughter; and kept long silence, whilst his heart had been hot within him. And now, at last, chance had tempted him too strongly; love had mastered prudence.

Let be!—for that one day he would be as happy as a king. Afterwards—why both would do the best they could, with God's blessing, the young ploughman trusted, thinking the same with a sigh, yet with brave humility and reverence. His Orange Lily had, in a manner, stepped down to his lower estate of her own will; otherwise, self-contained as he was, he knew not when, or if ever, his poverty-pride and dread of selfishness would have suffered him to have openly asked her.

So now, for another sunny half hour, they sat there among the gorse and talked. And yet, with the peculiar reticence of their northern race, little, if aught, was ever said about their mutual affection, as, till then, it had been barely mentioned. All that was *understood* between them.

"Would ye not nearly believe the sun up yonder was smiling down on the pair of us, and the whole country looking happy-like this day? Why, the very sea is laughing—look at the shine and sparkle of it!" said Lily, who felt again all the joy she had taken an hour or more ago in the sweet, faint beauty of the spring day, but in whom joy was now intensified.

"I'm thinking it's the mind within ye that just makes ye see it rightly the day," answered Tom, staring dreamily and happily over the land, every rood of which was so dearly familiar to him. "For the earth is always full of joy in the Lord, no doubt; though whiles, like winter-times, we'll not can rightly take up the notion of that. But, whilst each new spring is being wrought from within her, she seems to sing a new song of praise—'and the field is joyful, and all that is therein, and all the trees of the wood rejoice.'"

By and by both slowly rose and left with lingering feet that bonny nook, with its wood and whins, and rocks; then passed through the network of small fields before them, homewards. Now they skirted the marsh, and could just see opposite the chimney of Tom's lonely cottage; soon they would be at the Keags' farm.

The afternoon was drawing on. Shortly, too shortly, they must separate, and both go about their several duties; or, if they did meet again a moment, must do so in a common work-a-day manner.

Both, as by silent consent, paused, however, at a gate leading to the Keags' last hill-field, that marched with the Coulters' meadow—that field down which, as a little child, Lily had so often trotted to talk to Tom across the "gap," as he herded his father's cow, or else would help to "shoo" it home.

"Do you mind that Sunday in church, when it was read out about Jacob serving Laban fourteen years for Rachel?" asked Tom suddenly, seeming half ashamed of betraying any feeling that was out of the common.

"I do—well," replied the girl.

"Don't forget it," he impressively ended.

That was all; but, sure enough, she never did forget the earnestness and strength of purpose he put into those few words. Then they separated. The lassie would in her heart have gladly lingered; but Tom's duties of stabling the horses, feeding all the beasts, and seeing everything to rights before six o'clock, weighed so plainly on his mind that he was ashamed to show a sign of her wish. But they smiled in parting, and the face of each seemed to the other as its sun—and, when they turned their backs on one another to go their separate ways, some portion of light and glory seemed to have faded out of the evening sky.

CHAPTER XV

"All my life long
I have beheld with most respect the man
Who knew himself and knew the ways before him,
And from amongst them chose considerately,
With a clear foresight, not a blindfold courage,
And, having chosen, with a steadfast mind
Pursued his purposes."

SIR H. TAYLOR.

"Now banish'd from sweet Erin's shore,
O'er trackless seas forlorn I go,
In distant climates to deplore
My *Ulican dubh, oh!*

"Our flame from every eye to hide
With anxious care we strove,
For stately was her father's pride,
And I had nought but love.
Oh! woe is me, in evil hour
That secret love he came to know,
And I must fly to shun his power,
My *Ulican dubh, oh!*"

From the Irish—MISS BALFOUR.

NEXT day, down at the sea-shore, a cart and horse from every farm round the country was to be seen on the wet, gray sands. There had been a spring tide over night, and a strong gale, so that the surf line was all heaped with wrack, which the young men were busied collecting to cart inland for manure.

Among the rest worked Tom Coulter—hardest of all. The smell of the fresh seaweed, the salt breeze that blew strongly in his face, the sight of the heavy green waves rolling in, still tossed and troubled, were all welcome to him and invigorating.

During the past night he had slept little; but thought much

116

and long. A crisis, he knew, had come in his life, and he must act like a true man. After all, the lad was young, but gallantly tried his best to think over the matter wisely and rightly; and now by morning light he knew his resolve, which, if not altogether pleasant, he yet meant to stick to because right, and felt all the better man therefore. No more easy-going days; farm work that was a pleasure; habits, scenes, and companionship dear since childhood. He would go out into the wilderness and strive to earn bread for two by the sweat of his brow, relying only on his own courage and perseverance, and must wait with long patience. He must rise in the world—ay! higher than the best of his fellows here on the shore. He could do it. He would do it!

And he pitch-forked the wrack into his cart with such vigor, as if to prove to himself what power was in his strong, young arms, that the other men, in passing, called out rough jests to him. "Plainly, James Keag took his work out of him for the wages," they shouted; not that Tom heeded them a bit.

When Tom returned to the farm, he managed, in the course of his work, to meet his young mistress, likewise busied, and he whispered, shortly—

"I would like a word with you this evening"

She nodded, faintly reddening. All day she had gone about like one in a thrice happy dream, and only now, at his voice, roused up to any sense of reality at all. She had been verily mazed.

"In the byre, then, at milking-time?" Coulter hastily asked.

"No, no! The folk are running in and out so much," she interposed, with some vexation.

Her foolish little heart was set on spending those few minutes—however few—alone with her lover. But, whilst she would be seated on her creepie-stool, busily milking, Osilla, who was never happy away from her, would be, maybe, leaning on the crib, and the baby toddling in at the open door, and Hans and Henry-Thomas and Mistress Keag coming to and fro.

"I'll go there a bit later—after supper-time," she offered, in a bashful, pretty murmur.

Tom's brow wrinkled deeply with care.

"As you will, then," he reluctantly answered; "but I have a call" (a right) to be there at milking-time, and none later."

Duty was strong in him—so strong that her love felt jealous for pre-eminence.

And, all that day, Lily was even more tender with the children than ever before, and more helpful to her step-mother; she seemed to have opened her heart in love to the whole world in utter abandonment of self-seeking. Nothing was too disagreeable to her, no work too much, so that she could spare any one; she loved them all so much. Bonny and pleasant though she always was, that day she seemed a very house-angel; although now and again she would stand a second still—lost in a dream.

At supper-time the farmer was grave and preoccupied, and seemed hardly to notice how his gentle daughter at times did or said some little, foolish, loving thing to the children, with a happy face. But Mistress Keag cried out once or twice—

"Lassie dear! what has come over you? It's heartsome to see you." And the buxom, comfort-liking woman smiled on her, well pleased.

An hour later, when the March twilight had come softly over the land, when the cattle were housed, and the noises few, and rest had begun to brood over the farm and its buildings, two figures stood together in the darkening byre close by the farmhouse.

Outside the air was keen enough, but in here the three red cows were roofed snug and warm. Tom was saying, as in haste—

"I daren't keep you long, my own lass, for this very night I must make shift to speak with your father."

"What for, Tom—Tom, what for?"

"To notice him I must quit work here—the first day he can spare me."

"Quit?" the girl gasped, then remained dumbfounded, whilst Tom mistook her silence for sorrowful acquiescence, and went on more softly, betraying his own regret—

"Ay! ay! Well, labor is slack next week, and I know of a boy would suit him. I'd have gone many's the day ago," he added, with a half-sigh, "but I saw how he was thronged with work, and the wee boys too young to help him; and I feared none would do, in my place, all *should* be done. For the work is heavy, dear, and things thriving ill lately, and he's not as strong as he was; so I hadn't the heart to go—sooner."

"And must you go now?" she murmured, knowing well it was true that Tom had stayed at low wages, for her sake, and wrought like two men for her father.

"Would you have me stay on as his hired servant, and be courting his daughter unknownst to him? Would you be honest dealing?" returned Tom, his voice truly very hoarse, but the sterner that he knew all the determination for both must come from himself. "Lill, Lill, don't" (for, putting up her hands, the girl had silently hid her face in her white apron). "Don't hinder me from doing right!"

Poor Lily! All that day she had been so foolishly, indescribably happy; but now!—Tom himself had awakened her by those few honest words to remember their true relations to each other. Yet, O!—she had loved him since childhood almost without knowing it; so slowly had grown to know it that the knowledge had never startled her. He had been as one of themselves, "only far cleverer—all granted that;" that had balanced his inferior position whenever, on this matter, she had put herself through that most difficult process—thinking. And, even then, any vision of marriage was so far away! And always between came dreams that Tom's cleverness would make him rise, somehow, some time; she knew not how, but most surely; she thought not when, for she was very patient. And if even he were never as well-to-do as her father, she could yet manage. Although her father was but a very small farmer, at best, still that had never troubled his contented daughter. But now!—Tom himself made her feel that the man of her choice was, in the eyes of their little world, only her father's farm-servant. She was good and patient, but the sudden revulsion of feeling from foolish love-happiness to mortification brought the tears to her innocent gray eyes.

Neither had spoken since a wee while. The sweet breath of the milch kine was pleasant about them; the silence of the dusky byre was complete, save for the sound of the patient beasts chewing the cud as they lay, or the rattle of a chain, as a cow would turn her head to stare wonderingly at the human beings whose souls so troubled them.

Tom did not see the girl's tears, for he dared not trust himself to look at her face just then. With downbent head, and almost a dogged air, he was nerving himself to tell her all his plan—and have their trial over; for he himself found it worse to bear than he had thought.

"I'll engage to work up at the Castle for Captain Alexander for a bit; so I'll still see you on Sundays," he went on, assuming a brave air, and trying to cheer her.

See him on Sundays!—when it had been every day! The young girl winced, but suppressing all sign of pain, from a modest shame that rose in her heart against showing a greater wish for his company than he for hers, she only murmured in echo—

"For a bit—! Why, where else would you go? Is there a better place anywhere around here?"

"*Here!*—no. But I can't stay here! How could I rise—has a prophet, even, honor in his own country? No, no! Go I must, if ever I am to come back fit to claim you," burst out poor Tom passionately; tenderness for her, vain, wild regrets that fortune had dealt so hardly with him, honest young ambition, and above all hot love, all stirring so strongly within him that he felt well-nigh beside himself. But Lily could no longer restrain her anguish at the thought of verily losing him outright. It seemed as if she could far better have endured his being as poor as now always—but near her. It was all too much. She covered her face with her apron again, while low bitter sobs shook her whole body. Tom's heart was wrung. He caressed her, reasoned, pleaded, tried to comfort her; and so a few—a very few—moments passed.

Then the door beside them suddenly opened, and James Keag stood on the threshold, peering into the partial shadow of the byre, that was now but dimly lighted in the gloaming. Both started asunder; how they knew not. There was a silence so still it seemed *loud*.

The farmer spoke hoarsely then, in the voice both knew betokened that the slow-tempered, quiet man was roused to unusual anger.

"What brings the two of you here?"

No answer.

James Keag swore a big oath now.

"—! What call have either of ye here at this hour?"

Still both were dumb; only Tom groaned in heart—"What call indeed?" Had he not foretold that question?

"Did I see *ye* with your arms about *her?*" demanded the farmer again, leaning forward, with a dangerous quiet, but his eyes blazing in his gray, weather-beaten face on them both.

"You did," said Tom, brave, but still more intensely quiet; and he stepped up beside the girl as he said it.

She gave a little moan, no louder than the cry of a field-mouse in terror, and, leaning against the end of a cow-stall, stole out her hand to rest on Tom's arm, in mute appeal, as it were, praying—

"Help me—tell him."

At that beseeching (it seemed almost caressing) gesture, the father's wrath and disgust burst the dam of self-restraint. Did she demean herself by touching his serving boy before his very face, he vociferated with white, trembling lips, his love for and pride in his first-born, his Orange Lily, his heart's core, that were far deeper than any had ever guessed at, working in him to such wrath that she shrank back horrified.

Then he dared Tom to stand within a yard of her, to ever approach her again; but the latter never stirred. The lad's quietness had a stilling effect upon old James Keag for a moment, yet he stuttered as he went on—

"Beggar! viper! that we hatched unbeknownst to us! There was one told me this day that ye *daured* look up to my daughter, but I would not believe it of ye."

"It's true enough," said poor Tom.

In those few words he said all. They were so full-fraught with love, manly self-respect, steadfastness, but sadness—since cause of reproach might justly be found against him—that other ears would have recognized therein the whole pathetic tale. But even the lad's noble bearing, as he stood upright, with arms folded, as if to receive his sentence, only his head a little bent, his features lightly working despite himself—all in the unwittingly grand attitude of the peasant lad that must have appealed to all fair men—seemed to James Keag but impudence, and worse—insolence—defiance!

For one moment he was staggered at the bold avowal; then from his very soul he cursed the lad for taking advantage of being brought near her as their farm-servant, to ensnare the girl's affections. (No need to ask whether he had succeeded. One glance at the weeping, cowering, childish figure told that.)

"That is what I did not wish to do," most solemnly declared young Coulter, his eyes glowing with earnestness as he spoke. "It was but yesterday we said the word, and that, God knows, by chance; and I intended going this very evening to tell you I must quit."

"It's a lie!" shouted the farmer in his face.

"Oh! father," shrieked Lily, throwing herself between them,

"it's true—he told me so."

Her father turned and struck her.

....

That night, very late, Tom Coulter walked into his father's cottage.

"Where have ye been, my son?" asked the old man, dully rousing from sleep to greet his handsome boy, the one human being whom the poor, listless, lazy, but loving-hearted body apparently cared to keep still alive for, or who could keep him from the whiskey bottle.

"I've been out along the bogs, father, thinking."

A silence next. The father guessed something ailed his strong son, but, knowing his reserve, from apathy and a shrinking from ill news forbore to question him. The son could not speak it yet.

By and by, however, he sat down on the other's bedside slowly, as in his boyish days he had often done, when needing some of the paternal sympathy—which was all, indeed, he could reckon on—and using the old familiar term to a father he had long dropped, said—

"Da, we must flit the country—we must go to America. Dinna ask me why."

"Ochone-och! Must we so, my son?" sighed the old man, whose faculties of mind, always dull, seemed more obscured than usual by sleep, and perhaps some surreptitiously-obtained drink. Then—after some minutes, without surprise, but with dreamy patience, as if having well foreknown that his stirring son would not bide at home content, and that now some scrape, doubtless, had put him in fear of the law—he added—"Well, if we must—we must."

And thus they agreed upon it.

CHAPTER XVI

"Adieu, the simple, the sincere delight—
Th' habitual scene of hill and dale,
The rural herds, the vernal gale,
The tangled vetch's purple bloom,
The fragrance of the bean's perfume,
Be theirs alone who cultivate the soil,
And drink the cup of thirst, and eat the bread of toil."

SHENSTONE.

"When I am far away,
Eibhlin a rúin,
Be gayest of the gay,
Eibhlin a rúin;
Too dear your happiness,
For me to wish it less—
Love has no selfishness,
Eibhlin a rúin.

"And it must be our pride,
Eibhlin a rúin,
Our trusting hearts to hide,
Eibhlin a rúin.
They wish our love to blight,
We'll wait for Fortune's light,
The flowers close up at night,
Eibhlin a rúin."

DAVIES.

ONCE more the orange lilies bloomed beside the door of the farmhouse on the hill. Once more it was the eve of the Twelfth of July, and sweet dusk brooded over the summer land. But there was no gladness in the girl Orange Lily's heart, though her father was still the respected Master of Ballyboly Lodge, and though almost all the other lads and lasses in the country round were preparing gayly for the morrow's anniversary. To her, strong and young though she was, that glorious summer—with its unusually warm days, its brilliantly starlit night-skies, through which wandered a comet—was but hot, weary weather. Each scented summer twilight was heavier with longing and loneliness than the evening before. Each dawn was dead with the sense that one human presence—whose nearness again could alone have given back to earth and sky their sweet fulness of present delights, and joyful hopes of just such gladness still in future—was passing soon from out of the little circle of her world. So soon, she had of late counted the lessening hours with heart-sickness. For the morrow's sunrise was to see young Tom Coulter on his way to America!

Ever since the interrupted meeting between these two, on that March evening, Mistress Keag had kept, by her husband's severe orders, a strict watch that no such scandal should recur. Yet the days had been many since; and her vigilance naturally slackened. What says the old song, written we know not how long ago, or by whom, but as true of human nature to-day as then?—

> "Over the mountains,
>   And over the waves;
> Under the fountains,
>   And under the graves;
> Under floods that are deepest,
>   Which Neptune obey;
> Over rocks that are steepest,
>   Love will find out the way."

And so, nevertheless, they had met since, though but twice or thrice, and that but for moments. It was wrong, no doubt: but this is a history of what they did, not of what they should have done.

They had a strange love-messenger; a wrinkled beldam who lived alone, and who, as an object of popular dislike, and some superstitious fear, was known by the epithet of "thon witch!" The very same whose pet duck had once been accidentally killed by the Misses Alexander's carriage. This miserable old woman hated almost all human beings, excepting always "that decent lass o' James Keag's." Many a winter Lily's savings of scraps had kept life in her; and, though she seldom failed to grumble at the girl, she was attached to her after a strange fashion, while the latter, womanlike, liked the feeling that here was a creature utterly dependent on her. So, this July evening, the old woman crawled up the highroad, and found Lily awaiting her at the turn into the Keags' own lane. Then she paused, panted, and resting on her stick, said slowly, with apparently much complacency—

"Yon one says … they'll be flitting by sunrise the morrow."

"I know! I heard!" said the girl, catching her breath; "but how do they go?"

"'Ow?—by cart till Maghrenagh; then by steam-coach."

There was a little silence. The crone would speak no more awhile, but wheezed, pitying herself in grumbled mutterings for having come so far. Then Lily, though naturally so patient, at last clasped her two hands together and cried out—being able to wait no longer, though that was mostly wisest—

"Och! did he send no other message?"

"Ow, ay, he *did* that!" said the ancient messenger, apparently just bethinking herself of one, and watching the girl's soft, eager face with the maddeningly-slow, interested gaze of some ancient folk who seem to like dimly reviewing human passions as from a long, long way off.

Lily, though good and gentle, could have shaken her; could have cried.

"He said—ay! let me see … Would you meet him the morning, at the Whinny Knowe?"

That evening, when the Keag family gathered round the supper-table in the farm-kitchen, Lily, with difficulty, made a feint of eating; that night for certain she never slept.

ORANGE LILY

How hot it was in the closet she shared with Osilla, although she had set the small window-pane wide open! At times she dozed, yet seemed to hear the child's every soft, regular breath beside her in the darkness; and each time the big clock struck outside in the kitchen, the strokes vibrated through her sleep-dazed brain with a sick pain that always grew, like that of a wretch nearing the morning of doom. All through the short hours of that sweet summer night she heard the rose-bush outside fretting on the pane, though so softly you scarce would know it stirred. Though her eyelids were wearily closed, she seemed aware when the white dawn first glimmered over the farm-fields—to know how it lightened and spread till a small red rim of sun first rose out of the sea, just above the Majempsys' farmhouse, two miles away. Then she could wait no longer, and cautiously rising, so as not to disturb her small sister, the poor child (for, indeed, she was little more) put her head out of the wee window, and, looking, with sleep and grief-dulled eyes, abroad, felt refreshed by a tiny breeze that, blowing to her inland from over the sea, stirred the folds of her white gown and her hair. The dew lay thick on the single rose-bush outside, and sparkled wetly on the little close of red clover on that side of the house, enclosed by elder-bushes; the sunlight seemed busy hunting the shadows out of all dark corners; and—oh! but that was the time to hear what noises the small birds can make, before man is awake and up, and while the world seems all their own—what chirping, twittering, and trilling from early robin to lazier blackbird! The whole earth seemed full of gladness and joy—all but poor young Lily's heart! Still she had done with tears, she told herself.

She dressed now with hasty, yet cautious and tidy fingers, listening anxiously to the clock's ticks, yet taking time to tie her best white apron neatly over her common gown, and a bit of blue ribbon at her throat; and to smooth—then turn and touch yet again—the ruddy hair that framed her innocent young face. Poor face! It looked back at her so white, with such a dull, joyless expression, from the half-foot square of looking-glass fastened against the wall!

"He'll not think much of me this morning," she sighed, dispraising herself.

Then, feeling like a thief, she stole into the kitchen, trembling; heard her father's heavy snores in the parlor beyond; and, lifting the latch with faltering fingers, was out next moment in the newly-risen sun, the dew, and morning breeze.

On she glided, looking fearfully behind her, though not a soul would wake for nigh two hours yet—close by the beech-hedge whereon they dried the washing. Then with flying feet she sped across the open hill, past the cows that stopped cropping the wet grass to raise their heads wonderingly; into a coppice and along the headrig of a neighbor's green, rustling oat-field; then through a last thorn-hedge.

Here rose a stony, uncultivated little hill, forming an angle, round which the high-road passed, and—save for a brake at the top—all overgrown with scattered gorse, whence its name of the Whinny Knowe. This brake was the tryst; and here only Lily paused, panting, but more with agitation than from her run. Then she sat down on the grass, feeling quite wicked at being out there idle at that hour, instead of being still asleep or soberly working.

A long time seemed to pass then.

She began to wonder dully to herself how she could take all so quietly this last morning. She had dreaded that its anguish would be worse than even the daily pain of weeks past, when to her useless longing to see Tom had been added her father's averted face and utter silence, except when he was forced for appearances' sake to speak to her. Plainly her parents had resolved that none must be the wiser for what had passed—yet all the same the farmer's altered manner and his wife's broad watchfulness, that her honest but unrefined nature could hardly disguise—all made the poor girl as miserable as if her love had been cried aloud with contempt and jeers down Ballyboly village.

And yet this morning, when the heart-strings that had wound themselves, all her life, round Tom's constant presence seemed uptorn within her, and loneliness would replace that former sense, she yet could not feel—much; was only aware of being stupidly heart-sick. Once or twice she reproached herself; then again remained still, in a brainless, insensible way.

Minutes passed thus, when a fear, suddenly darting through her, roused her to consciousness of pain again. He was late, surely! All the household at home would miss, follow her! She would not see him now—and perhaps never again. Her heart began to beat once more painfully; the fear grew sharper. Creeping forward, she gazed continually at the bit of dusty road that was visible below the hill, strained her ears to catch the faintest sounds. Moments and moments passed.

Then—at last—far off! Yes, it was—the rumble of a cart.

That sound relieved her from a loving agony of suspense; thenceforth she waited with comparative calm again. Nearer and louder it sounded, strangely loud in the fresh morning stillness; at last came in sight with its three occupants. Even at that distance, she seemed to see how the old father was bent double, whether from grief or in usual apathy. And the aged aunt wept amid the household stuff they had left with her; and which she was taking to another home she had found for herself some twenty miles away, near other relations. But one young figure sprang energetically to the ground; and signing to the others that he would cross the Knowe by a short-cut common to pedestrians, gave the reins into the old man's fingers, and came up the brae with a strong step, while the cart creaked on. The sight of the young ploughman's broad shoulders again, and fresh ruddy face—although it being now a little downbent she could not make out its expression—seemed to console his former master's daughter at once for all her troubles; and she rose silently to meet him.

As silently he approached to greet her, his step heavy now and face firm-set, and took the hand she simply held out with strange slowness. And yet both heard the cart rumbling on that must so soon again draw them asunder. Then Tom just said, in a hoarse, almost gruff voice, as they gazed at each other—

"Well, lass, it has come to this." And she answered, as if her soul was dead—

"Yes."

There was an orange lily in her breast; and, after a while, without a word, she pinned it to his coat. In as stolid a seeming manner he let her do it. And yet, under that outward calm of their self-contained race, both were feeling pain with all the power of their natures; but too much pain to cry out! At their former meetings, tears on her part, embraces on his, had relieved their emotion; now both felt too sorely hurt to stir or make a sign. They heard the cart-wheels creaking round the hill-bend now, while as yet neither had moved or spoken; then the girl said, very low—

"Tom, do you think you'll ever come back?"

"That I can *not* say," replied Tom, with the slow emphasized manner of speech of his class now intensified. "But if I am living I will come, as sure as there is a God above us."

She answered quietly, "I'll wait." And the cart creaked slowly nearer.

The young ploughman turned away his eyes then from those dove-like ones that looked out of the fair girlish face with such unutterable, dumb patience into his. He made as though he were taking a last look away all round the wide expanse of level fields, and down to the sea, where the Majempsys' farm was like a white speck set in green that sunny morn; but a haze seemed over all, and now he could see nought—nought! They heard the cart stop. At that the poor lad brushed the back of his hand heavily over his eyes with a hoarse sound like a laugh; drew the girl to him; kissed her just once, and for the last time. Then he hastily ran down the hill on the further side, not daring to look back.

But above, Orange Lily stood immovable, gazing after the cart, that now recommenced its monotonous rumble, till it lessened and lessened to a mere dark speck still moving away. Then it passed out of sight round a corner, and she put her apron slowly up to her face—not that she was crying, but because her features were working convulsively. The peasant natures of both, transmitted through generations of toil-oppressed ancestors, seemed so used to hardship that they bowed their souls to it in silence. Yet even many others of their own class might have lamented their sad case more audibly. But Lily Keag had always been patient beyond others; while with Tom the oppression of circumstances, the thought of his inferior birth weighing on him since he had left boyhood behind, and known that he loved her, the obligatory suppression of his deep attachment, had all forced his stronger passions back into the secret keeping of his soul.

So, as he left his former playmate—afterwards the woman-child whose affection in their growing years had been all-in-all to the sisterless, motherless boy, his late young mistress, every hair of whose head he so loved, and set his face towards America, thinking, perhaps, never to see her more—Tom's heart felt ready to burst.

"Fate had been sore and heavy on them both!"—sore and heavy!

While he so thought, the girl he thought of was passing slowly home with dragging footsteps and white, still-set face, over dewy grass, and under the unheeded, laughing sunshine and waving branches. Her nature was one that, having endured all it well could, took instinctive refuge in a dull daze of bodily and mental semi-stupor. She might never die of any grief; but she might lose her wits, if too hardly overborne.

When she reached the farm its inmates were beginning to rouse; and by force of habit she went through her morning duties dumbly. And up and up mounted the glorious sun. Oh! but it was—even then, at five o'clock—a brilliant Twelfth of July morning.

Later on, at breakfast, Lily, once looking up, saw her father's eyes fixed with an unusual attention on her face; but next moment he withdrew them, and turned to pet the younger children with toil-roughened hands. These caresses she did not miss, since, with growing years, their affection had been mostly understood between father and daughter; yet, since March, he had hardly once looked her way, never smiled on her, and to those who knew his former silent but excessive fondness for his motherless girl this was terrible. Mistress Keag, to do her justice, had heartily tried to set matters to rights between father and daughter; although the untidy, good-humored soul had at times felt jealous of her husband's evident pride in her orderly, prettily-behaved step-child—but she only made things worse.

"It's well seen the daughter takes after the father for endurance and close-mindedness; they never give in," she gave self-praise, while clattering pots and pans.

"Dear be thanked! me and my childer takes things uncommonly easily."

Breakfast over, Lily mechanically rose and brought in from the garden-plot the finest flower she could find on her namesakes—the orange lilies. Since she could walk, she had never failed to bring her father one on this Twelfth morning; and now she offered it once more, but in silence. He took it in the same manner; then said, with an effort—

"You may as well change your mind and come with us the day; there is time still."

For, some days ago, Lily had ventured to ask her step-mother whether she might be left at home, instead of going to the Orange meeting; a request the latter approved of, as a properly self-inflicted penance.

"No, thank ye, father," said the girl, softly; "one of us must stay to mind the baby—and mother and Silla are quite glad to get going. They like it better than I do."

Without another word the farmer went out. How heavily he went down the lane, she noticed; how little cheerful was his face compared with former years! The poor child wondered was she the cause, and sighed; since many days she had only sighed for herself and poor Tom.

Night came; the hot, long working-day was over. The pleasure seekers had returned, weary, all but the women's tongues. Before the house was shut for the night, Lily slipped outside to be alone and at rest a few moments, and to cool her head. All day, without a moment's pause, she had of necessity been busied with the others' duties, besides her own; and now might well be tired.

She stood in the clover close, at the back side of the house. Above her head the white elder-blooms spread large and sweet unminded; unminded the soft gray moths danced up and down about her feet, and the sky's tender gloom was brightened here and there by a star-spark, as if the little boy-angels, who long ago she had fancied lit the stars up there, considered that was enough light for a summer night. With eyes fixed in the direction of the marsh, though in the darkness it could not be seen, she was thinking of the sea, of the big steamer ploughing now through the summer waves, leaving a milky track behind it in the darkness, while on its deck, fast being hurried on to a cold distant land, far from her and Ireland, was standing, no doubt, the man of all men she had ever known in her young, narrow-bounded life—the handsomest, truest, best she ever had seen or would see in Ballyboly, or in all the parishes round. And no doubt, too—no doubt—he would be thinking of her. The girl's heart felt bursting. Ay! he would be thinking of her, as in the words of the ancient and plaintive Irish song that she had heard sung in English long ago by her mother:

> "The moon calmly sleeps on the ocean,
>   And tinges each white bosom'd sail,
> The barque, scarcely conscious of motion,
>   Glides slowly before the soft gale;
> How vain are the charms they discover,
>   My heart from its sorrows to draw,
> While memory still carries me over,
>   To cailin beog chruite na mbo!
> (*To the pretty girl milking the cow*)"

Poor Orange Lily! The big tears rolled slowly down her cheeks in the dusk twilight, but by and by she felt they had relieved her heart. The summer night-breeze, too, blew softly round her temples like a bath of air, and was grateful.

Suddenly a heavy hand was laid upon her shoulder. She gave a great start, and saw it was her father, who had silently approached her over the clover.

"Lass," he said, quietly, an undercurrent of deep feeling being indicated only by the embarrassed sound and great gravity of his voice, "I'm thinking it's near time now for you and me to make it up together."

"I'm glad of it, father," she replied, half choked.

"I've been sore and bitter against you—but I was that deeply affronted," said he, low; and she knew he was looking away from her into the dusk and shadows, as if he could not bear to speak of this, and see her face, just because of his former great pride and trust in his child.

She murmured back—

"Father, remember he once saved my life!"

"That gives him no right to spoil it to ye now," said the father, with terrible solemnity. "*Better have left ye in the bogwater than demean ye to his level!* Well, well, we'll say no more about it!"

With a shudder the girl silently acquiesced. It was an ill revelation to her that the father on whose love she had counted always as her natural right, seeing even in his late harshness another proof of it, though a painful one, should yet prefer even the idea of her death to that of his pride being lowered with her social abasement. That was not how she loved; she had never thought before that people could love so unlike each other. But, at least, she was very thankful that her father was again reconciled to her.

CHAPTER XVII

"O'Rourke's noble fare will ne'er be forgot,
  By those who were there, or those who were not;
  Come, harper, strike up, but first, by your favor,
  Boy, give us a cup.—Ah, this has some favor!
  O'Rourke's Jolly boys ne'er dreamt of the matter,
  Till rous'd by the noise and musical clatter;
  They dance in a round, cutting capers and ramping,
  A mercy the ground did not burst with their stamping."
                              DEAN SWIFT, *from the Irish.*

THREE months passed; then "word" came to a friend of Tom Coulter's that the emigrants had landed safely—Providence be thanked—that Tom himself had got a little work, and hoped to do rightly.

When this was discussed through the country, at the village doors, or down the road, some wondered that old Coulter had gone so far at his time of life; others blamed Tom for not stopping quietly at home with his father, instead of dragging the latter out to America; while some again believed both had done right. Public opinion was so varied that it was well, perhaps, for the peace of mind of father and son that they had asked no man's advice previously, but had gone their own road. Only James Keag held his peace. When directly asked, however, whether he did not miss his young farm-servant, since it had attracted attention that the latter, though so strong, diligent, and superior to most, had yet rested content with small wages, Tom's former master would slowly reply—"He wrought well—ay, verily!—that no man can deny," and again became silent.

In a few days the talk died out again; so soon are people commonly forgotten, although young Tom had been a favorite with many, and had held up his head high to the rest.

Orange Lily was glad it was so. She had winced every time

ORANGE LILY

Tom's name was uttered, dreading lest Daniel Gilhorn had spoken of them both in his malice and jealousy to others besides her father, and so "talk" would arise—talk, the bugbear of all honest, modest girls like herself; since the village folk had too often tongues like knives, bearing out in their own lives the proverb, "Ill doers are ill deemers." But nothing was whispered as yet; so she grew to feel comparatively grateful to Gilhorn for doing her no more harm, although, indeed, his silence shielded the fact of his own beating.

Meanwhile, day after day slowly passed, and Lill seemed to herself only half alive, half awake; and many things around her went by as if she did or felt them in a dream. At first the poor girl felt almost (not quite) glad Tom was gone, seeing it spared her the sharp pain of knowing him near, yet sundered; later, she heavily thought that the mere chance of seeing him would be worth twice as much torment, one cheery, rousing word from him, bliss. Nevertheless, there was no outward change much seen in her. She rose even earlier, washed, worked, stitched harder, later, and more continuously than even before; that it was done in a spiritless way, few noticed—she had always been so quiet. If at times she utterly despaired, hope was more often still new and young within her. After all, it was not long since Tom had gone. It would, surely, not be very long till he came back again.

Soon after that Christmas came another letter from Tom Coulter to a different friend—this time briefer. Work was scarce, he said, and times bad; but they were going to Chicago, and hoped to do better there. None had written him a line from Ballyboly in answer to his previous letter; and he would like well to hear some word—that was all!

This news filtered through the talk of various neighbors, till at last it saddened Lily's ears. "Ochone!" she murmured to herself … "ochone!" Tom was unlucky, was "thinking long," and the strange longing and home-sickness thereby meant was dreaded greatly by all Ballyboly folk. But soon, according to her nature, she took a sober, very patient, but cheerier view. Her mind pondered and pondered over the words that he "hoped to do better," till Tom himself would have marvelled at their expansion. For in time they filled her with an ever-enlarging certainty that Tom had hoped to do better—*was* doing better—had fine prospects in view—would come home maybe next year, maybe in the one after that! All this while what he had written was but the brief expression of a deep discouragement the poor lad would not make further known.

At the new year time a neighbor, whose soul rejoiced over a new barn as his of the parable did in anticipation, gave an Orange ball[18], in the slated small-enough outhouse in question; and with the rest Mistress Keag and her step daughter were bidden. The barn walls had been roughly whitewashed and decorated with some bits of winter green; the earth floor was swept clean; two or three oil-lamps slung on a cord lighted the scene; and in a corner was the supper-table, set out with cakes and farls, tea-cups, and redolent already of hot whiskey and water.

First the supper was partaken of; then, when their hearts were warmed, and all felt full and satisfied, the dancing duly began. At these gatherings the guests were divided of late into two parties. One comprised all the older folk, who still loved to "foot" it on the floor, and who were anxious to dance none but old-fash-ioned country dances and reels; the other, the fashionably-minded younger ones, who had learnt polkas and waltzes by combining to pay for a dancing-master from Maghrenagh all last winter, and who naturally wished to show off what they had learnt for their money. The latter now carried the contest; and the fiddlers, who were perched on a little platform made of a shutter on two barrels,

---

[18] Orange Ball. A traditional country dance organised by a local lodge, beginning with a ceremonial and ritual 'folk dance' performed by members.

gayly struck up a polka. Away went the young folk dancing, not in a wild throughother jumble like the gentry at the Castle, but cautiously in a ring, six couples only at a time, doing their steps at every corner, and taking good care not to jostle each other, lest a kick from a hob-nailed boot should be given with applause, "to teach them to keep the circle."

Almost all were dancing except Orange Lily herself, whom no one had yet claimed. This was unusual, for she was considered one of the cleverest and genteelest dancers of the new-fangled dances, and besides, was held a beauty in the neighborhood, being thought pleasant-faced by all the men, and popular with both sexes alike for her "quietness"—the most esteemed quality in the north. Her placid nature had complacently accepted a fair amount of continuous respectful homage therefore, while the good maiden trusted rather pharisaically that she was not vain. Now she was conscious of an unpleasant surprise. For a time she told herself that many of her friends often fared likewise; but when the next and the next dances found her still seated on the planks ranged round the rough walls for sitters, her cheeks began to burn, and her eyes sought the floor.

"Woman dear! Are you beside me still? Well, this is new-uns!" (or something new), exclaimed her step-mother, kindly, but with a loud wonder that the poor girl felt ill-timed, since several of the young people near looked round and smiled. She began to wonder was there anything *queer* about her plain black dress and blue ribbons. Certainly many of her friends wore Joseph-garments, and some even displayed red arms through their thin muslin jackets, shocking her better taste; "but the men seemed to admire it," she thought, with a curl of her lip. Mistress Keag's remark had excited the good nature of their hostess, a farmer's wife, who bustled away, exclaiming, to the Orange Lily's mortification, "Dear! dear! I must get her a partner," and approached the youngest Gilhorn cousin, a young man whom most of the girls generally despised as loutish and ill-humored. To make matters worse, he seemed reluctant—he, who in general had no chance of such a favor as a dance with any of the popular girls. Poor Lily felt a mark for all eyes, and at that moment saw, with a start, a blue, piggishly small pair of orbs across the room, whose glance gave her "a turn" like the evil eye. Daniel Gilhorn was there! Home again—no doubt, on a holiday trip from Glasgow.

Back came the farmer's wife, apparently bringing the sought partner after her with difficulty.

"Will ye stand up, Miss Keag?" asked William-Thomas Gilhorn, but with such evident reluctance that the young girl, flushing, replied very distinctly—

"No, I thank you; I like better to sit."

"Well, I was bid ask you," he answered, rudely turning on his heel. And just then the dance ceased, and his cousin Danny passed by.

"Ah! Miss Keag, were *you* not dancing, that I never had the pleasure of remarking you before?" he cried, stopping, so as to arrest the steps and attention of a good many others.

"So you've lost our friend, Mr. Thomas Coulter. You must miss him very much," and he glanced round significantly at the bystanders, some of whom suppressed smiles.

A quicker-witted girl might perhaps have passed worse through such a sudden trial than the poor Orange Lily, who was so slow to understand that any one could wish to pain her that her dewy gray eyes gazed up wideningly at Gilhorn, utterly bewildered as to his drift.

"Oh, ay! We all miss him, of course," she slowly answered, bravely making her words quite distinct. "But my father has got another boy now to do the work."

No elaborate pretence of misunderstanding could have approached the excellence of that dulness. For Dan had so smiled and spoken in such a warm, friendly tone that surely, thought the honest child, he could be no enemy. Next moment the on-lookers began to discourse each other, as if by common consent; something indescribable suggesting that the young girl's answer had given an assurance for good to their minds.

On moved Dan, a sneer just raising his lip above his eye-tooth.

Then—then by degrees it began to dawn on the Orange Lily's mind that what she dreaded had happened … the "talk" had begun! Slowly, as the tide covers the flat sands by the Majempsys' farm-house, bitterness overspread her heart against the traitor who had done this evil to her. So his smile had been that of a wolf in sheep's clothing, had it? She thought indignantly, within her simple soul, that she would always know now what he meant by showing his white teeth like that. Alack! the more she thought about it, the heavier and sorer the poor lass felt her heart.

Just then, raising her down-dropped eye-lids, Lily perceived Big John Gilhorn, Danny's eldest cousin, staring at her. He was the same young man who, some years ago, had offered to back Tom Coulter in a fight against his own cousin Daniel; and now grown older, broad and burly, was as universally esteemed as his brother was held cheap in the Ballyboly parish opinion.

He slowly came forward now, dragging his hands from his pockets with a great visible effort, as if these much disliked be-ing called out for any other duties besides working or feeding. To Orange Lily's amazement, he asked her to dance with him; he whose steps made one think of an elephant dancing a reel—and who was seldom induced thus to divert the company, unless dragged up by his friends. But he was smiling at her so broadly, like a good-natured man-in-the-moon, and he was so well-to-do, even among the richest farmers, and respected, that she quickly said yes.

Great applause followed Big John's appearance, as he stood up with his partner in sign of his readiness to join in the company's diversion. A fire of jests was instantly opened upon him; but in a manner that showed he was the favorite, not the fool, of the merry-makers, and was held of consequence.

"What dance is it to be, John? A gallop, man?—a polka?" "You'll want the whole house to yourself, we're thinking; their's not many of your size will fit in." "Try a schottish, John!"

"Faith and I will *not*, then," quoth Big Gilhorn, decidedly. "None of your new slithery-slathery waltzes for me! What I like best is to see a man get up and take the middle of the floor—and foot it there for a good hour! 'The Soldier's Joy'[19] for me, if I may make so bold as ask that request; and I'll be bound there's a good few here will like to warm themselves alongside of me."

A perfect storm of delight from the partisans of the old dances greeted his declaration. The hostess smiled assent; the fiddlers scraped with an evident pleasure, in the lilt of the well-known old air, and Big John executed a bit of a breakdown by himself with much applause.

"Now, boys, off with your coats," cried he, as the couples formed with alacrity, more than one hale grandfather and grandmother among them, whose steps were the envy and admiration of their degenerate descendants.

In a twinkling the men were in their shirt-sleeves; and then, with an expression of glee contrasting curiously with the careful deportment of the new dancers, they started in the mazes of the vigorous reel. Big John did his steps with a nimbleness wonderful in such a heavy-looking man, finishing up every now and then with a solid pounding that made delicate-nerved folk like his cousin Daniel think it a "puffect mercy that he was on an earth-floor, in which holes were cheaply mended." All such jokes the big man took with smiling placidity; as if, out of kindness to his

---

[19] The Soldiers Joy. A traditional square dance still known and performed in County Down, and the origin of the American square dance of the same name and tune.

friends, he permitted them to make him their butt, yet knew how to keep himself respected.

After the dance, up came Daniel Gilhorn again (as might a gnat determined to sting, with his thin body and white face, thought Lily Keag, shrinking).

Well, Miss Keag, I'm glad to see you've such a fine partner at last," said he, with a laugh that disagreeably curdled what poor equanimity had been restored to his victim. "I'd have danced with you myself, but was afraid you would care for no partner after Mr. *Tammas Cowltert*," emphasizing the vulgar manner of pronunciation as broadly as he could.

The Orange Lily was now roused at last; the color of battle dyed her fresh cheeks redder, the light of war shone in her gray eyes as she turned upon him.

"You know well enough that I never danced with *him* in my life; although I have little doubt upon it that he could beat you in that, like as in other ways."

Her speech, always slow and deliberate, was unconsciously emphasized at the last words by her indignation. Daniel started, tried to speak; but could only produce a sound of anger that failed to be scorn, and with a vindictive glare walked away.

Big John thoughtfully worked about the contents of his pockets, and stared full in his companion's face.

"Wee Danny seems some way spiteful against Tom Coulter," quoth he, plainly. "Miss Keag, can you insense me into the reason for that? for I thought a great heap of that lad, now—in his own position."

The young girl was silent, with her eyes fixed on the mud floor. Her ears seemed to hate the loud laughter around, the stamping of feet, the scraping of fiddles, the close smells; she felt heated, heartsick, and only longed to be home that she might cry in quiet.

"Well, well, I'm not wishing to be troublesome," said big Gilhorn, kindly, if not very delicately; "but you're young, and

I'm sorry for you—that's the truth. And if a body *could* stop the ill tongues that are glad enough to give talk about a girl—"

He slowly ended, and gazed straight at her.

"What talk?" she asked, with a passion she had not felt since she was a little child, when one day the school-children had jeered at Tom Coulter's old clothes. "Mr. Gilhorn, there is nothing true to tell I could be ashamed of; anything else is lies."

"Easy, easy! Why now, I could have told you that; I was just convinced of that when I saw your face so open and innocent there a bit ago, when Dan was at you about it," cried the good-hearted man, jingling the contents of his pockets with a really glad air, for there was no evil joy in him, "and I'll say so to Danny, so I will."

"That would be like warning the thief that you fear there are robbers about," returned the girl, growing almost ironical in the bitterness of her soul. Then, because he looked so puzzled, she told him the whole story of how Daniel had once insulted her and been thereupon chastised by Tom, which was the origin of all his present malice.

When she had finished, Big John, who had listened in utter silence, only wagged his head, and said—

"Ay, ay, Danny has a cur'ous tongue!"

But the poor girl felt somewhat comforted; for in those days it was much to her to get a friendly look as his was, accompanying words that were at least not unfriendly.

During the week that followed, she sorely needed some such comfort; yet got none. For the gossip around had not failed to "acquaint" Mistress Keag what was surmised about a mutual at-tachment between her late ploughboy and step-daughter, and the good woman was very angry. A great gossip herself, she considered it a dire misdemeanor "for any one belonging to her to get talked about;" and good-natured though she was, her fibre was not fine, so she daily lectured her step-daughter on the past, in words that kept a constant raw sore in the latter's soul. Poor Orange Lily had always been proud enough in her quiet way, and held herself aloof from other girls of flighty manner and foolish speech. And now to find that, through a pure and honest love, which had begun unchecked in her childhood and but strengthened with years, never altered, she was considered to have disgraced herself below those others whose doings she had despised, was indeed wormwood and gall to her! But for that lesson, she had been in danger of becoming a good, nicely-mannered Pharisee of a farm maiden; that saved her. She took her moral medicine into a good heart, that happily sought and found in prayer its relief, then strength, hope, and very life; so it became a tonic to her, not a poison; and instead of growing bitter against those folk who so misjudged her, she humbled herself, and felt pitiful and sympathetic to all in her whole little world who were troubled, looked down on, and condemned for misconduct—"most likely wrongly, just like herself—just like herself!"

Lily worked hard, too, in those days, none harder; the good opinion of those she loved and lived amongst was like the very bread of her soul, and in this way only she could regain it.

"Och! ye do well enough now," said her step-mother one evening, after a long day, during which the poor young girl had worked "just out-of-the-common"—"well enough *now*. But if you had been as mindful in your ways last spring, it would have answered ye better."

"Let her alone," said the farmer's voice gruffly enough behind; so that both step-mother and daughter started, having believed him out at work carting manure from the till-midden. "Fair play is a jewel! And there is no use in casting up the past against her now, especially when *it can't change what's done!*"

It was a good thing that none dared tell Keag any gossip against his child; the reason being that the man was so easy-going and humorous that he was well liked through the country, but was known likewise to have a backbone of pride and stern anger in him that caused cowardly and ill-tongued folk to handle him cannily. Nay, not even his wife dared speak a word of it to him, had she been so minded; which she was not, however, "for when you get a quiet, decent man for a husband, it's well to keep him peaceable," she argued to a fireside friend. "And my one would just go clean demented if any one said a bad word of his Orange Lily, there—he'd take their life!"

Nevertheless, James Keag's daughter knew in heart, with sadness, that his pride in her was humbled; that he now looked on her with eyes no longer hard or angry, but dull, puzzled, and regretful. As the weeks wore away, however, so the talk slowly died, so the father began to look around again on his fields with a more cheerful face, and the forgetful step-mother became her careless, kindly self again. But never again could poor Lily feel as before she had—to her sorrow—caused such mortification to those whom she loved so dearly; never forget for a day that she had loved Tom Coulter, her father's farm-servant, whom she still believed worthy of her whole affection.

It happened one noon, at dinner-time, that her father startled her by remarking—

"There is a sough through the country (as I hear tell) that yon two Gilhorn cousins, Danny and Big John, have quarrelled out-right."

"What for—for any sake?" exclaimed Mistress Keag, while such a nervous dread stirred poor Lily that she could not speak. For unkind gossip had not hardened but made her so tender, poor thing, that she winced at the very mention of reports; wondering could Big John have said aught to his cousin about—herself.

"They had been rivals for the old grandfather's money this good wee while back," said the farmer, as he placidly ate his potatoes and bacon. "And they came to words, as folk suppose, about that, the last time Danny was over here from Glasgow."

So that was all! After all, Lily told herself it was foolish ever to think that a man's championship can stop gossip about a woman. And most likely Big John had never thought more of her—after his first good-natured pity at seeing a young girl (like many another!) grieving herself and taking it to heart bitterly that the world seized her name to make sport with, more from idleness than out of mischief. It seemed likely, indeed; for she saw nothing of him more that year.

CHAPTER XVIII

"When seven lang years had come and fled,
  When grief was calm, and hope was dead,
  When scarce was remembered Kilmeny's name,
  Late, late in a gloamin' Kilmeny cam' hame.
    And O, her beauty was fair to see,
    But still and steadfast was her e'e.
    ....
  Her seymar was the lily flower,
  And her cheek the moss-rose in the shower,
  And her voice like the distant melodie
  That floats along the twilight sea.
    But she loved to rake the lonely glen,
    And keepit afar frae the haunts of men."
                                            HOGG[20].

WHEN two more years had come and gone, a report was fitfully
and carelessly passed from one to another of the Ballyboly folk
that old Coulter had died out in America—"him, ye mind, that
lived down by the bog" (for Coulters thereabouts were as plenty
as snipes in the old man's marsh in winter weather). News of it
had come to his aged sister away in the next parish; and one heard
she took it so ill to heart that she had begun to fail, and was not
expected to last long.

Some few in Ballyboly regretted him as a decent, quiet creature. "Ay, verily! The best of that lot," said James Keag once, not
knowing that his daughter overheard him. Her heart swelled more
bitterly by far than his own, at that. For her part, although she

---

[20] In *The Witch of Windy Hill*, May Crommelin quotes from this 1813
'Bonny Kilmeny' poem of James Hogg. The ballad tells how a beautiful
young Scotch village lass, Kilmeny, is abducted by fairies and taken to
the fairy kingdom, where she is kept for seven years. She finally returns
to the mortal realm changed by her experience.

had never allowed herself to despise the dead man, because, as Tom's father, the loving little soul had tried to see only the best in him, she now secretly sided with those who replied that all his life long he had been but a "helpless body"—a dead-alive weight, that had to be supported by his brave young son.

Some wondered what had become of the latter, whose letter had said he was himself going further into the country; then he, too, after that vague mention, seemed as forgotten as though he had gone down into the grave.

After some more weeks, Lily Keag, carefully listening, but not daring to inquire, heard one say that the old aunt was dead too, and very decently buried. Then she knew that the last means of hearing news of the poor toiler, far away in a strange land, was gone. The friends he had before written to went away to work in England. Mr. Redhead, Tom's good pastor and patron, had got a better living. If he ever again wrote home, she never knew it; and doubtless any letters were unclaimed. Thenceforth she never knew whether Tom Coulter was alive or dead.

A change came over her whole life at Ballyboly after that. Instead of straining her soul, as it were, to hear some news of him—ever expecting, even hoping one day, only to dread the next, being often thrilled all through her foolish country maid's heart by such supposed auguries as the flight of three magpies for a wedding, a letter on the candle-snuff, or floating in the shape of a tea-leaf in her cup—she now subsided into an utter calm of mind.

After the inner restlessness, the hidden excitement of watching and waiting for two long years on some chance news, this seemed at first by comparison a rest that was good. Soon it would have turned to stagnation, but for the lesson taught by that previous pain: the grand lesson that some blessed few, like the child Samuel, seem to know from their childhood—that to far more it may be given to learn through excess of this world's pleasures, but that we of the vast human crowd, alas, are taught (doubtless perforce!)

by pain—that happiness for men and women *must* be sought in Him "with whom there is fulness of joy, and at whose right hand are pleasures forevermore."

So Lily Keag learnt her lesson; and came to know that of her own free will she would not have received this blessing … and was even glad.

Time passed, and the children at the Keags' farm grew bigger under Lily's sisterly eyes; the father perceptibly aged. Little fresh interests sprang up and died away—other broods of chickens, new calves, more crops to watch and reap and house; and the summers waxed and waned. Meanwhile, Lily herself apparently lived heartily, did her quiet work without flagging, ate well enough, slept well enough. That she seldom laughed caused no remark, she had always been so quiet; but the smile that more often lit up her grave, comely face grew always sweeter, till at last some thought it the sweetest they had ever seen on human face.

Big John Gilhorn was one of these; the rest no lovers.

Orange Lily, since she had grown up (even though the gossip about her first fresh youth was never revived), seemed to have had none; for, though she went to most yearly Orange-gathering, fairs, and the few farm merry-makings like her fellows, and took a sober enjoyment therein, and though on summer evenings she might, and at times did, join other maidens and young men strolling down the road, and was singularly well liked by both—yet so it was. Most often she herself never thought about it. But again, at times, when her step-mother would bluntly wonder aloud at the young woman's continued singleness, with intentional, if inconsiderate, kindness, giving her, unasked, the consoling assurance "that 'deed, perhaps, she was far better not to be caring about marriage like other girls"—in the next breath fervently hoping that Osilla would not take after her—at such times smiling doubtfully, Lill did feel something vexed that it was true, and that none seemed to desire her. Whiles she would, being an ordinary woman with some vanity in her still, say to herself with a half sigh, half smile that "maybe it was because she had just no heart that way;" then would go about her work again.

Little by little, Lily came in the succeeding years to be most highly thought of among the neighbors around. The parents praised her as the most hard-working daughter and God-fearing young woman they knew. The girls all liked her because she was so "quiet" (word of praise!); and because she sought no man's admiration. None envied her.

The younger men looked likingly on her from a little distance, but came no nearer; kept off by that very quietness and goodness which awed most, they knew not wherefore, with the sense of one superior to themselves—purified, they knew not by what—looking higher than themselves, although living like themselves amidst ploughed fields, and busied with like cares of seed-time and harvest, of cattle-rearing and farm rent. Some few approached indeed; but silently felt she was not for such as they, and passed away to other flames, unsinged and even more friendly. With the quieter and older ones she was best understood, and talked more freely, for there was hardly an unmarried man of middle age in the countryside. But, naturally enough, her heart could not be altogether satisfied with their and their wives' friendly almost reverent admiration, and yet—"Her heart was not in it; that was all!"

So the time slipped on, and she was fairly happy, like old folks in autumn; yet knew herself to be living but a half life—a dream-life, in which no wound hurt her deeply, and no joy gladdened her all through her soul.

Nevertheless, there was still mirth enough up at the farm, as of old; for the youngest children were still little, troublesome, and happy. James Keag, despite gathering wrinkles, could put away care for his crops and crack his quiet joke. The good wife was not a hair grayer, nor a day older, as she often lustily declared with laughter; and Osilla, who was now a lanky, dark young creature, with a child's face and a woman's figure, bid fair to be as merry and careless as her mother. The neighbors visited them readily; but most regularly of all, though at long enough intervals, came Big John Gilhorn. What he liked was to smoke quietly with the farmer; and what Mistress Keag liked was to retail him all her gossip meanwhile. And a quarter of an hour after some "quare joke," to which he had silently listened, the big man would astonish everybody by bursting into a great quiet laugh; having only then come to understand its merits. He let the children romp with him as they willed, being especially fond of Osilla, whom he called his own wee girl. But the eldest sister he only watched in silence year by year, as she moved about gently; apparently evermore busied in tidying up matters in the rather disorderly farmhouse.

CHAPTER XIX

"The youth had wit himself, and could afford
A witty neighbor his good word.
Though scandal was his joy, he would not swear:
An oath had made the ladies stare."

MALLET.

"An acquaintance, a friend as he called himself, entered;
An under-bred, fine-spoken fellow was he."

GOLDSMITH.

IT was six years after Tom Coulter had left the country, when, one Sunday afternoon in summer time, Big John sauntered over towards the Keags' farmhouse. All the family were sitting down below their own hill-field, by the marsh-edge, where was a sunny bank, and just below it a spring that bubbled out, strongly impregnated with iron, and celebrated thereabouts for its good properties, as the Spa Well. This was a favorite Sunday evening resort for the neighbors, who liked lolling on the grass, and had a firm belief in the strengthening virtues of "a sup of the water" for curing the ailments of the week. This day there were also there some cronies of James Keag's; one or two girls who were friendly with Lily; and two farmers' sons.

Big John was welcomed from afar by all. For, though owning a much bigger farm and better position than any of these, he was so "free" (*i.e.*, friendly) to every one, and not in the least proud, that all his poorer friends were as much at their ease when entertaining him as if he supped no better than themselves.

"You're quite a stranger—ay, verily!" slowly observed James Keag, with a twinkle in his eye; for, somehow, whatever commonplace remark was made by any one to Big Gilhorn was considered by the speaker as in some degree a joke.

"Well … how is everyone?" asked the new-comer, beaming a

wide smile on the whole circle; and (evidently considering it too much trouble to shake so many hands) only offering his broad palm heavily to the Orange Lily, to whom most folk showed their best manners. Everybody else felt that, somehow, as quite natural; and when he did not stay beside her, as any one who was paying her attention might have done, but stretched his large person on the grass beside Mistress Keag, who merrily invited him near herself, every one took that, somehow, as equally natural.

It was the children who always gathered round Lily's knee, while she talked softly to them, and kept them quietly happy in a wise, motherly manner, that it was pretty to watch. Now and again the others did so watch her with pleased eyes. If the bloom and soft roundness of earliest girlhood had vanished from her face, it had a sweet, steadfast expression of features, a tender, far-away look in the gray eyes, that touched some of them strangely. The men thought her a saint—and wished themselves were better. The girls thought her so good that—they were glad they were not quite as good! Perhaps they credited her with even more moral strictness than poor Lily truly had; not understanding why she cared so little for being admired by the men thereabouts, or should shrink from the somewhat unrefined compliments that other girls accepted from their swains—unless that she was just too religious!

Mistress Keag, having the giant so near her, like Gulliver among the little folk, now began to make sport for the rest with a most approved old joke.

"It's so long since we've seen you, Mr. Gilhorn, we just believed you were thinking long to be married, and was away courting. It's time for you, man dear!"

As the parish favorite was held to be a confirmed bachelor already, being shy of girls, this sally evoked much applause.

"Time enough," John answered, lazily staring over the marsh, green with flags and rushes, while here and there great creamy spikes of meadow-sweet scented the warm air. "I knew a man once

…" he began, slowly, in a story-telling voice, and every one looked up interested, for a story from John was a rarity indeed, and at no time a common possession of their own. Then Gilhorn went on: "I knew this man once; and there was a woman he liked very well. And he thought about it for five or six years, till at last he made up his mind till marry her. Well, he mentioned the matter to his father, and *he* was not agreeable. So the man just waited till, after awhile, the father died—and that was some years. And he spoke again to his mother; but she was someways disinclined for it, so he thought best to wait till *she* died—and, faith! She took a longer time about it. But at the last there was just him and woman for it!" (Here Big John artfully paused; and all listened attentively.) "So then he named it to herself; and she said that 'deed she was not just that ways inclined! She had her own house, and plenty to keep her, and was not to say young by then, nor in want of a change. Well, there were plenty other weemen would have taken the man, but he inclined to none of them, and just every Sunday evening he would walk down regular to see her; and did so still when I knew him afore he died, though turned seventy. And at the last, when he took bad, he said what came sorest upon him was missing that Sunday walk."

"And do ye tell me that he never brisked himself up to look out for another wife, but daundered on all his life?" exclaimed Mistress Keag.

"Just so! He was a quiet sort of man—like me," placidly replied Big John; and while the rest broke out in a babble of remark, most joining in Mrs. Keag's jeers, he rolled over on his other side near quiet Orange Lily, and chose himself a fresh grass-stalk to chew. She withdrew her eyes from studying the horizon, and said, softly,

"Mr. Gilhorn, I think I would have liked that man."

John's face broadened with delight.

"No, would ye—would ye, really, now? Would you, really?" he repeated, unable to express his satisfaction with variety, but hugely enjoying it all the same. In general he felt awed by the great moral and mental superiority over himself which the simple man rightly or wrongly imputed to Lily; her wits being, indeed, as a farthing candle to his rushlight. But just now she looked so gently and propitiously at him—put him so at his ease, unlike other girls, who teased him to attract his attention, that, after five full minutes' cogitation, he was about to hazard a weighty and different remark from his last… !

At that moment up ran Osilla, her wild head crowned with meadow sweet, and flinging herself down, began pelting John's nose with bits of flowers. Her mother burst out laughing, and cried, "Look at her!" Lill looked up perturbed, and just uttered one quiet, loving "Silla!" and the young sister stopped at once. She was a trouble to her thoughtful step-sister at times, seeming too unwilling to adopt the decorum of girlhood; and while as innocent as the youngest of the children, being, despite her added years, just as hard to keep in bounds.

"You're like one of the play-actresses at the show in Maghrenagh," observed John, grinning at his especial favorite, who always tried to monopolize him. "And I wouldn't mind" (with a great effort) "escorting you and Miss Keag to see them—if the mistress is willing."

"O ma! ma!—say yes," ejaculated Osilla, in an ecstasy.

"Mother dear, I've heard it isn't a nice place, indeed; thanking Mr. Gilhorn most kindly all the same," pleaded poor Lily, in dismay; for indeed the show was far from edifying, and John, looking at her face, could have bitten his tongue out.

"Och! now, don't preach at us, Lill! Sure I'd like to go myself. Plenty of respectable people does go," retorted her step-mother, half crossly, half in banter; for, being rather a rake in heart, the fat old soul was just dying to see it.

"Ay! but they say they are sorry for it," Lily softly expostulated.

"Well!— well!—well! I always let the womenkind fight it out;

and then I'm ready for whatever is finally agreed on," quoth John, in some haste, for he was an arrant big coward, as regarded feminine squabbles; then he rolled over to graze, like Nebuchadnezzar, in another direction.

"Just in time for a squabble among the ladies! The pretty dears will take to their nails in a minute. He! he!" said the voice of a new-comer from behind, with what, in Orange Lily's ears, sounded an evil sneer. She knew, at his first word, that Daniel Gilhorn—the only man whom she had ever looked on as an enemy—was back on one of his periodical visits to Ballyboly. Her old repugnance, almost hatred, since he had tried to harm her by his tongue, rose up and filled her heart so suddenly that the day seemed cold and the sun shadowed. Then, horrified at her own lapse, because it was her nightly prayer that she might be helped to forgive him thoroughly as all others, she rose with an effort, and was the first to hold out her hand with all the greater cordiality. But Danny backed from her with affected horror.

"Hold her somebody; she wants to scratch my eyes out! Miss Keag, I'm puffickly shocked—you that I thought had taken to religion with years."

Some of the more unthinking listeners laughed at this, as most greeted the new-comer; Lily Keag's sweet face slowly flushed. Danny, simpering at his own wit, placed himself as centre in the circle, smiling around, and began again.

"*Reelly, reelly!* it is quite dreadful to see the bad passions that exist among such dear creatures as the female sex. But though, no doubt, you have been abusing each other very badly, Miss Keag there knows it is a Christian duty to forget and forgive; though maybe she herself may not always practise it. Mrs. Keag—my dear madam—I know you are not the lady to stand up for yourself, unless you are just trampled down, but we must make allowances for your step-daughter, that is such a saint—nowadays!" (here Danny airily waved his hand). "These pious people like having their own way, you know. Now—what is this little dispute?"

"As you did not think it worth while to ask sooner, it is not worth while telling you now," calmly said Lily; her clear voice sounding before the rest had time to give their expected tribute of a general giggle.

Then she turned away to her youngest brother, an urchin that was dabbling in the iron-ooze, and staining his pinafore yellow with rust. Danny looked slightly discountenanced by her placidity, but tried fresh ground in haste.

"Well, Cousin John—haven't spoken to you yet—but no offence. I hope—he, he!—that you're glad to see me."

Up got John Gilhorn, stretched himself silently to his full height and breadth, looked down at his cousin, as if, but that he disdained touching such a worm, he would "knock him into smithereens;" and gravely said,

"James Keag … if it's agreeable to you … I'd be glad to go now and see your pigs."

At tea in the farm kitchen, that evening, Mistress Keag, who was as unobservant as she was good-humored, remarked, in a tone of triumph, when her husband and guest came in and sat down at the board,

"Ah! Mr. Gilhorn, I was telling your cousin Danny that Lill would not let even an old wife like me go to the Maghrenagh show—and he up like a man, and says he'll take me himself! Now you'll come too, with Osilla, quick enough."

Big John laid down the round of bread and butter he was just going to bite into, and said, emphatically,

"You'll excuse me, ma'am … but I'll not stir one foot! I don't speak to Daniel; nor will I suffer him to speak to me. And I'm—I'm queerly surprised that you bore with his impudence this very day."

"Hut! Danny must always have his joke! And very pleasant-spoken he is to me; although he and Lill seem to have some turn against each other," retorted the good wife, warmly; for she would never be too old not to be gratified by a young man's compliments. And neither she nor her husband understood well why Danny and their daughter were not on good terms; when he was so civil to themselves, some part of the fault was surely hers.

Keag now fairly roared laughing; for to see John roused, and his big face redden like a setting sun, was a rare sight.

"Ah! my boy, I'm feared Daniel has got the best of you with the old grandfather," he cried.

"Faith! and he has," returned John, with recovered good temper, biting his bread like an alligator, after that short fast. "I am 'the worst in the world' with the poor old man now—and Daniel is all in all! So I've not been near the farm this some time past—nor will go."

When tea was finished. Orange Lily silently collected all the broken bread; and her father, perceiving John Gilhorn's eyes upon her, said, half in apology, half proudly, in a whisper,

"It's to feed that old witch down the road there. My girl has kept her alive for years. I trust she'll be repaid in heaven; for faith! she doesn't even get thanks from her here."

The farmer's pride in his eldest daughter was as great once more, but curiously different from that he had felt years ago in the bonny lass whose manners so far surpassed those of her fellows. He felt now as one who had unwittingly reared a saint—an incomparable but rather incomprehensible daughter, who was doubtless praiseworthily but uncomfortably anxious to wash the feet of others not half so good as herself. The process of readjusting his good opinion of his child had been slow and puzzling; but at last was done. He judged her now as one of those blessed but simple-minded people in whom worldly wisdom is not to be expected; and only thought of her early attachment as a mental aberration, excusable in one whose conscience forbade her being a respecter of persons, and a proof that if such good people's friends were only properly determined with them they could save them from becoming utter fanatics.

The two men strolled outside to smoke then, while the good-wife was preparing the pig's pottage. She seemed always either preparing or dispensing; while, on the contrary, her step-daughter was as continually putting by broken bread, mending and tidying. For it often brought a thought-wrinkle on the latter's smooth forehead that in their family the mouths were now more, and the bodies bigger, to be fed; and yet crops had been bad and the rent backward, and her father, who had never been a strong man, was feebler now. By and by Lill went out and began collecting hens and chickens and ducks, to shut them up for the night; then Big John slowly approached her, and took his pipe from his mouth.

"I wonder, now, you don't make the children do that," said he, glancing with a newly-come disapprobation to where Osilla and her brothers were indulging in romps round the horse-pond—merry enough to watch, but no more useful in John's opinion, that moment, than the gambols of rabbits. "You are breeding them up to be lazy."

"Indeed, Mr. Gilhorn, I do try to do the best for them," answered the Orange Lily, somewhat perturbed at such an unexpected reproach.

"I won't gainsay, but you do," solemnly replied her self-made judge. "But you are like a new policeman; you do your duty, but you do *more* nor your duty! You are always for sparing them—and who thinks of sparing you?"

With increased surprise, Orange Lily could find nothing to say but "Shoo—shoo! now," to those most foolish of birds, the turkeys. John came nearer and cleared his throat portentously three times, each time pausing in a most ominous way to speak.

"And I wanted to speak … I have a thing to say … for I'm just heart-sorry now to have even named the show to you; and that's the truth! … And I ask your pardon for thinking *you* would go

… And—and that's all!"

"You could not say more; and thank you kindly," said the young woman, giving a gracious glance into his eyes, that seemed to him to go thence plumb down into his soft heart.

Then, after a few seconds of chicken manoeuvring—for it was hard to count them all on the roost—Lill, feeling encouraged to speak openly, and womanlike, enjoying the opportunity of preaching a little sermon to a man whose friendship and good-humor she reckoned on to make him take it not ill, said in her turn,

"And if you'll excuse *me*, Mr. Gilhorn, I was a little troubled in mind to hear you speak as you did of your cousin this evening. Surely you ought to forgive him;" and Lill paused with her hand on the fowl-house half-door, and looked up with reproach and pleading deepening her good gray eyes. "It's not Christian, you know, to bear malice; although he has, no doubt, ill-treated you … I—I had something against him myself once, but forgave it long ago."

Big John stared with a most troubled look at the comely, accusing farm-angel, who so arraigned him; and his whole body heaved with a reproachful sigh, like a breeze of wind.

"Well, now! … I never expected that from *you;* when it was about yourself, and none else, the first quarrel arose betwixt him and me, now five years ago … and six months! And a Christian I can be when it's only to forgive what harm he does myself; but I disremember where we are bidden forgive the harm done on those we care a heap more for *than* ourselves … ! O—just, I can never get over how ill he abused you!"

A thrill of pleasure vibrated through poor Lill one moment. The next she reproached herself for such a feeling sprung from the vain and baser part of her nature. Yet it was long—so long since she had had words spoken to her in such a tender strain! And the love of her family was only her natural right; the almost universal esteem of the neighbors she was used to, and gave it no thought; but this seemed to be a warmer, more satisfying tribute of respect, after all, to a lonely human heart—no more, of course! So she was amazed and rather glad, but ashamed to be at all thus moved; and fumbled at the door-hasp with awkward fingers and eyes soberly downcast. At last she murmured, "Indeed, indeed, I am not near worthy that you should mind that all this time, Mr. Gilhorn; but thank you very much." Then, with an irrepressible ejaculation of wonder, "And I who never thought you were such an' a friend of mine!"

"Who else, under heaven, did you think I came visiting here *for?*" returned Big John, in a deep, somewhat agitated grumble, meant for a murmur, churning the keys and coppers in his pockets hurriedly up and down.

Then he glanced with a rather piteous uncomfortableness at the farmyard, round which the children were racing, apparently bent on pulling each other's hair; whilst close by Osilla and her brothers were teasing the collie dog.

"It's a throughother place this. Won't you come down by the beech hedge a minute … ah do!"

"I can't. I must feed the pigs," hastily returned the girl, and she leant against the pump, as if glad to know that everything in the world was not unreal, nor changed strangely in the twinkling of an eye, like this, her acquaintance of years.

"Could you not speak here, please; if—you have really anything to say?"

Big John gave a sort of groan.

"Och, I *could* … and maybe it's as well said one place as another … but the long and the short of it is this, Miss Keag, though I've noticed rightly you've never been much on for marrying—*I am!!* … It came on me a year or two ago. And if you can noways make up your mind to have me, well … and … good! But, if you incline towards me, why—why—well and better!" And with a great effort he pulled both hands out of his pockets.

Lill felt almost giddy; her face paled, and she looked utterly dismayed and sorrow-stricken.

"O Mr. Gilhorn, I'm sorry with my whole heart," was all she found breath to whisper.

"Ay, ay, I was thinking as much," said Big John, very slowly, after a pause, during which both heard the ticking of his great turnip-sized watch; then he turned his back, and, staring at the barn wall, added, "You'll be like the woman I spoke of this very day—not just that ways inclined."

"There are plenty of others in the country, Mr. Gilhorn, better looking, and with more fortune nor me, who would be glad enough—"

"Sure I know—I know!—I *know!*" and John desperately waved his arm, as though implying they bothered his very soul. "But a woman's more plague than peace, unless I get a bit used to her, quiet like; and I've watched you this three years … ! Maybe, after another wee bit— Well, well! … Good-evening."

And away he trudged, while the children clamored after him. Orange Lily slipped into the byre alone; and sitting down there sadly, thought awhile of such another time nearly seven years ago.

CHAPTER XX

"Dust unto dust.
To this all must:
The tenant hast resigned
The faded form
To waste and worm—
Corruption claims her kind."
SCOTT.

SOME two or three years past, Colonel Alexander, up at the Castle, had "got married on an English lady with an estate and fortune," as the Ballyboly people expressed it. So more than half the year was spent by them across the water, although they regularly paid visits to their home in Ulster. But the twin sisters still kept their own rooms at the Castle at all times, owing to their younger brother's kindness; and yearly increased in gladness and in all good works, although Miss Edith's health had somewhat failed, and she required a donkey-chair.

One day, the Castle ladies were brought on a silver salver what seemed a begging missive, as was not unusual; dirty, and smelling of peat-reek. It ran as follows:

"DEAR MADAMS, with respect too youre owic ladyships and in the naime off the lord I umbly creaive the request of yez both to cum and spake a wored in private. I amm 86 yeares of aige and no more speedy att travalin and has none too seport me being a Dessolet orfant. So youre ladyships will see that theaire iss a call for a fire onn the harth too warem sum Drinks for a sickley hart and a soone Departing sperit.

"but i doo not craiv a Peneworth, onely too just say this one wurred too you afore i go. No more at present from youre umble tenent.

MAREY DEVVELIN."

The name was quite unfamiliar to the lady-sisters; but, on inquiry, they found it was that of the old crone who was generally regarded by the Ballyboly folk as Orange Lily's tame witch, whom

164

she alone by her goodness controlled (and that not always!) from overlooking their cattle and casting an evil eye on the children. Going down to her mud cabin, accordingly, with gifts in their hands—since they disbelieved in the pride of her letter—they were surprised to find the ancient woman as forbidding and morose as in the days when she had barred her door against them. Although she allowed them to cross her threshold, she took their alms without thanks; and neither time nor trouble seemed likely to elicit what she had really wanted, since on this point she would only grunt. At last, just as with worn-out patience they rose to go, she suddenly produced a tattered Bible; and politely remarking that she considered them the only honest people in the country, intimated that they were to be witnesses to her will, which was written, as follows, on the fly-leaf:

"I bestowe all i hae onn James Keag's eldest dochterr barring what iss to bury mee in the tea-pot."

"And the Lord knows, that's little," she added, glowering at the sisters as if fearing they might rob her. Considering that she had lived by begging and stealing, until of late Lily Keag had altogether supported her, the Misses Alexander by no means doubted the truth of that last assertion; and only wondered what miserable rags would be the reward of that poor old soul's good human angel.

Some three months later, however, the witch was found dead in her bed. And on Orange Lily going down with her father to perform out of pure charity what they now could for the dead, they found, to their unspeakable surprise, nearly five pounds in silver in that same tea-pot. Other and far larger sums were discovered secreted up the chimney, in the thatch, and under the mattress; forty pounds in all. So, since no one disputed the will, the ladies having told of its existence, Lill, seeking heavenly treasure, got a small earthly dower, and became an example of the rewards of virtue which set all the other young women of Ballyboly for some time crazed to support aged beggar women likewise.

One day the "old ladies," as they began to be called, came up to the farm to congratulate their young friend and former school-favorite in their gentle formal way; and the one asked,

"By the way, Lily, did you ever finish your feather-bed?"

"Just last year, Miss Edith. It was slow work picking up the feathers," answered the young woman, with a patient, apologetic smile.

"And now that I think of it, did you ever hear what became of your little playfellow of old, Thomas Coulter," the other twin added, being reminded of bygone days by her sister's question.

"No, Miss Alice."

"Och! he's settled and married out in America—or maybe dead. Anyhow, he has clean forgotten Ballyboly," lustily replied Mistress Keag, who never shunned answering on this subject, as if they had nothing to conceal; although, to do her justice, she had not once broached it herself for some five years back.

Clean forgotten! The words rang afterwards, in still moments, in poor Orange Lily's ears, like a far-off knell, which earth's noises mostly drown. Maybe, indeed, it was true; she could not tell! For now, most often, she seemed to herself waiting for one who yet she knew would never come; and yet could not but wait. If alive, she still believed—not daring to appoint times or seasons to the fulfilment of her thought—that he would return. But often another thought came that he was dead; perhaps long, weary months ago.

That was a trying autumn on old folk. They died, "verily," said James Keag, "as the ripe horse-chestnuts drop from the trees;" and amongst the rest the old grandfather Gilhorn was laid beside his fathers' graves in the full churchyard. Few were surprised, but most were sorry to hear that he had left all he possessed to Daniel Gilhorn, but not a halfpenny of his large savings to Big John.

"Och! it was the blarneying that done it," was the universal opinion through the country side; and although Danny swaggeringly promised to take a farm and settle in Ballyboly, foreseeing that he would be a little king in the country, but not much of a man in town, the neighbors would have preferred his cousin of few words to be a "big man," in both senses, among them.

CHAPTER XXI

"Blest be those feasts with simple plenty crown'd.
Where all the ruddy family around
Laugh at the jests or pranks that never fail,
Or sigh with pity at some mournful tale;
Or press the bashful stranger to his food,
And learn the luxury of doing good."

GOLDSMITH.

"One
Who thinks the all-encircling sun
Rises and sets in his backyard."

GOLDSMITH.

ONE evening, in the following spring, John Gilhorn came up to the Keags' farm to drink tea, and accompany them to a village concert at Ballyboly. This was got up by the good Alexander ladies, under the patronage of the colonel himself and his wife; while the performers were to be some guests who were staying at the Castle, and also the church choir.

When Orange Lily entered the kitchen from putting on her neat black Sunday gown, she saw an unusual stir, and her step-mother, with a jubilant countenance, frying something.

"Pancakes to-day, mother!—what day is it?" the little ones were clamoring, plucking at her gown, for these dainties were significant of a gala day. And "Pancakes—what has happened?" echoed Osilla, with a joyful sound, poking a wild black head out of the closet she shared with her sister, then blushed.

"O Mr. Gilhorn, I didn't know you were here, or I'd have come sooner."

"Ay! verily, it's for him the pancakes is. Oh, there's great news of him entirely! He's been at Maghrenagh fair, I'm thinking—haven't ye, John?" humorously observed James Keag, and winked at his sons.

As this was the great "courting fair" of the district, supposed to be peculiarly frequented by young folk "up for marrying," the two merry, gawky lads grinned from ear to ear, John's state of singleness being a standing joke, with a fine old flavor about it.

"Was it a good fair, Mr. Gilhorn ?" cried the mistress, merrily joining in the attack.

"Ay—for beasts," replied the embarrassed victim.

"But not for coorting purposes," rejoined the farmer, with the heartsomest laugh he had given for many a long day, having grown duller of late months. And yet I've a notion ye've somehow suited yourself—eh, John?"

Big John actually blushed.

"Och, James! Quit, James! … be quiet, James," he murmured, while a fine sunset effect was displayed on his broad cheeks as he devoured huge bites of buttered oat-cake, in the vain attempt to appear unconcerned.

"They are always teasing him, and it's a shame," hotly muttered young Osilla to her sister, being invariably John's devoted champion.

But something unusual in the well-accustomed victim's expression induced Lill to whisper by and by to her father, at a good opportunity,

"Is it true?"

"'Deed is it! Only don't let on to the rest," the farmer solemnly answered, but apparently having in his mind a well-pleased background of thought.

As for Orange Lily, her heart grew so light and glad she could have sung her usual grace after meat; and she gave poor John such a kind, sympathizing smile that it warmed him through and through. So, feeling gay, he made a great effort, and told them a story.

"Have you heard about my brother, and the church harmoni-um ?" he asked. "No? Why, that *is* a piece of fun—what you might call a 'big piece!' … For, the Castle ladies were wanting it up to the school-house for to-night; and he was laboring in his own field convenient to the churchyard, when the sexton called him, and says, 'William-Thomas,' says he, 'the ladies were examining this instrument, and I understood them to say it was out of tune, by reason of the cowld getting into its inside. So, after they left, I lit some fire, to give them every satisfaction. Now, how near it would *you* advise for to put her?' So, with that, the two consulted, and at last hoisted the harmonium right on the top of the big stove! ... But when the ladies came down awhile later, you never heard such a whullabaloo as took place! And the colonel's wife laughed till she cried, for they had it just *over*-roasted, she said! I ratherly think my brave brother will not meddle with harmoni-ums soon again."

The whole party went that evening together to the school-house, where Gilhorn placed himself beside the Keags, and among the smaller farmers, on the school-benches; though he had bought a dearer ticket for the front chairs, behind the Castle party, whence his cousin Danny surveyed with a supercilious air. Mistress Keag was overjoyed at this proof of Big John's condescension. Her step-daughter only inferred that his sweetheart was not present.

Now the Orange Lily had never once entered the school-house again since the days when she and Tom Coulter had gone there together, long ago. This night the walls were all decorated with flags and evergreens by the Castle gardener—yet still, there were the maps they had so often studied side by side; the black half-circle on the floor round which they had stood; the very form she sat on had been that of his class—the highest.

So she sat silent, and her heart grew tender thinking of those days, and the music melted her soul within her. In her opinion all the fine guests from the Castle sang beautifully, one after another; although Big John opined in a loud whisper, it was "just a wee thing too fine for him." When Miss Alice and Miss Edith, skilled musicians both, got up upon the little platform, and played a duet on the piano, his face took quite a pitying expression.

"Poor old ladies! Och! och! they're near done," he whispered again, close into Lily's ear, who sat beside him, clacking his tongue. "*To think that it takes the two of them to play one tune!*"

When the young woman, suppressing a smile, explained very low that it was not feebleness which prompted this fashion of piano-playing so new-fangled to him, the big man listened to her superior knowledge with respect; but, on a quartette being sung immediately afterwards, he barely controlled himself till the last note ended, and then burst out, in an under-gobble of excitement, "Well ... well ... well! You won't tell me *yon* was good music, anyhow! The one singing up and the other down, and none sticking to the same notes. Such a hash and a mash I *niver* heard!"

Next the choir were called up to perform in a chorus, the Orange Lily and her brothers among them. This received much applause, for almost every one had a relation among the singers, and, when they slipped back to their seats, Big John said with fervor,

"I could pick out your voice, Miss Keag, amongst the whole pack."

And Mistress Keag whispered in proud greeting to her sons, "I heard the bumming of ye both above all the rest of them!"

Thenceforward, having thus proved what *they* could do, the audience listened complacently to the gentlefolks' far less loud attempts, although occasionally uncertain whether they heard Italian or English. Big Gilhorn, however, was fascinated by his brother's movements, the renowned William-Thomas, who was fidgeting with some object he kept between his legs.

"What are you fustling with, boy?" he muttered, bending inquisitively forward.

"It's an opera-glass. They tould me it was grand for seeing with; but I'm something shy of using it," responded the unlucky harmonium-mender.

"Put it up, lad, put it up!" encouraged his brother, as just then young Mrs. Alexander herself stood up to sing. And thus fortified, William-Thomas slowly drew out a small-sized telescope, and applied it to his eye.

In a few seconds the singer's pretty face began to twitch curiously, and her gaze seemed spellbound to that quarter of the room.

"Can you see ony thing the better?" anxiously whispered John, while poor Lill felt a sort of amused but distressed shame, and two coastguardsmen near almost choked with smothered laughter.

"The deil a hait! It all swims," was the muttered reply, as the disappointed one dropped his optical instrument. And Big John imparted thereupon to his neighbor, with a sagacious nod, the song being ended,

"I've no great opinion of telescopes myself—for once I had a queer curiosity about those spots in the sun's face you read of in the newspapers. So I borrowed a spy-glass, and sat down under a hedge to have a good blink through it. But, would ye believe it—it burned me that bad that the divil a ha-porth o' sun could I see! and the useless thing spoilt my eyesight on me for a good wee while afterwards."

Going homewards, in the darkness, when about half way, Orange Lily found herself alone with Big John; since her step-mother had somewhat unusually called Osilla forward. She began to speak, therefore, with a shy, sweet voice.

"O Mr. Gilhorn," she said, "is it really true you are going to be married? It would make me so happy to hear it."

"No—would it?" muttered her big companion, after a doubtful pause, in a curious manner; and thoughtfully revolving in his pocket his huge door-key he there carried.

"Indeed it would! I am so truly glad to know you have given over liking me—or rather have found some one you like better," Lill made answer, a tender mirth playing upon her last words, while her congratulation sounded as truthful as it had been gracefully uttered.

"I'm—heart—sorry—to hear—that," slowly fell from Big John's lips; and although the words sounded lumpishly spoken, that very weight made them sink into his hearer's soul plumb, as if lead had dropped into her mind. She stood still, dumbfoundered. "Sure it was you, and none other, your father was joking about," he went on, with a slow heaving of anger within him, poor man! at her past want of understanding, and a kind of shame, too, mingling in his voice. "I was not for naming it again for a year or so, maybe, till give you time; but in course of business with James Keag this day, it came out, unbeknownst to me like, what a heap I thought of you—O he was over anything pleased, and the mistress too—and they both bid me to speak up, and have no fears!" he added, in dull explanation, his mortification becoming tempered again by his patience, and the certainty that after all reigned supreme in his soul that Orange Lily was too good and tender and holy-minded a woman to make sport of him to the world, or refuse him without high reasons.

Lill, alas! knew now why the pancakes had been fried, and that her father had been so jubilant, her step-mother so solemnly wise-looking at times, that evening, out of their wont. She began again to walk swiftly after the others; but, for the next half mile, what talk passed between them was most painful to her. Between pauses of five minutes, poor Big John, without plucking up courage again to ask her downrightly to have him, yet offered to give her a month—six months—a year, to think the matter over, and although she gently but steadfastly assured him it was all of no use, he still persevered, as one who kindly offers to lay by some sweetmeat till a wayward child chooses to take it. At last he began to press so weightily and persistently to be told her reasons for conduct that seemed to him so foolish and incomprehensible, passing even most "women's capers!" that poor Orange Lily, after striving to evade his directness of questioning, feeling distressed, perplexed, and driven into a corner, let escape her lips rather than knowingly uttered,

"Mr. Gilhorn—I am promised to another man."

"*No!*" ejaculated John, in pure surprise, after a long pause to draw his breath; then added, with bitter reproach for his wasted courtship, "And me after you—not knowing—all this time."

"I could not tell you, indeed," the young woman murmured, grieved and humiliated that he thought himself treated unfairly. "It's maybe best to tell you all about it. It is to—Tom Coulter."

"*To your father's farm-servant?*" uttered Big John, as if he could not believe his ears, his pride stung to the quick on discovering such a rival.

"Yes, Mr. Gilhorn, just so. Now you would sooner look at the dirt under your feet nor me," she answered, with a sort of sad satire, but the minute after began softly to cry. Now, if there was one thing on this earth which reduced the big man beside her to deplorable weakness, and shore him of his locks of strength, that was a woman's tears. Before they had gone much further he was trying to console in his turn the comforting angel of all distressed Ballyboly with sighs, and clacks of his tongue, and pitying ejaculations. And so, between her tears, the saddened soul, being a little relieved to have a listener at last, told the whole story.

"But will he have enough to keep you, if he does come back?" practically inquired the disappointed rival.

"He won't come back unless he has."

"And if he never comes—it'll be gey and hard upon you."

"Whatever God sends me will not be too hard, Mr. Gilhorn," Lill replied, drying her eyes at last, and with a sweet and cheerful assurance composing her voice again.

"In course not," assented big Gilhorn, as to a proposition he could not dispute. "And yet whiles one thinks things might be as well for us *easier!*—when bad weather comes—or disease among the cattle, like."

"Nay, I feel sure now that even the hardest times were best for me," the poor soul said fervently, a thrill of such living conviction vibrating through her voice that it impressed the man more strongly than many a sermon.

Then she went on, gazing up at the changeless stars, and more as if pursuing her own train of thought, than seeking to persuade her hearer:

"Little by little I have come to understand it. When not a sparrow falleth but He knoweth it, and even the very hairs of my head are numbered, is it out of reason that a loving Father should order all the events of my life for my good, when I am of more value than many sparrows? I feel it ... I know it, because I have asked and been answered! With fuller happiness, I would never have been forced into looking higher than this earth for my best gladness."

Then she added lower, in a voice of which the low, fine tone fitly brought to the world outside the secrets of the innermost holy place of her mind,

"Maybe I am not fit, not worthy for the happiness and responsibilities of other women; maybe I would have worshipped my husband over much till have rightly served my God."

"Plenty of rare bad ones gets married anyhow," bluntly argued John. "And I wouldn't be much of a one to be worshipped, if you took *me!*"

"Most likely it is the only chance of making the bad ones better," calmly replied Lily Keag, as if on ground she well knew. "And, if they cannot rear their children to godliness, the little ones may teach them the way to the kingdom of heaven."

Then neither spoke again till they reached the top of the farm-hill, where, through the darkness of the night, they could dimly descry the figures of the farmer and his wife waiting for them.

CHAPTER XXII

"The farmer's thoughts? and were they something sad,
And did pale Conscience put her horse-hair on?"

BUCHANAN.

"The sea of Fortune doth not ever flow,
    She draws her favors to the lowest ebb;
Her tides have equal times to come and go;
    Her loom doth weave the fine and coarsest web;
No joy so great but runneth to an end,
No hap so hard but may in fine amend."

SOUTHWELL.

"WELL" called out Keag and his good mistress, cheerily, "when will the wedding be?"

"We'll discourse about that, maybe, another year," replied Big Gilhorn's voice, with ponderous gravity.

Both the parents cried out; and the farmer, who, in his great amazement, was almost tempted to scent in this a sniff of popery, the abomination of all sound Protestant Orangemen like himself, demanded passionately, with that terrible doubt in his voice,

"Lilyun!—don't tell me, your religion would drive ye to be a papish nun!"

"Hoot, James, you're a fool! It's only to be an old maid she wants," jeered his wife.

"Listen now, the two of yez … I want no woman dragooned intil being my wife!" broke in Big John, stammering in his earnestness, but impressing them all therewith nonetheless. "It is her and me for it!—and noan else need meddle betwixt us. But—but if she's nagged at on this account, *we're off our bargain, James!*"

And, having thus gallantly delivered himself of his sweetheart's defence, he made off down the hill with great strides, rattling door-key, knife, picker, tobacco-pouch, and the other furniture of his pockets, in an agitated manner.

Those left behind dismally entered the farm-house. Osilla had vanished; but the boys were encircling the peat-blaze they had stirred up again on the kitchen hearth, and looked up with bright curiosity. They were harshly bidden begone upstairs to their beds in the garret by their father, and slunk away in wonder at such unusual severity. James Keag mutely beckoned to his daughter, then, to follow him into the parlor. Mistress Keag might have gone with them; but was too daunted by her husband's manner, which boded, in her experience, a rare but all the worse outburst of wrath. When such storms had, in late years, fallen upon herself, she had been used to invoke her step-daughter's shelter, whose gentle influence with the father for peace was irresistible. But now, weakly deserting her helper in the hour of need, the good-wife murmured to herself, with blame, yet pity for the victim, "The dear help her—he's fit to kill her!" and remained in the kitchen stirring the pigs' food in the big boiler on the fire ostentatiously, as if every one must know she had to see to that; yet, to satisfy the cravings of curiosity, stealing on tiptoe every few minutes to listen at the parlor key-hole, since they had shut to the door.

Inside the parlor, the farmer stood looking at his daughter. His face was gray and so strange in its expression that, with a sudden fear knocking at her heart, she put out her hand with imploring gentleness, saying,

"Dear father, don t strike me. You did so once, you know, and I—I—never could quite forget it. Only, don't do that … please!"

His gaze turned, at that, to one of such grieved reproach that she saw at once her error; but, before the words of quick atonement could cross her penitent lips, he had sunk down on a chair and laid his grizzled head upon his crossed arms on the table.

"My girl—my girl!" he groaned, "this is a bad night's job for me."

All his daughter's fears of him had fled; but alarm for him took their place. She had never seen the easy-going, humor-loving, practical man like this before; and a good father he was to her, and dearly beloved, although as rough and hard on the surface as a nut's husk.

She knelt down beside him in haste, putting her hands beseechingly on his knee.

"What is it, father? … Father, you don't, surely, want to turn me out to a man I don't care for? Have I not wrought hard enough, that you would wish to get rid of me?"

"My poor lass! Better turn you out to him than to the workhouse … ! I'm clean ruined!"

"Ruined!" repeated the poor girl, with a low, quavering cry; then, raising her eyes involuntarily, the prayer came from her lips as naturally, and only a moment later than that cry, "O my dear Lord—help us."

The farmer put out his hand to caress her head, and went on more soothingly,

"Maybe it's not just so bad … ! But how can I hold up my head till John Gilhorn, and you not marry the man, when I owe him nearhand fifty pounds?"

Orange Lily's amazement was great! She knew, indeed, that things had gone badly with them of late; but her father was too reticent to let even her know how matters truly stood with him—much less his wife. Now, however, she coaxed him and besought him, till little by little, in low, broken sentences, he told her how small debts of long years' standing, with their exorbitant interest to the petty usurers who fatten in the country as in towns, had never been paid off; how the last flax-crops had brought less than she guessed; and, as she already knew, the pigs had been diseased.

"And, if your mother had lived, things would never have gone so far astray with us," he said, sighing. "But, with your step-mother and me it has always been, 'take things easy,' and 'trust to luck.' Then I told Big John there, near two years ago, how the very life was just sucked out of me with these wheen wee debts and their awful interest. 'Faith,' said I, 'that money borrowed was like leeches, that, after curing, should stick on and kill you.' And, like a good friend, he offered to lend me what would pay off the whole rick-me-tick!—and ask only fair interest as an honest man. Then, to-day, we met to speak on the subjeck, and I said if I had but ten pounds more to buy a beast at the morrow's fair, it would answer me well; but, as it was, I had nought to pay him off with yet, forbye that I was sold up, and quitted this roof I was born under, and that I brought your mother to." (James Keag's voice choked). "'God forbid,' says John, and let on (intimated) there was one in my house he liked more than his money, and would gladly swap the whole kettle of fish with me for—only that, as a prudent man, he could not rightly afford it." (Here the farmer gave a small shrewd smile, which his daughter was glad to see again)." But he offered me the money for the beast on the spot, and would take no denial."

"My money! There is mine in the bank," exclaimed Lily, in pure wonder that he had never asked her for it; and with a great sense of relief to find the matter not so hopelessly bad as the fear of ruin had implied. But her father drew his sleeve across his forehead, and answered slowly, with painful emotion,

"I feared that was how it would be, my wee Orange Lily. Take *yours*—that I've thanked the Lord for on my knees many a night, thinking it would still keep you from the workhouse, if all the rest of them went there."

The girl sprang to her feet, and, touched though she was all through her at this evidence of his exceeding love, felt a quiver of indignation, none the less, that he should think her capable of possible meanness.

"Then I swear, father," she said, laying her hand on the big Bible upon the parlor table, "that I will give it to the rest myself, whenever they need it. And if any of us must go to the workhouse, I will be the first!"

ORANGE LILY

The poor father sighed, and rubbed his wrinkled brow, whilst his gaze travelled round the little parlor, resting on the best bed, the big clock-case, the mahogany-painted drawers, the glass corner-press, with the china tea-set inside. They were all dear to his heart from old associations; yet he would have sold all sooner than do this thing, which seemed robbing his child. Long she pleaded with him; long he resisted; but at last she prevailed.

Coming out victorious, as the young woman opened the door, somebody large jumped away from the other side with the lightness of a feather bed.

"Och, Lill dear," whispered her step-mother, ingenuously. "I had my ear at the keyhole half the time, but I'm getting that deaf I could hardly hear a word. What did ye both say?"

When her step-daughter had sufficiently satisfied her curiosity, and caused her to moderate her astonished bewailing of the ill news of their debts by the consoling and repeated assurances that this need no longer signify—and that now they would all start almost unhampered in their joint struggle of life again—the good-wife sighed—and, brandishing the ladle, stirred the pigs' food and sighed again.

"Well, you are a good daughter to us both; and that I always will allow," said she. "But to refuse a man like yon is just throwing away the gifts of Providence" (and she rattled the crane to relieve her feelings). "At least, none can say I'm a jealous woman, or would have grudged seeing you drive past me in your own gig—not, indeed, but that John's one is a tottering ould shandhrydan! But there is Osilla, too, crying her eyes out at the very notion of losing you. A soft-hearted big baby, at her age, as I told her; but maybe you had best go in and comfort the poor wean."

"Silly child!" said the elder sister, tenderly, entering the sleeping-closet, wherein young Osilla was giving vent to small sniffling sounds in the darkness, stooping as she spoke to kiss a face buried in the pillow. "You are not going to be rid of me yet, if that is what vexes you."

"Are you not going to marry him?" cried Osilla, bouncing upright, her elf-locks hanging about her.

"No, no. Not yet—if ever," answered Lily Keag, slowly; bethinking herself, with an uncomfortable remembrance, of John Gilhorn's last words, which seemed to foreshadow yet future efforts on his part. Then a dread crept over her mind, as if that "*not yet*" had been a prophecy her unwilling lips had uttered. If she slept ill that night and dreamed strange things of bygone times mingled with the present it was little wonder! For a host of sad, sweet old memories had been aroused from their partial oblivion by the stirring emotions of that night, and fluttered in her brain like the light-winged ghosts of former living glad facts.

CHAPTER XXIII

"Noon—and the north-west sweeps the empty road,
The rain-washed fields from hedge to hedge are bare.
....
Shalt thou not wonder that it liveth yet,
    The useless hope, the useless craving pain,
That made thy face, that lonely noontide, wet
    With more than beating of the chilly rain."

MORRIS.

TWELVE months had passed away; another year was gone.

It was a soft, spring day in Ballyboly. The skies above were like a great sponge that was trying to blot the parish out of the province of Ulster; already the outlines of the more distant hills and trees were blurred out, and horizon and sea along the coast seemed merged together in one watery, gray island-setting.

Up the high-road, two young women, huddled in shawls, but not much protected thereby against the insinuating rain, were dejectedly picking their way, side by side, through the mud. It was wet overhead; it was wet underfoot. And their eyes were wet too, for both were softly crying, as if since many a day (like the weather) they had got into the way of it, and did not now mean much more than usual thereby!

As they came in sight of a long, cleanly whitewashed farm-house,—with only a low wall, and a strip of garden two yards wide, along its front, separating it from the road—the elder said,

"There is his house. We must dry our eyes now, Osilla, and make the best of it ... Dear child, won't you—won't you help me? I would rather cut my hand off than ask him!"

"We are like beggars—the pair of us!" replied the other, with a momentary flaring-up, it seemed, of a passionate emotion that had nearly exhausted itself. "Ask him yourself. You have only got to marry him, if he says—yes. Is that a hard thing?"

The elder sister sighed.

Just then, as the women passed the out-buildings flanking the farmhouse, Big John Gilhorn met them as he came out of his yard gate, and lustily exclaimed,

"Is it yourselves? Bless my heart and soul, James Keag's two daughters! And where are the two of yez going this soft day?"

The young woman glanced entreatingly at the girl; the girl avoided her elder's beseeching gray eyes. Then Lily Keag said, with a great effort,

"My father has sent us with a message to you, Mr. Gilhorn."

"Step inside, step inside," cried John, hospitably; and taking two strides through his garden, he threw open his house-door and ushered them into the kitchen. Here he made them take off their wet shawls before they spoke, drew chairs up to the fire for them, while he himself only shook his big body like a dog fresh out of the water, and sitting down exactly between both sisters, with his hands on his knees and a broad smile on his face, presently began to steam in patches.

"What a—a nice kitchen you have!" said Orange Lily, making a manifest effort to say something, and gazing dully at the coal-fire, which was an improvement on their own plain hearthstone for peat at home.

"Well," said John, slapping his knees and looking around with an air of some exultation, "It's the first time you've been in it, Miss Keag; but I hope … but I hope—!"

As this plainly implied a tender declaration, both girls became even more embarrassed; and there was a silence. It was a pleasant kitchen, if dark, compared with that of the Keags' home; there were geraniums in the little windows and muslin blinds; a well-filled dresser and good chairs betokened carefulness and comfort.

Big John now asked heartily after Mistress Keag.

"Is her foot better yet, of thon scalding?" said he, slapping one knee.

"She's very lame still, or she would have come herself, murmured Osilla. "Still she put treacle enough on it at the first."

"Ah! treacle—treacle is the thing for a burn," returned John, slapping the other knee. "And how is your father?"

"He's far from well—he's very ill, or *he* would have come! It was the red cow done it on him," again replied Osilla.

"How? Did she toss him?" cried John.

"No," interposed Lily—"she died last night."

"Ach! bad scran to her! She could not have done worse! … I never had a good opinion of that beast, now," slowly observed John, scratching his head as if meditating over the iniquity of the red cow; then, being accustomed to show sympathy, like his neighbors, by dwelling on the sorrows of the afflicted, he added—"Well, well, well! You have had troubles, indeed, this past twelvemonth. One thing after another; ay, ay!"

"Bad weather and bad crops," said poor Lily; who, like others, also felt consoled in rehearsing her miseries, and hoped likewise to attain her end circuitously hereby, since she could not find courage to speak it openly. "And my poor Osilla, there, ailing since last spring."

("There was nothing the matter with me," muttered the young girl, almost crossly, but her pale cheeks and wistful dark eyes contradicted her.)

"Yes—yes. And worst of all, poor Henry-Thomas being banished, as you may say, to America; just when he was grown to be a man, and able to work for your father," chimed in Big John, comfortably crossing his legs. A sudden burst of sobbing came from Osilla. "Bless my soul!" John ejaculated, and rapidly uncrossed them, as if they were to blame.

"Don't take notice on her, please Mr. Gilhorn—she'll be better soon," said Lily, soothingly, and wiped her own eyes very quietly. For on the last Twelfth of July their part of the North had been the scene of the worst party riots remembered for years;

and Henry-Thomas, who loved the Orange cause not wisely but too well, had taken a hot part therein, having gone up express-ly to Belfast to stay a week with a cousin "for the fun!" Being young, and indiscreet, and excited with several days' fighting and stone-throwing, he and some others "went further nor loyal Orangemen should" as his father euphemistically explained the matter—which was merely the killing by accident of some Roman Catholics who tried to kill *them!* Some of the lad's comrades were captured by the police. He himself escaped, but thought it wisest to betake himself quietly to America. In the Keag family such an occurrence could hardly be considered any disgrace; but it was a sad misfortune.

"And now my father so ill the-day!" resumed the Orange Lily, after a pause. "He's breaking his heart about the cow—! And—and he was in arrears with the rent last November, Mr. Gilhorn." (The last words seemed spoken quite small and fine, and a thrill of exceeding pain shook them.)

"Ochone—oné! It's far easier to find the way *into* debt than the way out," said John, moralizing, and kindly clacking his tongue with fellow-feeling. At that moment even Osilla thought him stupid, as the two girls looked despairingly at each other. Then the young one cried out,

"Oh! Mr. Gilhorn, *don't* you see—he wants to know, will you help him? For tomorrow week is the rent day, and he meant to sell the cow, before then, at Black Abbey[21] Fair … and, if not, we must leave the farm, and—!"

---

[21] Black Abbey. This is the name given by the author to another local novel she published the following year (in 1880), set in the neighbour-ing village of Greyabbey. The sequel is anticipated here. By royal patent of King Charles I, Greyabbey was still holding two annual fairs, one on 28th March, and the other on 29th October. There is, mid-way between Greyabbey and Ballywalter, the site of another medieval abbey in the townland of Blackabbey, with no visible remains.

She covered her face with her shawl; her sister had already done so. But Osilla sobbed violently, the elder was still as death.

"Don't, now—Och! don't!" exclaimed poor John, in almost ludicrous terror, jumping up and walking round and round the kitchen to relieve his mind, that could never endure women's tears. "Silla—Miss Keag—sure I'll do … I'll do … what I can. But for *any* sake stop crying."

After a little, Osilla did again control herself.

"And you will help my father," she murmured, her sister being still silent.

"I will *so!*" said John emphatically; then a shamefaced smile stole gradually over his round face, and he added, But … but … but—I like to be sure of my money's worth."

A quiver of pain and shame tingled through poor Lill at that. She started, roused up from her dulness, and gazed with piteous earnestness at him.

"Indeed—indeed, Mr. Gilhorn, we can pay you back—surely! Do you think we would let *you* suffer … I spoke to Miss Alice the other day, who was wanting a maid; and I could pay you myself out of my own wages a wee-thing at a time, in two years at the worst—"

"Hut-tut," interrupted Big John, in a mild agony, from where he had propped himself, buttress-fashion, against the dresser, wrinkling his forehead, and waving one arm like a windmill sail to express that she did not understand him rightly at all, at all! Then he worked his hands frantically in his pockets, as if searching there for new modes of expression; and, lastly, looked round in much reproach at his old ally, Osilla.

"*You* understand … Och! now, can't ye speak a word for me?" he exclaimed. "Sure, now, *you'd* marry me fast enough if I asked you."

"I *would*," returned the young girl, hotly, her cheeks flushing crimson, and her eyes lighting up. "Lill, can't you marry him and have done with it? You owe it to him, if we take his money—my father told you so—"

"Naw—did he?" cried John, in a rapture. "Och! Silla, you're the girl to stand up for me. Miss Keag, listen till her."

Lill turned her head slowly. She never spoke; but looked at them both with a dull, patient expression, and eyes as if she was hunted. Both somehow turned silent at that look, although hardly thinking there was much wrong with her, being neither close observers nor fine-fibred folk. They only waited, feeling uncomfortable, till at last she said, under her breath, as if to herself,

"Ay! … he told me it was but fair; and that all the rest would suffer if I did not give up my own wishes to yours and theirs. I've heard nought else this year past!" then, with a touch of passionate emotion, "And yet to stand up beside you in church, Mr. Gilhorn, with a lie in my mouth—"

"Hut-tut. Easy now; take it easy!" interrupted Big John, with a broad grin of delight he could not suppress, evidently treating her last words as he would the freaks of his young mare when put in harness at first. "No fears! you'll take kindly to it yet," and he began patting her on the shoulder, and uttering soothing sounds suggestive of the stable.

Osilla, who had been watching them both anxiously, sprang to her feet at that, as if stung with nettles.

"Mr. Gilhorn," said she, "I think—I think I'd like to look round your parlor, if you please."

"Ay—ay—ay!" cried John, and he winked and nodded broadly from behind Orange Lily's chair in vast approval of the young girl's tact in leaving them alone. "There's a very nice bunch of wax-flowers there, that I'm sure you'd like to see." Left together in the kitchen, however, with Lily, the big man's courage began to ooze, and before it vanished he had only time to ejaculate, "Ah! now, Miss Keag—you will have me? Ah! now, do … Ah, now!"

Poor Lill put up her hands to her head. It was so dazed and

heavy with long thinking and night-vigils, and the way every one talked at her, that she longed—tired soul!—for stillness. Her face was whiter than ever, and her gray eyes pale and wild—then her hands dropped, and looking up at John as if she were pouring out her whole soul before him, she cried out—but low,

"O, Mr. Gilhorn, if I only knew what was right to do! *but I don't know!* There are my father and mother and you, all wanting me to marry you and make every one happy, they say; and, on the other hand, it presses on my mind day after day and night after night that it would be a sin for a wife not to love her husband better nor I can you—though I like you very well. I am in a sore strait—a sore strait! And surely one path must be right and one wrong; but I have been so sinful and foolish most of my life in not using the wits the Lord gave me to discern betwixt right and wrong that now I can *not* tell one from the other—and that is a sin in me, too. And I have prayed to be guided in this—it is my whole life that is to be decided—but I have had no answer." (Her voice had died away at the last; then she collected herself again.) "Mr. Gilhorn, my good friend—say you understand me."

"Troth! and I do *not*—not one haporth!" quoth John, plump and plain, with a most determinedly puzzled air. "Women's capers beats me entirely." For a moment he seemed in doubt whether to consider himself aggrieved or not; but then his goodness of heart triumphed. Besides, the young woman was so plainly at a loss for right judgment that he waxed in wisdom at the very sight. And, his good humor restored by feeling his own superiority of mind-weight as a man, with pity for her feminine wits that went all to scatterment at a pinch (like butter for the market in summer-time), he seemed to enlarge his breadth of shoulder and swell his voice, as he went on, in kindly condescending expostulation—"See now! Is there another man ye like better—in the country?"

"No."

"Isn't—*thon one*—out in America most likely dead or married?" John continued, so eager to unroll his argument, he absolutely forgot that she did not consider that a good riddance, too—like himself.

"Most likely," she just murmured.

"Then what's to hinder us? … Come along; take me and try me, and I'll hould you, you'll like me!" cried John, triumphantly clinching his argument with a sounding clap on his thigh.

There followed a considerably long silence, most painful to the sorrowful girl, most surprising to the overjoyed man; then she pleaded low, never once looking him in the face—

"Give me to the next Twelfth of July. And then, if—if he doesn't come back—"

"We'll be happy thegether!" gallantly ended Big Gilhorn; in his amazing satisfaction, overlooking kindly the foolish feminine scruples that alone withheld her from being blessed with such an excellent bargain; then wiping his mouth on his sleeve with preparatory enjoyment, he came slowly nearer.

"And now," he grinned, "we'll seal the agreement."

Lily Keag sprang up.

"Not now; not now—not till then! Silla, are you *never* coming back?"

In came Osilla with her eyes fixed on the floor and a guilty look, as if curiosity had kept her behind the door, although consideration for them had taken her away.

"Well," said poor John, annoyed at being baffled, yet always good-humored, "Please the pigs! I'll—I'll have a kiss, anyhow; so, Silla, if your sister objects, I'll be bound you won't!" and with a most brotherly air he loudly verified his words with a sounding smack on her cheek.

The young girl turned upon him with hot anger; and that for the first time in her life, since he had made a favorite of her from her childhood.

"Leave *me* alone! What have you to do with me!"

"The dear help a man betwixt the pair o' ye!" exclaimed the ill-used lover, in chagrin, unexpectedly rebuffed here, also. "Why, Silla, you're but a lump of a child! Leastways, that's how I still consider you."

At this, Osilla, who was proud of being grown-up, showed a strong disposition to re-melt into the tearful state in which she had already passed most of her visit. Her elder sister had to remind her, in a hasty whisper, how much they would now owe to John Gilhorn. This succeeded—and both feeling, in truth, the kindliness the man had shown when acceding to the request they had made in reluctance and grief, thanked him, before leaving, again and again in trembling, mingling voices.

Poor John's complacency, which had suffered some severe shocks during the visit, was now completely restored; and the smile which they lured out again on his round visage grew broader and broader. Even their utter refusal of his wish to "convoy them home" was not unpalatable; since, they assured him, the matter coupled with their visit might cause too much talk among the neighbors.

So when they gently, and as quickly as they could, said good-by and stole away, John, with his thumbs in his waistcoat arm-holes, filled up the doorway and gazed after them with a jovial air. After which, looking forward with placid satisfaction to the coming Twelfth of July, he began whistling to himself "Boyne Water."

CHAPTER XXIV

"I gang like a ghaist, and I care na to spin.
I daurna think o' Jamie, for that would be a sin."
                                        LADY ANNE LINDSAY.

"Meanwhile Hannah … had closed and fastened the shutters,
Spread the cloth, and lighted the lamp on the table, and placed there
Plates and cups from the dresser, the brown rye loaf, and the butter
Fresh from the dairy, and then, protecting her hand with a holder,
Took from the crane in the chimney the steaming and simmering
        kettle,
Poised it aloft in the air, and filled up the earthen tea-pot."
                                        LONGFELLOW.

THE weeks passed over, and warm, passionate June came, seeming full of present gladness and pleasant promise; a June bringing soft winds and glorious sunshine, bean-flowers and birds' songs; such a June, farmers said, with a perfect content for a wonder! as had not been for years—if it lasted. But Orange Lily neither seemed warmed nor gladdened by it, like others. The now few days that had still to elapse before the Twelfth of July, seemed to press upon her with such a sense of shortness that she could not breathe. She saw all her family looking at her with smiling eyes, for although it was considered best not to hurry her in any way—she being so unlike other people—yet every one took it for granted that her marriage would soon take place; and she knew that, and felt forced, and at times half thought she would have preferred more open force, against which she might have cried out and relieved herself. At other times, however, she tried to be just to them and to remember how much all felt they owed to John. He—a blissful swain!—now paid daily visits and hinted with awkward pleasantries, and kindly if shame-faced smiles, of the preparations he would soon be making—for two. One thing the young woman did ask,

191

that none of the neighbors should be told about the matter, and this she gained; her family agreeing together that, on account of her goodness, they must respect her harmless whims.

So while the warm days slipped on, and most evenings John strolled up to the farm-house, Orange Lily would sit quiet near him and stilly listen to his few remarks. At rare moments, stealing a look at him with the thought that soon she must be his wife, a sudden dislike would dart through the woman's heart, and it would sink low. Then again she would chide herself; remember all his kindly deeds; count over his virtues in her secret mind; and almost passionately tell herself that it was ordered clearly for her that she should marry him, and therefore must be good for her!—if otherwise, some way of escape would be surely made plain. For Lill believed, as utterly as do fatalists in their predestination, that though free to use her own will, and though liable to mistakes, yet that all things must work together for her good; because the Master she served had plainly promised this, in return for her willing love. And so, feeling herself but a weak woman, with little wit, she prayed for divine guidance in this as in all other matters, imploring that she might not be suffered to sin from lack of judgment; and simply having faith without a shadow of doubt that she would be thenceforth guided. She knew she was bound to use the understanding given her to her best ability; but now, strain it as she would, she could noways decide. Her soul was troubled, her brain dazed; it seemed at times selfishness not to sacrifice her mere private wishes for the preservation of her family from social degradation; at others, a sin to force her conscience. So she waited on—patiently prepared to accept this coming change of life, as a duty—yet yearning for a sign against it.

But none came.

"Deary, deary me! but that girl's wits seem all gone to water! Osilla, it's changed times when you are the wisest of the lasses; but Lill, there, reminds one of a sleep-walker these days," said Mistress

Keag one day, out of many when she had likewise spoken. For her home-grown mind was lately as surprised at her hard-working step-daughter's musings, as if she had learnt that her patron saint, King William III., was also a foreigner and Dutchman—truths that had never yet come under her observation. "It's truth I'm telling, that she spent a right half-hour by the clock on her knees scouring and scouring out that back kitchen yesterday. And when I spoke to her, she only said, in a dazy way, 'I like to have it clean.' 'Woman dear,' I cried out at her, 'it's just wasteful to wash like that! *Sure you'll wear away the stanes!*'"

Osilla moodily replied, with a slight superstitious fear of impending trouble,

"Ay! and she nearhand swept one of the crickets into the fire yesterday, she was brushing up the hearth so hard. By good luck I saved it, but if she had—!" (Crickets[22] were sacred at the farm fireside, and showed their ungainly shapes safely. What evil would avenge their molestation was more than Osilla knew!—more than she wished to learn through experience, so she averred.)

"But, och! the crown of all was last night," quoth the good wife, laughing, shouting her secret behind a sheltering hand. "She made me promise not to tell on her—*but I'll just tell you!* She was lighting me in the parlor till I put my Sunday gown by; and what does she do but puts the candle in the press instead, and leaves us both in the dark! Well, well, says I, it's easy seen you are as bad as other lasses when they're foolish with coorting, for all you cried out so sorely against having John Gilhorn. She must be greatly taken with him now, Osilla." And the stout body looked vastly relieved at this satisfactory explanation of her step-daughter's behavior;

---

[22] The presence of crickets in an Ulster farm-house was considered lucky. Indeed, if a house lay vacant, neighbours would keep the kitchen fire going in case the crickets would disappear and the 'luck would leave the house'.

her own cares seldom troubling her long, and, naturally, still less so those of other people.

"Oh, she *likes* him well enough," blurted out Osilla, adding, with a touch of bitterness, "But I think she ought to like him a good heap better." For the young sister, for the first time in her life, strongly disapproved of her elder's ingratitude in not being ready to go down on her two knees to John Gilhorn, for offering "to bestow his fist and fortune on her."

As for other matters in Ballyboly parish, Miss Edith up at the Castle had rallied in health during the last year or so, though Miss Alice had grown slightly feebler. It seemed as if, having been born together, they meant to go hand in hand down life's hill and die together. The Colonel and his lady came over oftener, and in winter she gave balls and parties, and he hunted the Ballyboly harriers.

Daniel Gilhorn was making a mess of his trial at farming. His new and pleasant home by the seaside was going all to wrack and ruin, as James Keag often said, with a farmer's grief at seeing fine land so sorely mishandled; while Danny himself was continually to be seen in the Maghrenagh public houses, and, while admired loudly as "doing things in fine style" by the still thoughtless young men around, was condemned by the elder under their breath as "going clean to the bad."

"Verily, some dance gayly to hell, and others step sorrowfully to heaven! It's a queer world, if a body thinks about it," said James Keag.

"It was a very good world once, father; and there will be a very good world again," reverently answered his daughter.

One day work was over, and the Keags were sitting down to supper in the evening cool, having been joined, as was now usual, by Big John, when one of the children called out from the door that Daniel Gilhorn was coming up "their road," as any lane was always civilly called thereabouts. Daniel entered soon with a jaunty air, a round hat, like a gentleman's, perched awry on his head, "as if it knew it was out of place," thought Lill. He also wore two coats (a light one flying back loose over his other one; dear knew why one was not enough for any man—and the evening so warm too!) He had a swaggering "how-d'ye-do-clodhoppers?" manner as he greeted the company, while superciliously tapping his boots with his stick, that made the little children shrink small and the colley-dog growl from between James Keag's legs.

The farmer himself was not over-fond now of this visitor, who, as he had slowly come to perceive, was not quite as civil as he should be to the former's favorite daughter, his retiring, tender-minded Orange Lily; and there must be a bad drop in that man's blood who could not abide goodness, he was wont to say. But Mistress Keag, whom Danny always blarneyed with compliments, greeted him warmly; and John gave him a labored but friendly welcome, because, as he now always observed, "He wished no man to say he bore his cousin ill-will about their grandfather's money."

Lily Keag, in her heart, held John should be a little more above public opinion, seeing all knew well that he thought as little of Danny as before; and she secretly distrusted the latter's apparent responding warmth, his condescending rib-pokes, and patronizing fashion of addressing Big John nowadays, when the two met by accident.

In general, they avoided each other's company, by common consent. "You'll sit down and take a drop of tea with us," cried Mrs. Keag, hospitably, preparing to press upon him big oatmeal farls and hot griddle-cake that smelt excellently. Danny smiled a disagreeable smile, and withdrew his chair from the table.

"Please excuse me—I've reelly no appetite."

"Are ye ill?" asked Big John, simply, with a concerned and ready fellow-feeling in his voice, as he paused with a saucer full of scalding tea in one hand and a well-buttered farl in the other, midway to his mouth.

"He, he, he! No. But tea at this hour would make me so,"

replied their guest, with much inward diversion apparently.

Both Lill and Osilla glanced meaningly at each other, for they, like other such-like lasses, had sharp noses for the smell of whisky, and avoided those men on whom it was habitual, and now they knew well enough that Danny had been in the Ballyboly public-house.

"Humph! Changed times!" growled Keag, with vast scorn of the degenerate days in which his latter years were unhappily cast; then directly addressed his guest. "I'll hould ye now, you eat flesh-meat more than wunst a day, which was good enough for your father, decent man! and far more nor many an able man has been reared on—and should be—in these parts."

"Ahem! "Well … simpered Danny, "I am used, I confess, to something tasty for my supper; and then there's bacon at breakfast—"

"Bacon! Blatheration! What do ye stuff yourself like that for, man alive, and no more good work comes out of ye, for all the food ye put in ye, than your ancestors had to show." ("The dear knows, not near the hundredth as much!") "Now my grandmother used to tell me," went on Keag, pushing back his chair and crossing his legs the better to lecture the young folk, as all parents except Adam must have done on the better practices of their forbears—"she used to tell me how many an early summer morning, in *her* young days, they shore a sheaf of oats and would put it at the back of the fire-place in the logie to dry, and then would put it again in a sack and thresh it with sticks, and grind it after that in the quern and make stirabout of the meal for that very morning's breakfast! Ay! … she did so," and he glanced round the circle till his eyes slowly fell upon Daniel—with an expression that bid all take *that* to heart and avoid sinful luxury.

Up jumped good Mistress Keag now, and brought a dish of buttered pancakes from the peat embers.

"Well, anyway you'll taste these," she eagerly cried. "These are what your cousin there likes; and to let out a secret, some one made them especially for himself, too."

"I'll hould ye, I know who," Big John remarked; slowly turning a friendly I'll-eat-you-boys! eye on the cakes, then smiling gratefully to his understood sweetheart.

But Lill blushed, with a pained expression, and answered quick and low,

"It was not I … it was Osilla. She always thinks of what people like." (And yet, in general, it was she that merited such words, and not Osilla; who, though soft-hearted as wax, was still too thoughtless, and somewhat slow-witted, to think much of most folks' wants—although her boisterousness of childish behavior had vanished.)

After some jests about the pancakes, which much resembled gibes to one ear more fastidious than the rest, Danny remarked, with a would-be careless air,

"By the way, I had a visit yesterday from Mr. Redhead."

"Him that was church-clergyman here, and went over to Black Abbey?" asked somebody; then everybody added,

"Yon was a queer and nice man."

"Ya-as," said Danny; as if to be on terms of friendship with such persons of good station was now a matter of commonest occurrence with him. "Quite the gentleman! He said he had been wanting to call upon me this long time past, but could never get over—very polite of him."

That was a falsehood all present guessed; knowing that Mr. Redhead spent too much time among the sick and poor to trouble himself with visiting a rich young farmer as his equal, who lived far from Black Abbey parish[23]. So all were silent; while Danny, slapping his boots with his light cane, again observed, airily,

"He was pressing me very hard to know could I be induced

---

[23] Greyabbey Parish.

to give up the farm … Has a friend of his own in his eye for it."

Big John let fall his knife with a clatter. "And would ye—?" he ejaculated, staring open-mouthed.

"Well, r*ee*lly, r*ee*lly! … he was so pressing that to oblige him—I r*ee*lly hardly know, said Danny, mincingly, his vanity apparently having gone to his head of late, and much affected his weak brain. "Certainly, as he remarked, farming is not as gentlemanly an occupation as I am fitted for" (lie, number two) … "No offence to present company, he! he! he!"

"There'll none can be taken, if none is meant," gravely answered Keag; "and I trust heartily we are content with that station in life in the which it has pleased God to place us."

"But what would ye *do?*" inquired Big John, practically.

"See life in town … There's a friend of mine, there, has a secret for making a man rich in no time, if I become a partner; then we'll make the money fly, eh, John?" And Danny playfully treated his cousin to a rib-poke.

"Well, if it flies—I do not see that there would be much of a gentleman left about you," simply answered the big man.

Although the remark was plainly not meant to carry any sting, an irrepressible smile broke out on James Keag's face, and on that of Orange Lily. Up got the guest very soon and took leave.

"Hi, hi! …" suddenly bawled Big John, from the doorway, after him. "Does the friend that wants your farm come from hereabouts?"

"No," sneered Danny. "There are few here could afford it, I should think … He comes from a bit further than Maghrenagh, Mr. Redhead says: if you *want* to know."

Big John stood puzzled and plagued-looking, scratching his head; then very heavily he followed Lill to the dairy, where she was putting up some butter for Maghrenagh market next morning. He stood silent for almost a long while, watching her, whilst she felt nervous and longed that he would but go away. During their now frequent interviews the poor young woman counterfeited no affection for John, beyond the respect and esteem she really felt for him. But it had begun to dawn upon her that he was somewhat troubled by and discontented with her too cool regard. Plainly to-night this was the case, for by and by he said—"I'm going now. Good-evenin'."

"Good-evening," said Orange Lily.

"Well, I *must* be going, he repeated emphatically, after another short pause; then—"I'm half feared at times you don't like me very well—yet."

"I always liked you fairly, Mr. Gilhorn."

"Well, said John, again, with a sort of gulp of determination. I'm willing to do for you, what I'd do for noan other."

He looked as if he fully expected some caress, or affectionate token of thanks for this weighty announcement. But the young woman only answered as if in a dream, with a cool voice and a little sigh, "Thank you kindly, John Gilhorn."

As John went down the hill he had to remind himself by some rib-thwacks of the coming Twelfth of July as a consolation on being again disappointed of getting any sweet signs of affection from his promised bride, beforehand. And being a placid man, he fairly succeeded.

But the next day was to show what new-born thought had been in his mind, when he had made those particular inquiries of his cousin, and that obscure offer to his sweetheart. In the early morning, since the sun was shining with the promise of a full week or more of hot, almost too hot weather, all the Keag family was busied in mowing and making hay in the low marsh field. In June, still, it seemed full early for this; but since ever the farm had been his father's, James Keag had known two crops of hay off that water-meadow, bad or good; though in some wet years the second set of cocks had stood there miserably into winter-time almost. So the men's scythes were swishing down the meadow's pride in swathes that were here and there thickly yellow with buttercups, or in damp parts pale-lilac with ladies-smocks; while the women in white sun-bonnets went tossing out the hay. On a sudden Mistress Keag called out—

"There is Danny Gilhorn driving in to Maghrenagh market, in his brand-new, second-hand gig."

"It verily gives me a turn to see such a fool," muttered her husband, pausing a moment to wipe his forehead, then went on again with his toil.

When it was late afternoon, and they were a good deal more than midway across the meadow, they heard the wheels of a gig again; but this time saw, to their amazement, John Gilhorn's black, battered and aged "shandrydan—" in which he was carefully driving home his cousin Danny, who was plainly incapable of supporting himself.

"Tipsy!—ay, verily," muttered Keag, as the cousins passed, John sagaciously nodding, whilst Dan wildly waved his hat. Well, now! If that doesn't beat all!—boys-a-boys! They must be quite friends again—that is 'newuns,'" ejaculated Mistress Keag, stopping to stare with her arms akimbo.

This gave all the family in the hayfield something to speculate about, as was agreeable, till late evening. Then only, when the meadow was all cut, and the hot weary workers were loitering by the hedge, taking a last drink of butter-milk in turns from the solitary can, John drove up again; and leaving his wise old horse to graze along the roadside, came up, evidently so full of some piece of intelligence that he could not long contain it, for already it was escaping in awkward smiles and curious contortions of his body. Being assailed with questions, he gave them, bit by bit, to understand that, going to the market in the morning, Danny, through careless driving, had smashed his own gig; whereupon John, driving by, had rescued him from his predicament. Here he nodded at them slyly, with an air implying that—for all his guileless looks—there was a world of cunning in him. And afterwards he had "stood" his cousin a glass or two in Maghrenagh.

"Ay! and bigger news nor that! ... I—I—I'll hold you all, I've played a queer trick on yon chap from beyond Maghrenagh."

Hereupon Big John slapped his leg, and laughed outright; and then shook his head, as if ashamed of himself for such an ebullition of self-delight, although apparently none-the-less conscious he merited all praise for astuteness. To the renewed volley of questions that now buzzed about his ears, from all but Lill, who stood by silently, he slowly replied,

"I got round Danny ... and a slow business it was, and took a good deal of whiskey ... to promise *me* the first offer of his farm."

An outcry of amazement came from all; then expressions of congratulation, mixed with wondering looks, for John was usually considered so prudent, and even close, in his dealings, that it was conjectured he must be getting a cheap bargain; and yet Daniel was known to be greedy enough for others' coin, though he spent freely on himself. But John only buried his head in the tin can, hoarsely gurgling, "I'll drink till it," and finished the butter-milk.

Although much pressed, he would not go up to the farm, averring he had "lost his day already;" but, with a newly-confident smile, asked Lily to step just as far as the gate with him. She consented silently, and the rest discreetly trudged homewards. When the engaged sweethearts came to the gate, the young woman leant her arm on it, and Big John remarked to himself how very white her face was.

"Mr. Gilhorn, why did you do it?" she asked, with strange emotion. John smiled broadly. "I heered it slip from your tongue onst, you had had a fancy to live there since you were a wee child?"

The poor girl looked at him in a sort of dumb dismay. She could not say, "Yes, yes—but with another man; not you!" Meanwhile John went on, in half-regretful meditation.

"I've been turning it over in my mind a good bit past, for your sake—and it's fine land, too! Well, well, it's a grand bargain, but I'll be queerly sorry to leave the ould home; and I'd do it for noan other living woman!"

"But you might repent of it. It's not too late. O think twice of it," she urged, with all the pained awkwardness of one to whom a proposition intended to give great pleasure is secretly hateful.

Big John looked at her with quite a downcast expression stealing over his face, like a cloud across the moon.

"It's done now, for Danny swore he'd be off with the other man, and it was all for you I did it—just to make you like me a wee thing better."

The young woman's tongue was tied at that; could she tell him that the thought of thus realizing, indeed, her childish wish seemed the last straw to the burden on her meek spirit. She forced herself, poor soul, to think only of the goodness of this man whose wife she would soon be; and listened, as a debt of gratitude she owed him, to how, for once, Esau had got the better of Jacob, till the big man's heart was uplifted again—and finally, at parting, with shyness, and many abortive attempts at making his speech he prayed to be repaid for the day's work with a kiss.

Lill did not feel spirit enough within her to refuse him; maybe she owed her lover that much. She felt sadly and utterly vanquished now by this last proof of his affection. But, though he kissed her cheek, she seemed so still and passive that poor John could not feel as great a victor as would have been delightful; and somehow, as he drove home, he doubted whether he had not best have waited a wee while longer; for she was a saint, and such a sweetheart, of course, could not be wooed in an earthly and humanly affectionate fashion, like other women. Nevertheless, with all his reverence and almost awed admiration of her, Big John found a hankering in his foolish heart for a more vulgar display of affection, and less chill spirituality and strictness of manner, as he interpreted it in his woman divinity.

CHAPTER XXV

"The laborer with a bending scythe is seen,
  Shaving the surface of the waving green;
  Of all her native pride disrobes the land,
  And meads lie waste before his sweeping hand;
  While with the mounting sun the meadow glows,
  The fading herbage round he loosely throws;
  But if some sign portend a lasting shower,
  Th' experienc'd swain foresees the coming hour;
  His sunburnt hands the scattering fork forsake,
  And ruddy damsels ply the saving rake!
  In rising hills the fragrant harvest grows,
  And spreads along the field in equal rows."

GAY.

THERE was naturally much pride in James Keag's heart to think that his favorite daughter should be going to sit down as mistress in the finest farm in the countryside, as the Majempsys' former home was held to be. And the rest of the family were all more or less excited on the subject, though Osilla stoutly declared, against united opposition, that she thought John's own house far the most homely and pleasant-like to her mind. Amidst all this talk and congratulation Lill remained so quiet, humbler-looking, instead of being elated, that in their hearts all the folk in the household marvelled at her. But she felt like a wild creature that knew it was being silently snared with nets—she could hardly breathe! One day, John solemnly asked that his promised bride would walk down with him to the sea-farm.

"For," said he, with a wink, "I thought it just as well yesterday, since Danny is so agreeable, to drop a hint of how things is between me and you; and if ye could take a survey of the house, and see any changes you would like done—*beforehand!* it … it would be mighty convenient."

"So you told him! And what did your cousin say?" asked the young woman, slightly shrinking.

"You never saw a man so taken aback at the first!" replied John, with a great haw-haw. "And then he seemed pleased above anything, and shook hands, and wished me luck. 'O bring her down,' says he, 'I'll be ready for you both the morrow,' and he went away laughing to himself, fit to split. I believe, in my heart, that drink has made him mad."

So the Orange Lily put on her Sunday clothes and went soberly down the well-remembered solitary lane leading from their hill to the sea-farm with John, trying all the way to keep her thoughts from straying uselessly back to that sunny summer day long ago, when she and Tom Coulter, a pair of happy weans, had travelled this very path, and in the evening, returning, had plighted their troth. She was a foolish creature; she would not think about it. Was not her wedding-day coming so soon?—the thought choked her!

The day was unusually hot, although they neared the sea, and dark. There was thunder in the air, and rain seemed threatening as at last they reached the whitewashed farmyard. The gate, the only entrance here, was padlocked, to their surprise; so John hammered thereat, and shouted loudly to attract the attention of some one. After some time Danny Gilhorn's voice was heard from a stable close by, cursing and asking who was there and what they wanted. Then he himself appeared swaggering to the gate with his hat all awry, and two surly bull-terriers with him.

"We want in; and there is a shower coming," shouted Big John, briefly enough, being ill-pleased.

"Then I'm afraid you'll get wet, he! he! he!" sneered Danny, with a malicious leer, from the other side of the gate. "For you won't get in here; will they, my beauties?" and he stooped down to pet the bull-terriers, who growled at the strangers.

"Did you not ask us down?" inquired Big John, with amazement, supposing there was surely some joke in the matter.

ORANGE LILY

"Is it *I* ask the like of you two within my door? It's like your impudence; *you asked yourselves, ye beggars!*" sneered Danny, with drunken insolence; then grinning at his woman-guest from behind the strong bars of the gate, added, "Miss Keag, I wish you joy! though you don't seem as fond of John as you were of your father's farm-servant—he! he!"

"Come away—come away," whispered Orange Lily, hastily laying her hand on John's arm, while her face grew as red as a rose. But the latter seized the gate with all his might, and shook it.

"I'll thole sitch capers no long-er! … Did you not say that you would be ready for the owner to-be?" he bellowed, wrath beginning to boil in him.

The dastard inside shrank back a second; but seeing the gate was high and strong, and that bluster was safe, now treated them both to a variety of insulting grimaces as a garnishing to his speech.

"And so I am ready for the owner to-be; my own friend from beyond Maghrenagh who is coming down the road immejently. If he catches you here, he'll just murder the pair of ye, I can tell you, you big gawk! … yah! So you thought you had come round *me* with your blarney, did you? Did ye ever see such a pair of fools? O Lord! It will kill me with laughing," and holding his sides Danny indulged in a weak cackle, and such extravagant gestures of mirth that John thundered—

"*Are* you going to let me have the farm, or not?"

"I am not—!" returned Danny, with a horrible curse upon them both, as the two human beings—bar one!—he hated the worst in the world. Then he gave an exclamation, and darted back to the shelter of his house-door, for Big John had taken hold of the gate again, like a second Samson at Gaza, and was wrenching and shaking it till he seemed likely to burst it in. In a twinkling the coward had bolted and barred himself inside, yelling he'd take the gun—he'd take the law on them.

After a few minutes, like an angry bull that no longer sees the object of his rage, John Gilhorn desisted from his fruitless efforts; and, listening at last to the continual entreaties of his gentle companion, allowed himself to be led down to the sea-road that ran past the front of the farm along the beach. But, on turning the house-corner, to Lill's sore vexation he broke from her restraining clasp; and, rushing back a few steps, sent a well-directed stone whizzing through one of the windows. That done, he returned and drew a long breath, like one satisfied.

The young woman had purposely drawn her angry lover on to the high-road, although that was a longer way home, because a terrible thunderstorm was plainly about to break, and the lane was quite without shelter. Now she tried, for this reason, to persuade him to hurry onward till they should reach a cottage. But Gilhorn was almost unmanageable, and heeded nothing but the sore and shameful ill-treatment he had just received; recounting it all again and again with palsied speech, white lips, and body trembling with rage like a drunkard, or a man in ague.

All his sweetheart's well-tried qualities of sweet reasonableness and soothing persuasion were now called on and taxed for some time, to their very uttermost. With her hand laid on John's arm lovingly (as she had never before there placed it) she reminded him continually, putting the idea in every different shape imaginable, so that his mind might but some way receive it, that he had felt sorry at thought of leaving his own home—that she herself had been secretly grieved to think he had made the sacrifice for her—so that now they had both only to rejoice.

Tenderly, with most sweet womanly insistance, she pleaded, too, with him to control his passion; to be a man, and a Christian man. Yet so long was it in vain that her soul sank; and having no foundation of great affection for him on which, though beaten by his obstinacy, she could fall back, thinking, "Yet, with it all—I love him!" she found her heart suggesting how purposeless was this man's anger, and what unreason in his babbling outpourings.

He vapored too much and performed too little, it seemed to her; and though that only proved his harmlessness, yet comparing him with another man whom she had once known, who had stronger passions, but governed them, Lill trembled at coming so near despising him, with all his goodness. Then, growing impatient with both herself and him, she cried out—

"Ah, now! John, tell the truth! You're only angry at being made a fool of! It's not for the farm itself; it's that Danny has tricked you. Och! sure the disgrace is his own! You have acted as an honest man, and can hold up your head with the best. Indeed, I am vexed for you … but not sorry for myself."

"I am angry at losing the farm. It was to please you I wanted it," John repeated, and all her assurances of relief of mind were just wasted on him. Then Lill's heart burned, and said she—

"It is better to tell you the very truth, John Gilhorn. I am glad with my whole soul not to go there when I marry you," and, standing solemnly still, she pointed back to the farm, over which a dark cloud had gathered. "For when as a little child I had the vain wish to live there, it was with—another man."

Gilhorn's jaw fell slightly, and he turned a blank, gloomy stare on the young woman's face, that was visibly thrilled with emotion; while her eyes, full of sadness but utter honesty, met his without flinching—no, not to the quiver of an eyelash.

As if subdued either by her words, or a superiority he dimly felt and thus acknowledged—bred in her by suffering and displayed in patience, self-control, and love to all—the man, in sudden therefore strange silence, resumed his walk; and as mutely she stepped beside him.

A little while past, an unnatural darkness had begun to creep over the land; the dull, close afternoon had become hotter. From northwards, over the sea there, jagged black clouds came silently but swiftly moving across a background of dun. There came now deep murmurs in the distance, as if earth and sky were muttering to each other; then some few rain-drops, warnings of what was coming. By instinct each bird, beast, and insect was hidden; there seemed not a living thing left on the face of the land, and "Run!" both the man and woman ejaculated to each other, seeing a cottage near—and gained it none too soon. Quick, terrible flashes of lightning came in the east; the sky in that quarter was all cracked with flame; and mighty peals of thunder rolled, rumbled, and crashed right above the roof. Light and its brother sound seemed mocking mortals' fright, and urging each other to deave and dazzle poor old earth, worse and worse!

The only cottage inmates seemed two women, crouched, crying, and quaking in terror on the ground, with their heads under the bed-clothes, as was the usual practice in Ballyboly during a thunder-storm. In vain Lily Keag tried to comfort them; she could not make either listen; so at last turned away and gazed, with awe and admiration in her face, out of the window, at the mighty and glorious show.

"Are you not feared, too? I've heerd tell often of lightning coming down the chimney and killing people dead," said poor John Gilhorn, breaking his sullen silence at last.

"And if it did—!" came, as if she could not stop the words, from Lily's lips.

"Why?—what!" gasped Big John, shocked as at a blasphemy; and that from a saint. "You don't surely wish yourself *dead?* I've never heard the like of that from the lips of living soul! but just some wretches too miserable to care what happened till them … but, Lill!—you! held to be so religious—!"

But the young woman smiled a strange but beautiful smile, as if not caused by aught on this world; and her face seemed lit up by that holy and reverent expression as she answered—

"You don't quite rightly understand me, Mr. Gilhorn. I am willing to live while the Lord wishes me, but will be far more glad to die. Life is good, but death is just glory! And often I think what a darling thing it will be to lie down and be at rest—when He calls to me that I have finished my work for Him, here."

As she ended, a little child in a cradle, which they had not noticed, awoke and wailed. Lily took it to her arms, nursed it, and hushed its cries. Between the next two thunder-claps she heard John Gilhorn say, quite low, looking outside as he spoke,

"Lill … what do you think has become of that other man … of Tom Coulter?"

"I think he must be dead."

Another peal of thunder; then he said again—

"And—tell me … Do ye *really* still like him better nor me?"

"I like and respect you above most men, and, since you took the promise from me, I will try to be a true and good wife to you," Lill sadly answered; "but I loved him with my whole heart. And if he were to come back to-morrow as poor as he went—(which he never will)—God help me I I should feel just the same to him."

Neither spoke again to each other. The darkness outside was lit still by flashes, but only to appear again the denser. Then heaven's sluices seemed to open, and down full on earth, with the rushing noise of a waterfall, came the big rain, dark and drowning, hissing and flashing up from the ground, and turning the high-road into a water-course.

After a while the fierceness abated; there came a few more forked gleams, lessening rolls of heaven's artillery behind time in the concert; and there was peace again in the little house. The two women had recovered themselves; and one of them accused herself for never having heard her child cry out in its fright.

"But you quieted him well, Miss Keag. He seems as happy with you as me," she added, with gratitude—yet a touch of feminine jealousy.

"Still a mother's breath is aye the sweetest," replied Orange Lily, quoting a country saying; and gave her back her infant with that pleasant smile which made most hearts turn to her like flowers to the sun.

As she and John Gilhorn went homeward again by the high-road, they were silent all the way, except once when the young woman suddenly stopped, and cried out, "O—our hay!"

The water-meadows, which had been so recently cut and made into lap-cocks, had already had one severe soaking, so that this very morning the hay had been all spread again to dry. If, in that state, the thunder-shower had come down, before there was time to save the crop again—"Och, och! it would just be ruined!" as Big John, with the groan of a good farmer, made sole reply. But, lo and behold! as both came in sight anxiously of the low, flat mead, it was all dotted again with little lap-cocks; and Lill felt most thankful, for the hay would have been a severe loss, truly.

As they went up the lane together, Lill at last spoke again, and very earnestly, to entreat Gilhorn to say at first nought of what had so lately occurred, but let her gently break the matter to her people. And to this he silently nodded consent.

Inside the farm every one was at tea, and received them with such high spirits and eager tongues that both found themselves pushed into seats, and made to eat and listen, before either had courage to say or show that they carried ill news. Mistress Keag—of course—first taking up the word, declared that a special interposition of Providence had saved the hay. ("Ay, verily!" came from her husband.) For, as they were all hurrying, foreseeing the coming shower, and despairing, and working—dear help them, how they had worked!—a kindly man coming up the road, seeing their distress, had called out he would give them a hand's turn; and jumping the hedge, accordingly, seized a rake and wrought like nine men. ("Ay, verily!")

But for him the lower half would have lain there under that most outrageous drenching! ("Ay, verily! … And all the words ever he said was, when the lightning came, 'Bid the weemen go up to the house, for they will be skeered,' but himself just worked on," put in James Keag, dryly, with admiration.) When he took shelter in the kitchen at last, went on the goodwife, she had urged him, all her able, to stay for tea—such a handsome, fine man as he was, too! (A chorus in approbation of the stranger came from all the younger members of the family.) But he would noways be persuaded, saying he had to go on and see Daniel Gilhorn.)

"What! …" exclaimed Big John, striking his hand on the tea-table with a crash that made them all jump. "Where does he come from?"

"From—the dear help us!—from … I asked him from where, and he said from a good bit further than Maghrenagh."

"That's him," stuttered and spluttered Big John, scarlet now as any turkey cock. "That's the very man that has gone and cheated me out of the farm; for—for—for Danny has given it till him behind my back!"

Such a hurly-burly of voices arose at this that for a long time the gentle Orange Lily could not make herself heard in favor of peace. When the calm followed, however, she did speak up, to take in fairness the man's part who had so proved his kindness of disposition; who most likely knew nothing at all of Daniel's treachery; and who—they should all remember—had asked first for the farm, before John had ever thought of it.

Her words made some little impression on the men, notably on her father; although they would by no means acknowledge it. Yet, to her last remark, her young brother warmly, and John more tacitly, averred that a Ballyboly man ought to be preferred for a Ballyboly farm—be his rival never so good!

Mistress Keag and Osilla showed themselves, however, inclined to side with their homely farm-saint, who had appealed to the generosity of all present; but they were so manifestly stirred on this point by the remembrance of the stranger's good looks, that the men voted this a matter in which "wee-men had no call to interfere—" and retired with dignity to consult together, outside; for, "verily," said James Keag, "the female mind first goes the one way and then goes di-reckly the opposite; for all the world like the pendulum of a clawk."

The women, however, being all the more free to talk, bore up under this treatment; and Osilla, bridling and blushing—since she was plainly smitten—recounted to her elder how the man had asked her had she a sister as pleasant-looking as herself, for, if so, he would like her very much, he was certain sure.

"And I told him you would most likely be coming up the lane; and he directly after went down it—what a pity you missed seeing him!"

" Yes, he seemed greatly taken with Silla. Who knows, lass, but if poor Lill does miss the sea-farm, you'll maybe be mistress there?" merrily cried the mother; who, though heartily sorry for her step-daughter's supposed vexation, now took a brighter view of the case. "Oh—ma!" cried Osilla. half modestly, half with a vexed air—but pleased.

Before bed-time that night they learnt the result of the men's private discussion, however. It had been agreed among them that on the morrow morning Big John should go to the Colonel, and just let him know how ill his tenant for the sea-farm had behaved; it being shrewdly guessed that then Danny and the new man would be at the Castle.

"He'll be staying this night with Danny," observed eager young Hans, as though he had something to suggest anent that.

"Not he", interrupted Mistress Keag, "for he asked me what time the long-car to Maghrenagh[24] would pass the sea-farm. 'In

---

[24] Maghrenagh. A fictional name used by the author for the nearby market town and sea-port of Donaghadee, largely owned by her Delacherois relatives and close to this 'sea-farm' with its view "facing the white strand and the broad sea across to Scotland". Maghrenagh is anticipated in May Crommelin's first book, *Queenie. A Novel*, published in 1874.

an hour,' says I. 'If you do be wanting it, you'll not have many minutes with your friend.' 'Quite time enough,' says he, smiling; and by that I judged he was no such an' a great friend either."

James Keag, it had been settled, was to accompany Big John both as friend and witness; but that night, worse luck, took rheumatics so badly, owing to a partial wetting in the thunder-shower, that he was obliged reluctantly to abandon the idea in favor of Hans, his son, who most willingly undertook to represent him; secretly thinking that young blood, in these matters, brought matters to a more glorious issue, even when defeated, than did the sluggish, sober minds of his elders.

CHAPTER XXVI

"By this, the sun was out o' sight,
 An' darker gloaming brought the night;
 The bum-clock humm'd wi' lazy drone;
 The kye stood rowtin i' the loan."
                                                    BURNS.

"Since there's no help, come, let us kiss and parte:
 Nay, I have done: you get no more of me:
 And I am glad, yea, glad with all my heart,
 That thus so cleanly I myself can free!"
                                                    DRAYTON.

THE women and the sick man at the farm saw, with vast interest, their two spokesmen set out for the Castle; and watched eagerly, and with still greater curiosity, for their return. But two hours passed—and only at noon, when they were sitting down to dinner, did Hans enter with a slow step and a dubious, almost dejected air, very different from his ardor of the morning—and alone.

"John would go home his lone," were his first words, "but bid me say he'd be up this evening, maybe."

The rest easily perceived that the young lad had no great news to tell; so, not to humiliate him, his father repressed the mother's eager inquiries as to whether the Colonel had not been rightly angered by their tale, and bid Hans help himself to his food first, and then recount the morning's doings in his own way.

Hans did so; and first remarked, with an air of chagrin, that there was little to say. However, said he, to their surprise, when they reached the Castle, and, after some delay, were shown into the justicing room, Danny was not there, but the stranger alone—so well-dressed and "troth! so much the gentleman!" and the Colonel seeming quite familiar with him, that the light left their eyes, as Hans expressed it, and both felt quite abashed.

John, however, was obliged to speak; and had no sooner given them, albeit dully, to understand that he had received his cousin's promise of getting the first offer of the farm—but now found himself cheated—than both his hearers seemed surprised.

The stranger spoke up bravely, like an honest man, as Hans must acknowledge; and bid them both believe he had never known that any other man wanted the farm, let alone himself.

"You know that is so, Colonel!" he had said, appealing to the landlord.

"Certainly," said the Colonel, who stood lifting his coat-tails before the empty fire place with one hand, and stroking his moustache with the other, as Hans described him; "and more than that, it is nearly a fortnight since Daniel Gilhorn sold his farm to Mr. Redhead, who was acting for his friend here, Mr.—"

"Lee," put in the stranger.

"Whom I agreed to accept," went on the Colonel, smiling, "as a fit and proper tenant."

At that John and young Hans gaped, open-mouthed; but, before they could speak, the stranger again took up the word, adding—

"And your cousin was so eager to get rid of the farm that, although I never expected to come into possession of it till November next, when he would have got in the crops, he offered to make it over immediately; which Mr. Redhead, on my behalf, accepted." Upon hearing, and at last thoroughly understanding, how, from first to last, his cousin must have been fooling him, John went clean mad, added Hans; and in his wrath blurted out the whole remaining part of the history of his ill-usage—"and why you had gone down to Danny's house with him, Lill—plump and plain!"

At that the Colonel looked rather queerly at the stranger, but stroked his moustache still, and held his peace; while the other never said a word either, but looked straight out of the window. At last he turned round in a rather sudden manner, and asked

Colonel Alexander to allow him kindly a few minutes' private conversation with John, when he hoped they would come to a friendly understanding. The Colonel seemed at this not surprised—(which much surprised Hans!)—but agreed with an air of great kindness, and had the two men shown into the dining-room; whilst Hans—having no more business to transact—had been obliged to go out into the waiting-room, where he had cooled his heels, said he, for a good half-hour.

When, at last, the rivals did come out, John seemed quite daundered and silent, and refused to vouchsafe to his young companion one word of explanation of what had passed betwixt himself and the stranger. All Hans—who was disgusted at being treated in this childish way—could remark was, that, on parting, Gilhorn and the latter had shaken hands; the man called Lee observing that all that afternoon must be spent by him in having the goods and chattels at the sea-farm valued, since he had agreed to take them wholesale—but that he would not spend the night under the same roof with the mean cur who still owned it. Would he come up to his house, then, Big John had said. And the other hesitated, then replied that would depend upon what Gilhorn himself would tell him by evening.

This gave the whole Keag family much cause for discussion and surmises, and altogether unprofitable and puzzled talk; so that they all tarried longer than usual round the remains of their meal.

Hans, with a young lad's hastiness to condemn his elders as slow-paced and dull-eyed, declared that Big Gilhorn had shown himself "soft" in the whole matter; and should let him, Hans, teach all Ballyboly how Danny should be treated according to his deserts. Osilla still more warmly defended the absent John from this charge. Upon which, her brother replied that it would be more fitting if she let her elder sister, with whom he never quarrelled, because of her reasonableness and gentle temper, say all that. The father had to quell the rising war of words by ordering his son outside to work; while Lily had some ado to soothe poor Osilla's incensed feelings. Before he went, Hans, however, took occasion to whisper to the former,

"Big John bid me tryst you to meet him down the lane—after supper."

So that evening found Orange Lily down the lane at the appointed time; with no joy in her heart, yet no sharp sting there either, since now her dread of having to live at the sea-farm was removed. Yet she had loved well its view facing the white strand and the broad sea across to Scotland, so blue and fair to gaze on up and down in the summers; so fresh, and changeful, and living a sight with its ebb and flow even in winter-time—when the small, bare fields around John Gilhorn's home, like those below her father's lane, made the country's face like an ill-pieced, deplorably ugly patchwork quilt. It was late now; yet she never looked down the lane for her lover, but was industriously working at her flowering[25]—as the white embroidery, which was well-nigh the sole means of gaining a livelihood known to the women in those parts, was called. Farmer Keag's daughter did not, of course, depend on the few shillings to be gained by even the finest needle-work, like others; but having the reputation of being the daintiest needle-woman in all the country, she had never to beg work, like many whom part of her earnings went secretly to console. Now she plied her shining needle through the little "hoop" that stretched the work, as if her sole thought was to finish a delicate flower-sprig before the red sun went down.

But the sun set, and the glory of the west faded to a golden gray; a mist rose up over the marsh down there, then blended with exhalations from other low-lying places into a tender, almost

---

[25] *flowering*. The domestic, white-on-white embroidery also called 'Ayrshire Lace' was commercially organised in the Ards by Scottish agents based in Donaghadee.

imperceptible veil over the land; and still she worked on—and he did not come. She had waited by a bit of fence, to gain more light than under the hedge. Across the field beyond lay the Castle woods, over which the moon was rising; seeming to her so like a beautiful silver thing hung there in the sky, that every summer and ever summer's night seemed a new and exquisite sight, that she raised her eyes to admire it, awed—and, then only, became aware that John Gilhorn was almost by her side.

"I'm feared you've been waiting long," said he, approaching.

"I was working; so that the time passed quickly," Lill tranquilly replied, to reassure him. But he answered with a downcast air, to her surprise—

"I'm thinking, if ye cared much above the common for me—ye would har'ly make that reply."

Orange Lily knew not what to say; never hitherto having credited John with much sensibility or delicacy of perception in such subtle matters as a maiden's mind towards a man; but even while she hesitated he went on, looking downwards at his strong brogues and speaking steadily, as if reciting a speech learnt by heart—

"Those words you let drop yesterday have wrought queerly in my mind since … And I'm come this evening to say … that if it is your wish to be set free from your promise to me—I'm agreeable!"

To save him pain—and that meant much to her!—the young woman could not have prevented the great wave of relief, the sense of lightening that thrilled through her whole being. Yet she did not know how it had lighted up her face, till, raising her eyes, as if to see whether he truly meant it, she saw a vexed expression on poor John's ordinarily unemotionable, kindly visage. Hastily—for him—he answered himself—

"There, there! … It's easy seen that is good news to you."

"Indeed, Mr. Gilhorn, I do think it will be happier for both of us," she softly pleaded, grieved to have grieved him, yet knowing it was better so; and, above all, thinking how the blessed deliverance she had longed for had so unexpectedly come! It was wonderful! it was wonderful! so wonderful she could not realize it!

"Well … well … well," said John, half turning on his heel, "I'm not angry that ye don't like me better; for that should come natural … and if you haven't got it, ye can't help it. But I cannot but say I'm sorry, too, till give up a notion that has been in my mind this wee while back. You're as good as gold—as good as gold! but maybe, as I thought to myself this day—ratherly *too* good for me!"

Seeing he still waited, Lill murmured—with a touch of feminine curiosity for details—but with real sympathy, too—

"When did you make up your mind to it—was it last night?"

"No—" replied her late lover, truthfully, "I went to sleep. But since some things that happened this morning, I lay all day at the back of a ditch and thought upon it, and for a long time I said nought but drat it! drat it! drat it! to myself, and then I took a turn for the better. Well, good night," and he moved away.

"Will you tell my father yourself?" asked the girl.

Big John turned his head and looked at her, as if petitioning a last favor.

"Och! for any sake, could *you* not let on to them? And don't blaze it out, to create a ruction between us, but let it slip from you softly."

"I will so," kindly assured his late sweetheart.

And with a slow and very serious good night, he went down the lane. But she, with a heart off which mountains seemed raised, went home, and took occasion to tell her parents that the disappointment about the sea-farm had put off John from thoughts of marrying yet awhile; at which, though plainly vexed, they were silent, and, knowing his tardiness, not surprised. Poor Lily's brain was quite giddy, she felt so light-headed with relief—though ashamed, and almost grieved, to be so glad, so very faithfully, humbly thankful.

Young Hans had gone out, none knew whither.

But that night to Osilla, in the retirement of their joint little chamber, the elder sister was fain to confide all that had passed; feeling need of her present sisterly sympathy and future support—yet a little dreading her censure. For, in all matters relating to John Gilhorn, his old favorite, though almost torn asunder by her allegiance to both, took his part even before that of the sister who was, otherwise, her incarnate ideal and living example. To the other's astonishment, soft-hearted Silla cried out, "O Lill, Lill! … I am so glad!" then melted into a rivulet of tears of joy. Drying her eyes hastily, however, with a scarlet blush the lassie protested that these foolish drops arose solely from the excess of her gladness that their home comforter was spared now a marriage that she had strangely never "*rightly conceited*" (however fair-seeming to others!). Her elder sister acquiesced in the truth of this assertion, the young girl plainly believing it true; but, even whilst she gravely kissed and quieted her, scales had fallen from Lill's loving eyes, and she saw a thing plainly which before had been hidden from her, and still was dark to simple, young Osilla herself.

CHAPTER XXVII

"The heavy hours are almost past
    That part my love and me:
My longing eyes may hope at last
    Their only wish to see.

"But how, my Delia, will you meet
    The man you've lost so long?
Will love in all your pulses beat,
    And tremble on your tongue?"
                    LYTTELTON.

"And will I see his face again?
    And will I hear him speak?
I'm downright dizzy wi' the thought,
    In troth, I'm like to greet!"
                    MICKLE.

THE next morning there was some stir in the country round. For it was told at the public-house and discussed at the smithy, and before noon the word had passed to most of the farms, that Daniel Gilhorn had taken French leave of the country.

Young Hans Keag knew as much of the matter as anybody, and told his knowledge to his family; but that rather sheepishly, for it did not add to his credit, he felt. It seemed that, burning to resent his sister's wrongs and gratify his own ardor to engage in a good row on any decent pretext, he had urged William-Thomas Gilhorn to join him as his brother's champion and go down in the past evening to Danny's house to give him a beating. To this William-Thomas willingly agreed; but the misfortunate creature's ill-luck stuck to him even in this, as Hans added with deep disgust. For, being such a sieve that he could keep no secret above an hour, and likewise thinking it a pity not to let some more friends join in the spree, he had gabbled about the matter to some other young men. His old farm-servant overheard him, and, being of a magpie nature, forthwith sent secret word to Danny's ancient housekeeper, a crony of her own; lest the "crature would be scarred" out of her wits! To add to her transgressions, it seemed that Big John, on quitting Orange Lily in the lane that evening, went straight to the churchyard, where he had a tryst (as was supposed) with the stranger who had bought the sea-farm—and who had been waiting for him there for near two hours, sitting by a grave. Both, after some talk, had started to go back for the night to Big Gilhorn's house like good friends, when, passing William-Thomas's door close by, his brother stopped to look in. Then, murder and turf! the whole job was blazed out by the tongue of "that ould ijit," as Hans unkindly designated the confiding granny; whereupon John, pressed thereto by the stranger, set off at a run to the sea-farm to keep the peace.

Meanwhile, the conspirators, after battering at Daniel's gate in the dusk of that sweet summer's night, forced an entrance only to find their enemy had given them the slip, and escaped. This crowning act of sneakingness on his part, bringing to nought their well-laid plan of retribution, roused the indignation of these punishers of evil-doing to such a pitch that they proposed and were just about to execute the wrecking of the house, when John Gilhorn and the stranger arrived and spoiled all the sport. The new-comer made himself master of the situation at once, as Hans was bound to acknowledge. He quieted them, reasoned with them; and when he made them finally understand that he had already paid down his money for the house and furniture, which were therefore his, they left him in peaceful possession, and departed. But that next day the gnashing of teeth among the small shop-keepers of Ballyboly, the smith and miller, and all to whom money had been owed, or from whom it had been borrowed, by Daniel Gilhorn, was great; for all that could be traced of him was that, having received a good sum from the in-comer that afternoon—he had slipped away like a thief in the night.

In the late afternoon, Orange Lily, who had been "misrested," as the expression was, during the night by the revulsion of feeling and consequent excitement in her mind, asked her step-mother to spare her for an hour or two from work; and by way of holiday set out to visit a sick woman down the back-lane that ran towards the sea. Seldom, indeed, did she go abroad except on some such errand; for she had a great fear of wasting her time, and a mere idle walk such as other farmers' daughters many a time took, would have been almost a sin to her—though it did not seem to her a sin in others.

She never judged her neighbors. But, this day, she was some-what severely anxious to judge herself, although hardly knowing wherein she had erred. She was troubled without knowing why; glad of freedom, yet feeling a void; ready to blame herself for not yet having told her father of her *dis*-engagement—although conscious that she had been eager to snatch any good opportunity of doing so all day, and had only refrained because none had yet come, and she shrank from increasing the pain he would, surely, anyway feel.

The sick woman was unmarried, lonely, and such a sufferer that she could seldom creep further than her door for fresh air. The farm-maiden crossed its threshold now, like light to her eyes, said the poor soul.

"And, oh!" said she, as, after comforting her a good while, at last Orange Lily rose to go, "Miss Keag, dear—may God bless you and send you a good husband and children of your own, that you may never be left a lonely stick like me."

As Lill went out, she hesitated an instant or two whether or not to turn homewards; but at last strolled slowly onwards down the solitary lane. The walk further was perhaps a luxury, yet that day she felt she wanted it; really needed a little time for thought; was glad of the solitariness and silence. Foolish, inconsistent feminine heart that hers was, the sick woman's parting wish had stirred up too many dead longings, vain regrets within her bosom, which should have been only glad of deliverance, that day, from unwelcome marriage. She chid herself soberly, trying to reason fairly with herself. "Are you never satisfied?" she asked, as if this weak loving nature within her was another woman. "All you wanted lately was not to be John Gilhorn's wife—now you have your wish, why be fretting again because you are likely to be an old maid; because you have no future but a blank after your parents go to sleep quietly in the churchyard, and when the wee ones will all be grown-up and married? Put away thought of that long-past time when you were loved and loved again." Still Lill found herself quietly, regretfully weeping, for all that. But when the tears had washed her cheeks, she felt lighter-hearted again, and began to call pleasanter thoughts into her mind with a pale smile; putting by the sad remembrance of how complicated matters at home still must be, whilst her father's debt was a mill-stone round his neck.

Daniel Gilhorn's departure from the country, for ever, seemed to lift a cloud that had always hung in her otherwise clear mental horizon; and a little hope also lovingly crept about her sisterly heart, small as yet, but with much likelihood of one day becoming a great and joyous fact, that Big John might be consoled for loss of her, and yet find a more loving wife than she could have been to him, in the old farmhouse at home. Lily herself would, of course, now be a spinster and a "regular old maid."

Thus musing, Lill took off her white sun-bonnet to let the sea-breeze play about her brow that pleasant sunny day; and since also the old lane was utterly solitary for a mile around, so no neighbors would be surprised at the indecorum of a farmer's well-to-do daughter walking bareheaded a mile from home. The sunshine lit up Orange Lily's warm-hued tresses as with an aureole. What tears still glistened in her eyes only made them the brighter, like dewdrops on a spray. Her face was now like that of an angel—holy, heaven-turned, and hardly sad—it was so still and gentle.

A few steps further, round a sharp bend, was a pleasant bit, where the high banks were topped with furze above and made a grassy seat below; and where once, long ago, two little children, coming home at evening, after a long day's pleasuring by the shore, stopped to share their sea-spoils and to plight their troth with the rim of a limpet-shell.

The lonely poor soul had a wish—a foolish yearning to see the spot again.

Coming round the corner, the young woman found herself close beside a man already standing there. At that, taken aback, Lill stopped. The thought flashed through her that here was the new owner of the sea-farm. A man with full, dark, curling beard and ruddy complexion, strong-limbed and broad, who stood as if lost in reverie; his arms folded—now he turned. Three or four seconds both stood gazing at each other; then the earth seemed reeling under Lill, and the sky vanishing. "*Tom Coulter!*"—she shrieked, and would have fallen, but that the man, with a great exclamation, had already caught her in his arms—and was straining her to his breast as if two beings, whom supposed death had sundered, should meet again in full love and life on this side of the grave.

....

The first exquisite rapture of that meeting passed words. Neither could utter them. Yet each knew what the other felt; but it seemed as though they must not squander the knowledge on the vagrant tell-tale air around.

The afternoon passed; yet they had only stirred to sit together in close embrace side by side on the bank, as they had sat when far more youthful lovers. Time seemed as nothing to them, and their shadows on the sun-dials of their lives to have gone backward ten degrees. Often they looked in each other's eyes, the soul's windows, as if to see down into those very souls; and questioned each other's faces to know what change time had wrought; or again felt both hearts and souls stilled in the calm of utter bliss, not to be stirred with even unspoken asking. They were like beings of a better world than ours in the perfectness and purity of their happiness—and in that they took no reckoning of past years, and only felt humanly mortal when, again and yet again, they kissed.

In Tom's eyes, as he told her, Lill was not changed, but perfected. His girlish Orange Lily of eight years ago had only become fuller-blown, a gracious woman. To her, poor thing, Tom seemed just the living impersonation of all her proudest hopes and wildest dreams for his possible future. That he was, indeed, the very owner of the sea-farm, his lips told her; that he was well off his coat alone answered for; but now she asked to hear all the rest—the whole of his life and adventures since they so sorrowfully parted years ago.

"That will take the most of the rest of our lives in the telling," said Tom, smiling fondly at his love with the old tone of mastership of their childhood so dear to her, perforce dropped later. "But come!—to give you a rough notion (like the wee maps I had to help you in drawing at 'schuil')—I had a harder time of it after we went out than I would have had folk at home know. It was for nearly two years like fighting hand to hand with fate—and feeling you'd be beaten! Then my poor father died; and though he was aye a burden that was dear to me, still I felt the better able to struggle on single-handed. Till then, though I am thankful to think he never wanted bread, yet many a day I had none; and I never knew how long still he could be fed. Ah! my lass, I was often glad you never knew it … !

"After that, I went off to California to the diggings, and had a rare run of luck. Everything seemed to prosper with me. The money seemed to turn up under my spade. I had a clever, fortunate partner, too, and was the envy of many another poor fellow.

"And then I would not write home to you; for first I feared you would not be suffered to get a letter, and next I said to myself it was best not to write till soon I'd have enough money made to start home, and surprise you—and the whole parish besides, that had looked down on the farm-servant. I was so uplifted with self-confidence that I said in my soul any man with a sound mind and a healthy body can get on in this world, and needs no help *but* himself. There was no more confident, masterful man ever walked God's earth than I was during those months; only it seemed to me more man's earth than His, handed over to us for the strongest to make the most of … Then I was suddenly struck down with a bad illness, and lay for days between life and death—and, when at last my senses came back, it was to find that my partner had, meanwhile, robbed me of every farthing, and made tracks clean away!

"At that, Lily—I own to you—I laid down my head and cried. I was as weak as a little child in mind and body; and far poorer than when I started out from here. My pride was utterly broken; and all my trust in my own strength rightly humbled; but the good that hard time did me," Tom added, reverently and quietly, "I am now grateful from my heart for.

"Then, seeing an opening, back I went to New York, and became a clerk. My old education came in useful, and I worked at nights and picked up a good deal more. Often I used to go down to see the emigrant ships from home come in, and watch whether there was any face I recognized; and so once I saw young Henry-Thomas.

"He knew me too—this beard was not full-grown then—and told me about all in Ballyboly; but the only one I cared to hear of was you, and when he said how you were still unmarried, and a blessing to the parish—I cannot tell you, dear, what I felt.

"There was as yet no hope for me of going home for years. Still I was able to take the boy back with me, and give him a helping hand; but bid him not mention my name when writing to Ballyboly."

"O, but—" cried out Lily Keag, with eyes that, though wet, shone with such a gladness and light as they had not known for many a day, "he did speak of having met a kind friend. And we, who never guessed it was you—"

Tom let her say no more.

"Only a month or two ago," he resumed, "our junior partner in the firm—an old man, though—died. He had taken a fancy to me, and asked my history; and as he reminded me something of my dead father, I told him it—all. It seemed he had risen himself from being a mere clerk; but had not what I have—one, at least, in the world, dearer than myself. No living being was much more to him than another, poor old man! He spoke little to me afterwards, but seemed kind; and when he died—to my astonishment—had left poor Thomas Coulter a fortune!"

"And are you rich, then?" his old love cried; dwelling on the word, with a surprise the greater that this exceeded even her dreams for him—"well-to-do" having been their utmost limit.

"Not rich in the sense of gentle-folk; but three—four times as rich as your late lover, poor Big John," cried Tom joyously, again embracing her.

The rest of the tale was soon told.

Even before he had left for America, his good friend, Mr. Redhead, had known most of his history; on the chance that he was still in that part of the country, Tom wrote again, telling him all. At Coulter's earnest request to know whether the Majempsys' farm was to be had (young Henry-Thomas having told him how that Daniel Gilhorn was wrecking it fast), the good pastor had successfully applied for it.

Tom quickly followed his letter. "On that day of the thunder-storm I was coming straight to see you," said he. "Seeing none of your folk had recognized me in the field, I stayed as short a time as I could, and talked most to Osilla, knowing she could not remember me; for I would not betray myself till I should meet you—and was sorely disappointed to miss you down this lane. Next morning I called first to see the Colonel, who remembered me rightly when I told him who I was, (though they all say I am wonderfully altered, too). And his kindness to me—even though good Mr. Redhead had told all my story in his own way, and dressed it up till it seemed romantic—his great kindness, even considering that, was far more than I deserve. But when your young brother, that I had so often carried in my arms, and John Gilhorn, came in—O, when it was talked of, quite naturally, by both that, after all, you were soon to become his wife ... Lill, dear, it went badly with me for a few moments! Well, we spoke alone together; and had all out. Poor John got a start when it suddenly flashed across him who I was. He said little about whether you were attached to him—you know his way; but I could guess pretty much how it was, and had some glad and selfish hopes again.

"Will you give me this day to turn it over in my mind," said John at last, "seeing she is promised to me, and I like her very well? Maybe I'll free her from her word ... not being a hard man. Maybe I will not ... for a bargain is a bargain. If she takes you without my consent, it will be a bad day for us all ... but maybe by evening I might come round, for peace is peace. And a woman may be the best under heaven; but, if she doesn't take kindly to you, a man might be happier with the second best."

"And before we left he said he would not wish me, after all, to have had worse luck in life—having always had a kindly feeling to me, although it came ill upon him ... poor old John!"

And, in return," went on Tom, "I offered freely to give him up the farm, and leave the country for ever, if you found you liked him better than—"

But at that the Orange Lily reproached him with a hasty, joyful, loving ejaculation, and then a timid caress, for she was almost awed still by this outward-seeming stranger; and so the rest of that sentence was never finished, Tom being only too delighted to be thus diverted from it.

It was, indeed, no great wonder that he had been unrecognized by those who in former days had looked on him with indifferent or unappreciating eyes; for even the girl who loved him had not discerned all the possibilities of fine development in his character, and had only known its unpolished sterling worth. The ruddy plough-boy they had known had become a somewhat weather-beaten, bronzed, and bearded man; his coarse clothes were changed to as good a coat as the richest farmer around would wish to wear on week days; voice, accent, manner, were all refined and improved, so as to escape the memory of those who had not, like his sweetheart, kept the true spirit and meaning of them constantly in mind since years. And she now recognized them, but with gladness and wonder as transformed.

It was allowable enough, indeed, that young Hans had thought the stranger almost a gentleman. Travel, with eyes that saw and perceived, experience and self-education, though only fed on scraps of time and crumbs of knowledge, had made of Thomas Coulter a thoughtful, self-respecting, fairly cultured man. So the young woman knew, with a natural discrimination heightened of late years by the habit of looking with weary eyes at the other men in the country around—unconsciously asking herself whether any had such qualities as could please her mind or satisfy her soul. So she sat, hardly able to take her loving eyes an instant off the man's manly face, except when she dropped them with modesty and overweening gladness—or because Tom caressed and praised her with such extravagance (as she thought, being meek and moderate) that she could not look up.

But why had Tom called himself Lee, she asked; and how had Danny been persuaded to sell the farm to his enemy? Tom laughed with glee, the sinner.

"I am Lee; it was the poor old gentleman's name, and he wished me to take it with his fortune. And, as Thomas Coulters are as plentiful as blackberries, how was Danny to know that the rich Mr. Coulter-Lee—whose history good Mr. Redhead did not think it a gospel duty to tell him—was the poor little chap with his elbows out of his jacket, that Dan used to sneer at in school!

"That day of the thunderstorm, he was too drunk, when I did arrive, for him to recognize me. All the business was already done; though yesterday I thought it time to give myself the pleasure of watching his face when I disclosed the fact."

"What was it like?" asked Lily, almost ready to pity the poor wretch for such a deep mortification.

"It was a treat!" dryly remarked Tom. "But he had not been drinking, and there was no gate between us—so he was very cowed. He forgave me in the most warm and humble manner the beating I last gave him, and was inclined to weep; and tried his utmost to cheat me into paying double what his furniture was worth. Well, he is gone anyway; and his memory go with him! … See, dear, it is getting late; and I want to walk back with you and make friends with your father again, and all the dear people upon the hill there, this very night."

CHAPTER XXVIII

"O fortunate, O happy day,
  When a new household finds its place
Among the myriad homes of earth,
Like a new star just sprung to birth,
And rolled on its harmonious way
Into the boundless realms of space!
So said the guests in speech and song,
As in the chimney, burning bright,
We hung the iron crane to-night,
And merry was the feast and long."

LONGFELLOW.

IT need hardly be told now how the Keag family were reconciled to the new owner of the sea-farm; how, after recognition, astonishment, and wonder at his history, they at last settled down to a complacent feeling that Providence had thus rightly favored their former farm-servant, in order to bless themselves—in the person of their Orange Lily—in a roundabout way, with his riches.

"Verily! it is remarkable, most remarkable—but I'll not disallow a marriage betwixt them now," quoth James Keag, with a dry smile, to his neighbors, when Tom's origin was discussed. And his friends, who knew how this future son-in-law could buy all Keag was worth many times over, smiled too.

And, a few days later, on the Twelfth of July, Tom Coulter-Lee—(or rather Coulterlee, as the folk all took to calling him)—and his sweetheart at last realized their childish agreement of long ago, and walked together proudly with the Ballyboly lodge to the meeting-place of the Orangemen of the countryside. And the very next day they were married; while all the village street was still strung across with arches of orange lilies,[26] twice as many as on most Julys, in honor of the double rejoicing; and the little path up to the church, likewise.

It was the biggest wedding ever was seen! And, to make it more noticeable, as the merry procession went along, the Colonel himself, and his little son on a pony, came riding by. Their landlord stopped on the road and called out such good wishes to Tom and his bride that no wonder the latter blushed, and her bridegroom looked a proud and pleased man that day. And more by token, the very evening before, the Colonel's lady herself, with her two little daughters and the twin old ladies, had all gone in their carriage to the Keags' farm. "Six ladies in all, bar one; and he was the *futman!*" quoth William-Thomas Gilhorn, who had watched them go by, recounting the matter to the curious.

The Colonel's wife brought Orange Lily a cuckoo clock so quare! that—but this is anticipating—her children and Tom's wonderingly admired it, as would their children's children, no doubt. But the good spinster sisters gave a great Bible; telling their favorite farm-maiden, with gentle, earnest voices, that no match in all the country round had given them such pleasure for years. Miss Edith and Miss Alice, dear good ladies, had indeed—by dint of mildly observing to each other how suitable such a union seemed between their two school-favorites of some twenty years ago—begun to believe they had always foreseen it, and at last that they had had some hand in this glad ending.

Such a bright wedding-day as it was! And such a fine crowd of friends!

Every man at the wedding wore an orange lily in his button-hole, and every woman in her bosom. One of the happiest

---

[26] 'Orange Arches' were originally simple constructions made by suspending bunches of flowers (Sweet Williams and Orange Lilies) from lines of string or wire between temporary poles.

faces there was that of the master of the Ballyboly Orange Lodge—whose pride in the social exaltation of his idolized daughter, and pleasure in watching the happiness of her face, "Verily," said he, "made just a fool of him."

Mr. Redhead married the young couple himself; and John Gilhorn, like a kindly man, swallowed his disappointment and came bravely to church with Osilla, to whom he was heard to confide with a sigh like a wind-blast, and plenty of sound in his whisper, "that he had grown used to herself, like; though most young weemen were the biggest plagues in life! … Her sister, the bride, he would always uphold to be a saint on earth, but—but …" He was then seen apparently struggling to find in his pocket some words for expressing to the young girl an idea that was not yet quite clear to his own mind; but that seemed to have arisen by dint of gazing at her blushing face and listening to her murmurs of sympathy.

It may here be added that a short time later Daniel Gilhorn was heard of, as having fallen off drunk from a car at some races, and being taken to hospital, where he died without recovering consciousness. There was no great mourning for him. Big John, his cousin, inherited after him what was left of the old grandfather's money; which, as Mistress Keag truly remarked, was "a powerful consolation!"

And on that wedding-day was seen a grander sight than had gladdened the Ballyboly gossips for many a long year. For no less than one carriage and five inside cars took the bridal party gayly on the usual wedding-drive round the country, instead of mere "outside" ones. And when, that golden evening, they halted at the married couple's home—and the farm looked smiling and neat by the blue sea as any heart could wish—not one, far or near, in all the country-side but wished the new-made husband and wife from their hearts good-luck!

When all the rest had left, Tom and his wife, standing on the threshold of their own home, held each other's hands; and looking over the pleasant farm on either hand, and the fair sea in front, turned and looked next moment in each other's eyes—smiling.

And Tom, with a steadfast face, said—

"We have kept our word to each other."

"Ay!" said his new-made wife, gently; "with God's blessing."

And thus it happened after all, to the astonishment of Ballyboly parish, that Orange Lily, Farmer Keag's daughter, married her father's farm-servant.

THE END.

THE WITCH OF WINDY HILL

CHAPTER I

"To hear an open slander is a curse:
But, not to find an answer is a worse."

OVID.

IN the North of Ireland—the Black North, as the hot-blooded southrons[27] call the province where the sun shines less warmly than with themselves, and Protestants and Presbyterians and Scotch-speaking descendants of Scotch-bred colonists abide[28]—there lived some years ago in one of the districts furthest from towns and civilization, a widow and her only child. This only child was a girl.

The widow's name was Daly; and she and little Mary lived in a poor enough cottage, with two fields attached to it, on the top of a little hill so bleak, bare and solitary, among surrounding lowlands, that it was known through all the country simply as "The Windy Hill."[29]

Just below the hill, however, in the valley, was a farm of rich land—richer indeed than most of the holdings around, and Dennis Ryan, the young farmer who owned it, himself still almost a mere lad, and alone in the world, besides being young, was strong, handsome, and comfortably off. Through the valley ran a little stream, and where the high road crossed this by means of the bridge lived the carpenter and his wife. These two were thus the next nearest neighbours to the Widow Daly; but not any the more welcome for that, since the carpenter's wife was a shrew and

----

[27] *southron.* An archaic term for a person from the south, formerly used by Scots to describe the English. Here the author uses it to refer to people from the south of Ireland.

[28] *Scotch-speaking.* The 'Ulster-Scots' tongue was known by its speakers as 'Scotch' throughout the 19th century.

[29] *Windy Hill* appears to be located between Carrowdore and Greyabbey (the 'Ballyboly' and 'Black Abbey' of *Orange Lily*).

a gossip, with a bitter tongue in her head.

Some years ago, Widow Daly had come to take up her abode at Windy Hill as an utter stranger. None knew whence she came or wherefore. The peasants round, naturally after a while, went up the hill to visit her from curiosity, although somewhat harsh in their ways and more outspoken than polite.

But the new neighbour was a "stand-off"[30] woman they all afterwards separately declared. Plainly not from those parts of the country, though as to where she did come from they got very little "satisfaction," as they expressed it. They all were displeased, more or less, at being thus baffled; and some said she was proud and unfriendly; and some even said she was a suspicious character. The truth was, the widow was so sad a woman, and one who, with bitter reason, had so sore a heart, that she shrank from the faces and questions of strangers, and would rather have lived alone with her grief, her soul at first refusing comfort.

The little daughter, too, was unlike other folk's children since she was dumb. A dumb only child, and a strange woman who avoided giving any history of herself, and shunned neighbourliness! That was enough to make the pair on Windy Hill seem strange in the opinion of the countryside. Nevertheless, since human beings were never meant to live solitary lives, by degrees and with time the widow's heart and manner softened; and although the peasants in the few and distant cottages around, from want of habit, never now thought of going up to see Widow Daly, still she had to come down to them sometimes, in especial to the wayside grocer's shop. Here she weekly came to buy her slender store of tea and tallow-candles, salt and sugar, flour and soap—little more. But after so coming for months she was persuaded at times by the good-natured mistress of the shop to stay and drink a friendly cup of tea, and rest herself and the child.

---

[30] *stand-off* = standoffish, cold and reserved.

THE WITCH OF WINDY HILL

Little Mary was the apple of the mother's eye, so for her sake she would at whiles[31] stop. The dumb child was so pretty, with a beauty of raven-hair and deep-blue eyes, common enough in the southern parts of the island, but rare in the north among the sandy-haired, raw-boned type of folk[32] round Windy Hill, that the grocer's wife honestly praised its looks.

"But what does she blush up like that for, and hide her wee face in your apron, woman dear? Dear bless us, Mistress Daly, ye don't tell me the *dummy* understands what I'm saying?"

"Hush, hush!" said the poor mother, with a warning glance, while she caressed the sensitive little creature, who was then about eight years' old; then added in a burst of confidence, with tears in her eyes: "You see, she was not always like this. She's no *born* dummy[33]; she could speak like any other child till a little while ago—till it pleased God to afflict us sorely, when she lost her voice."

"Deary help us! but that is over everything! How did it come to her? What made her dumb anyway? Would she no' mend and get back her speech ever again?" cried out the grocer's wife.

But at that little Mary broke into such a passion of tears (she had been trembling all over before while the talk about her went on), that the mother, alarmed by her passionate agony of emotion, hushed, caressed her, and finally hastened with her homewards, giving no more explanation.

The grocer's wife, however, naturally gossiped about such a curious fact as little Mary Daly's strange and recent dumbness to many of her customers. Among others, the carpenter's wife heard

---

[31] *whiles* = sometimes, at times.
[32] *sandy-haired, raw-boned type of folk.* In *Orange Lily*, the local folk are described as "… the fairer-haired, purer Scotch race which King James had planted …".
[33] *dummy* = a deaf-mute person.

the tale, and as a rival gossip she hastened to put a shawl over her head on the first spare convenient evening, and hied[34] up Windy Hill, for the express purpose, as she declared, of hearing all details about the cause of this phenomenon.

But, to her the widow Daly would not vouchsafe a word. She disliked the carpenter's wife; and she was busy, her cow being sick, and her potatoes unweeded. Also little Mary had a nervous horror of strangers and of her calamity being talked about, that made the mother dread a similar outbreak on the poor child's part to that in the grocer's shop.

Down Windy Hill, accordingly, the carpenter's wife had to come "with a flea in her ear," as she expressed it to her cronies, and with a strong dislike to "thon[35] queer, wee, witch," as she called little Mary.

"She is not like any other child, but so cranky and petted that the mother never dared tell a word about her dumbness before me, for fear of her crying herself into fits."

The carpenter's wife was right in saying that the child was unlike others. Not only was she delicate and more sensitive and nervous than older and coarser minds could well understand, but besides, the only child led a frightfully solitary life on the top of the hill; not a life certainly to make her forget the terrible sorrow and affliction that had nearly crushed out her young life.

The widow seeing this, tried the experiment of sending the little one to school. But the other children either jeered[36] at the dumb child and her signs; or, if less coarse-natured, looked on her with wide-eyed wonder. This last was almost as unendurable to the speechless young soul among them, who, in her silence had thought so much more than any of the far older ones; felt more;

---

[34] *hie* = to hurry, rush.

[35] *thon* = that.

[36] *jeer* = mimic in a hurtful way.

had, alas, more terrible experience of life and its ways already.

So she passionately entreated her mother after a week's agony and humiliation to send her to school no more; clung about the widow's knees with gestures full of meaning—and wept.

To see so young a child weep so much wrung the poor mother's heart; so little Mary gained the day.

She never went again to school, but was taught to write and read by her mother, who was a woman of some education, above that of the surrounding class. She seldom saw any of her school playmates, or if by chance they met her in any lane near the cottage, it was with her only companion, a black cat in her arms or on her shoulder, and little Mary would shrink away to the side of the hedge as the urchins bawled out, "Look, there is the dummy! the dummy!—chase her cat;" or else they would cry, "Look boys, here is the wee witch of Windy Hill."

For the carpenter's wife having once given the child the epithet, it had pleased her own fancy and she often repeated it, averring without meaning very much by the remark—that the little Mary was uncanny. The carpenter's children who went to school, naturally repeated their mother's remarks, and called Mary "the witch." Other children took it up, and so their parents again naturally said that all the children called wee Mary a witch, and said she was uncanny. This came round to the ears of the carpenter's wife, who, slapping her hands together declared, "See there—! Just what I always thought, not that I said anything or knew much about her. The very children don't take to the little crowl[37] kindly."

All this was little enough cause of dislike, however, and would very soon have been lived down and forgotten, as Mrs. Daly recovered good spirits again and the child gained in health. But there came to these two poor souls a worse trial.

---

[37] *crowl* = an undersized person.

CHAPTER II

A PEDLAR crossed the bridge one day, and stopped to show his goods to the carpenter's wife, she being always ready to spy any passer-by, and delighted at the chance of chaffering, if not of getting a bargain. He had just come down from Windy Hill, he said, having sold nothing up at the cottage, however—little wonder! The moment he had clapped his eyes on Mistress Daly and her dumb little girl he had recognized them, and on his saying so, the widow had been so vexed, she had shut the door in his face.

The carpenter's wife could not contain her curiosity at that. With eager lips she inquired more, and with itching ears listened to a strange sad story, told with equal relish by the pedlar.

Widow Daly's late husband had been hanged for murder a year ago!—ay, for murder: no less! They lived down in the West at the time when he was said to have done the deed, and was taken and tried for his life. And his own child— this same child, little Mary—was brought up as a witness and swore the evidence that caused her poor innocent father to swing. "Ah! innocent"—repeated the pedlar with unction. Who could doubt it, for did not her tongue turn black in her mouth the moment after she said it, and she was carried in a fit out of the court and never spoke another word after; as those he knew, who were bystanders, could affirm.

"Never?—no never!" cried the carpenter's wife.

And the pedlar, in reward of his marvellous tale, was asked to spend the night in the cottage, and after supper repeated his story to several more eager listeners. And each time he told it, it grew by help of additions, till at last it seemed as if the pedlar had himself been in the court-house and seen all the sad scene between father and child; whilst an impression began to gain upon himself and his hearers, first begun by the idle surmise of one among them, that the widow must have been at enmity with her husband, else how could she have allowed her child to swear away his life.

THE WITCH OF WINDY HILL

This was certainly the supposition only of the most ignorant among Widow Daly's neighbours. Some few were found to take her part, in fairness—all this being still unknown to the poor woman.

But, nevertheless, the story, after it had passed from mouth to mouth for a month through the country, ran somewhat thus: that the widow was shrewdly suspected of knowing who had done the murderous deed, and had taught her child to help in screening the guilty, thus bringing about the death of its father.

At last all the neighbourhood around Windy Hill thought so fiercely of the unsuspecting lonely mother and child, that some mutterings of the black storm brewed by slander against them, alarmed poor Mrs. Daly. The grocer's wife told the widow, kindly enough, that there was ill gossip going which she herself would not entirely believe. Nevertheless, unless Mistress Daly could contradict it, it might be better to keep away from the shop. For, though a good customer, and one who paid with the most careful exactness, still other customers objected to her presence.

In alarm and grief poor Widow Daly went straight to the minister of the parish, and, entreating him to take her part, at last told out all the sad story which till then had never crossed her lips.

She said—what he found out to be the truth—that her husband had been indeed guilty, and the grief of knowing this she must bear to her grave! But poor little Mary had in nowise been even the innocent cause of her unhappy father's execution; since the child, although examined could tell but little. It was the evidence of others which had been damning, and could not be disproved.

The awful misery of mind felt by the tender child, who had been much attached to its father, was, however, so intense beforehand and during the trial, that when it came to her own share in the latter she fell into convulsions, and in this state had to be removed, as the pedlar said.

Instead of recovering, the little creature grew only the more ill, and no one knew rightly what ailed her. She would hardly ever speak, scarcely eat, and in a last attack of her nerves the power of speech seemed altogether to leave her. A good Samaritan, a doctor, saved her life, and said he believed that any great shock would give her back the use of her tongue, and she would then speak as well as ever again. But, alas! meanwhile, the child remained dumb.

The minister took up the cause of the widow and the fatherless and spoke sternly to many; so that after a while those in the cottage were again better thought of, and the scandal came to die, or at least it hushed, and no more harsh human clamours reached the ears of the lonely dwellers on the hill-top, who seemed to themselves nearer the sky there— more beneath the very eye of God.

Two or three years had passed, and one there was who thought well of both mother and daughter—the young farmer below the hill.

Mary Daly, the dumb girl, had grown up so fair of face and slender of figure that she was, though little seen, sometimes the talk of the country-side. The jealous raked up at times the old story; but young Ryan thought he could judge best. Who, of course, so unprejudiced, he thought, as a young man judging of a pretty girl. He was no relation, and impartial; not a woman, therefore not jealous; not an old man, therefore not indifferent.

So many a dusk and many a gloaming, when Mary Daly came out to search for the calves to house them, she would see young Ryan come up the narrow dark path lined with tall ashes that led up the hill, to tell her how the calves had broken into his young corn on the right-hand field here, or had strayed down to his meadow yonder—not that he minded the damage done a bit. Then he would help her to bring them up to the bleak hill-top, and stop to lean over the gate at the lane end to say some parting words, and watch Mary's pretty gestures answering him back, and her "speaking face."

THE WITCH OF WINDY HILL

At last young Dennis told Mary he would rather have whatever her face said to him than any other woman's sweetest words. So it was settled, and soon known in the country that these two were going to be married.

Many a mother had wanted Ryan and his rich farm for her own girl. They wished the widow to her face joy of having got so good a son-in-law, but behind backs they talked bitterly of how she must have entrapped him. The old malice broke out afresh.

But young Mary Daly became like a new creature; she that had never laughed, nor hardly smiled—the timid girl who seemed just stepping out of a joyless childhood with regret, as if fearing older years meant added sorrow, seemed suddenly to have seen the sun and be glad! She was like a young bird fluttering happily out in the great green world— like a fresh opening flower.

Her mother trembled lest it was too wonderful and blessed a change in their lives to last.

And indeed too soon came up a small cloud in their clear blue sky, for the mother fell ill; so that till she grew better the wedding must wait a bit.

They said it was all for the best; since a black-edged letter came from America telling young Ryan of the money left him there, which he must go out and claim. So he sailed out in the next vessel westward, and his last words to his sweetheart were: "Now, Mary, lass, don't ye be carrying on with any other man, for it would break my heart."

Days passed, and other young men truly enough saw Mary Daly, and tried to get her to walk with them, and quarrelled together about her; but she never heeded them. The carpenter's wife watched for gossip against the girl like a cat for a mouse; and whenever any young man seemed to admire dumb Mary, if the lass only gave him, in passing by, the smile of an acquaintance, that was put down to her discredit in the old gossip's memory as in a black book.

But young Mary knew nothing of all this, and walked innocent of harm to others or malice from them.

She was happy. Her childhood, if lonely, speechless and delicate, had yet been not altogether sad. Gleams of mother's love had brightened it; mother's constant care and support had kept it free from the worst fears and trials of orphaned childhood, although childhood's keenest joys had likewise been unknown. Hers had been a tender twilight existence, like that of Kilmeny, who was brought up by the fairies, in their land, whose day is lit by the moon; so the maiden's

> "Beauty was fain to see,
> But still and steadfast was her e'e!
> ....
> . . . She loved to rake the lonely glen,
> And keepit afar frae the haunts of men."[38]

Now the sunlight had uprisen, flooding all the heaven of Mary's young existence. She was utterly, unutterably happy during these months, nigh a year! Too happy—!

For when Ryan had been gone some weeks there came a dark day for the poor young soul he had left behind in Ireland.

---

[38] A quotation from 'Bonnie Kilmeny' in *The Queen's Wake* (James Hogg, 1813) "… And O, her beauty was fair to see, / But still and steadfast was her e'e! … But she loved to raike the lanely glen, / And keepèd afar frae the haunts of men". The ballad tells how a beautiful young Scotch village lass, Kilmeny, is abducted by fairies and taken to the fairy kingdom, where she is kept for seven years. She finally returns to the mortal realm changed by her experience. In *Orange Lily*, May Crommelin introduces chapter 18 with several other verses of this poem.

CHAPTER III

"Oh, richly fell the flaxen hair
Over the maiden's shoulders fair!
On every feature of her face
Sat radiant modesty and grace;
Her tender eyes were mild and bright,
And through her robes of shadowy white
The delicate outline of her form
Shone like an iris through a storm."[39]

It was fair-day at the little town, or rather village[40], that lay nearest to Windy Hill. Fair-day, coming only once in the summer, was a great event in the neighbourhood.

All the girls, far and near, put on their best bravery and went off to the fair gaily, to have a pleasant day with their sweethearts, after the business was over, and to be given presents or "fairings"[41]—all but Mary Daly.

Several young men had come and asked her to go, but she smilingly shook her head with a pretty refusing gesture at them all and stayed. Had her mother even been well, Mary did not care to go in Ryan's absence to any gaiety; it was always fair-day with her only to think of him. But her mother, who had been ill since before Ryan's absence, was not better, even rather worse that day, although the dumb girl knew it not; the mother being always anxious not to frighten her.

Towards mid-day the Widow Daly called gently to her daughter, who was busy at some household work, and who was never

[39] From 'The Watch-fire' in *The Salamandrine; or, Love and Immortality* by Charles McKay, 1842.
[40] Greyabbey (the 'Black Abbey' with its Fair Days in *Orange Lily*). Greyabbey's Fairs were held on 28th March and 29th October.
[41] *fairing* = gift from a fair.

far from the great straw chair in which the invalid dozed away her time. "Mary dear," she said, "I am vexed, after all, that ye did not go to the fair and have a little fun like the other girls. For I see just now that my medicine-bottle is nearly empty, and I would like to have it filled again before the night."

Should she go still—and hurry; hurry back, the dumb girl asked in eagerness, by expressive signs.

"Yes, dear, I wish you would go—and ask the doctor to stop and see me as he drives past the hill this afternoon—but there is no need to hurry. Don't go too quickly and tire yourself," said the sick woman.

And as Mary quickly put on her common straw bonnet, and left the house, the last words she heard was the affectionate entreaty, again in her mother's loving voice, called after her, "Mind— there is no need to hurry now, my dear one."

How could poor Mary guess that there was need indeed, as the mother feared; that the message about the medicine was only a pretence in order to get the doctor; but that, above all things, the loving spirit behind there feared frightening the young creature, or that she might in anxiety over-exert herself? Nevertheless, in her eagerness to go down to the village soon and get the sooner home again, Mary sped quickly along the road. She had some fears for the dear good mother behind there, who was half her world of love, Dennis Ryan being the other half; she was not very uneasy, but still a misgiving at times seized her.

The dumb girl walked so fast that in little more than an hour she was close to the village. Most of the people were already in the fair; still she now overtook one of the young men who were reckoned among her admirers, and the best and truest among them, John McConnell the blacksmith.

On his surprised inquiry she told, by a few gestures, pointing homewards and showing her medicine bottle, what she sought. Mary's ways were indeed full of speech, as Dennis Ryan had said

often. But for this, and the extreme beauty of her blue beseeching eyes, and the raven's-wing gloss of her dark hair, the dumb
girl would have stood a poor chance among her many rivals.
Nevertheless, perhaps, many of the men may have thought with
shrewd and caustic reasoning that her affliction might be none
to a husband, since

> "Silence in woman is like speech in man,
> Deny't who can."[42]

The crowd at the entrance to the fair was so great that naturally
enough Mary Daly was glad when the blacksmith offered to escort
her safely through it.

Who should see them both together just then, however, but
the carpenter's wife! "Ho, ho!" thought the crone, "so that young
witch has come down to the fair on the sly, after all, and is keeping
company with John McConnell while Ryan is away. And yet her
mother said yesterday she never cared to go anywhere till Dennis
came back. Wait now, if I don't tell him!"

To Mary's sorrow the doctor was found to be absent when she
inquired at his door, and not expected back till the afternoon; so
what could be done but wait. McConnell tried to comfort her,
saying she must only be patient, and her mother would be none
the worse for waiting he was sure. And to spend the time he proposed that they might just look into the show opposite. "There's
a snake lady who charms three big snakes and winds them about
her, and shure such a sight as a snake hasn't been seen in Ireland
since St. Patrick banished the last big wan! All the world is seeing
her," he pleaded.

Mary Daly was strongly tempted to see the great sight; and
why not go? She could do no good to her sick mother by keeping
away from it.

---

[42] A line spoken by 'John Daw' in Ben Jonson's *Epicoene, or the Silent
Woman* (1609).

251

So they too joined the crowd, when the carpenter's wife spied them again, and followed them close to see what fun they were after.

The afternoon came on, and the performance was just ended, when a gig drove by. It was that of the doctor! and on seeing Mary he stopped his horse, while she came up eagerly to him to ask, by signs, for the physic.

"Go home, my poor girl, as fast as you can," said the doctor. "Never mind the medicine. As I drove by the Windy Hill, an hour ago I went up to see your mother, and found her very ill. Hurry back to see her, there's a good lass; it's all you can do."

"She's dyin', and ye've left her lone. Shame on ye—shame upon ye," cried the carpenter's wife, who was standing by. But Mary seemed not to hear the cruel thoughtless words. She looked only at the doctor's face, and gave a strange hoarse cry—the cry of a dumb person—then turned and ran.

She heard calls behind and noises, but she never stopped.

On and on swiftly, out into the country by the steep path up the hills young Mary sped. Thunder muttered in the distance; then a storm came on. McConnell had foreseen this, and called after her to ask leave to go with her; now he followed but lost sight of her at times in the hills, for this track was seldom used, being dangerous from shaking bogs. Sometimes, bewildered, the dumb girl got among these, and had to jump from grass tussock to tussock, but her steps seemed guided as by some blessed higher Power. Slipping, panting, wet to the skin, she yet ran on under the driving deluge, that seemed as if it would beat into the ground this young thing that defied it. Jagged lightnings leaped down before her, thunder crashed through the dun sky above her head; but the terror in her mind was worse—far more awful!

Would her darling, her blessed mother, be living? Would she still speak—still know her?

Now Mary dragged her way by the water ditches in Ryan's

meadows, the only living creature to be seen out in that wild weather. The Hill rose before her and she tried to climb it, and twice fell flat with her face in the wet grass with exhaustion, and twice again rose and clenched her teeth and caught by bushes and branches to help herself along by the lee of the steep hedge. At last she reached the cottage, and stumbled wildly in over the threshold.

All was dark and very silent.

She gave a loving little dumb cry, and stopped panting.

No other sound!

Then she crept over like a thief to the straw arm-chair, seeing her mother's figure in it; felt in the half-darkness for her hands; put her face to the other quiet face. Her mother was sitting dead!

Ah! silent misery! voiceless, dumb despair! That night, when the storm clouds rolled away, and the moon shone out, it looked upon a desperate young heart on the top of Windy Hill, watching the beloved dead, as if believing it would yet move and speak again to her; a girl laying her warm cheek to a stone cold one, or writhing in dumb agony on the floor. Then within her poor voiceless soul Mary was crying out for the two she loved to come back and comfort her—on Dennis, on her mother! She thought her heart was broken. But she knew no better; it was not broken—yet.

There came some one and knocked at the door. Why Mary should be frightened any more *now,* she herself knew not, but she sprang up from the floor straight and white, and trembled like an aspen leaf. But it was only McConnell, who had taken shelter till the storm was well past, and now came out of his way to see if he could help. He sat up with her through that awful night, to wake the dead, silent as herself.

The news of the death went through the country none knew how, and by cock-crow the carpenter's wife was up to have a sight of the corpse, and more followed her. And some said, when they left, McConnell was kind and good to have stayed by the lone young creature on such an awful night. But the carpenter's wife said it was queer *he* had been with her at the fair too, and wondered would Ryan like it, and thought of her own rich niece who had a fancy for Ryan.

Days passed. The grave-mould lost freshness. The orphan girl got on as best she could, but life was terrible, except for the hope of seeing Ryan soon. For the story that she bad been "disporting herself" at the fair, and had left her mother to die alone, had gone like wildfire through the country, spread by tongues unknown.

Every one said they thought it but natural that the mother's death should be out of the common, seeing the father's had been so shocking; and when Mary Daly had helped to hang her father, it was not held over-surprising that she should show herself unnatural to her mother.

The first curiosity past, the unhappy girl was shunned like the plague, and her childish ill-name was revived. Folk said, "Have you heard the story of that young witch up at Windy Hill, and how she deserted her mother?"

No living soul but Mary herself, the minister, and the sexton, was at the funeral. John McConnell's courage failed him too: he thought best bide a bit till the storm of reproach blew over, though he knew partly how innocent the poor girl was.

However, one day he came.

But the dumb girl gave him gently to understand, writing the words on a slate she had, that she thanked him; nevertheless, for a while yet, would think it more friendly if he stayed away; for she thought of Dennis Ryan's last words: *"If you take on with any other man, it will break my heart!"*

But it was a bad time for the friendless young creature. She knew what was said, well; knew even the cruel epithet "the young witch of Windy Hill," since folks thought it their duty to tell her. But none thought it a duty to interpret her passionate gestures and wretched entreating looks. So she wept till she sickened, and after two days and a half that no one saw her, they went up to the hill-top and found her lying alone in the solitary cottage, ill in fever. One single woman was found to nurse poor Mary, who meant to make her pay for it too. But hope of a ship coming home was in her heart. She recovered, though only after tedious relapses and long stretches of illness, during which all her mother's little hoarded money was spent and the cow had to be sold.

One spring morning she was well enough to go outside; then she saw smoke curling up from the farm chimneys below. She pointed to them, her face flushed up.

She asked the woman who tended her, plain as words, "What does it mean?"

"Ryan's home since a week," said the woman.

Home since a week! and Dennis, her lover, had never come up the lane to ask after her!

CHAPTER IV

"O waly waly up the bank,
    And waly waly down the brae,
And waly waly, yon burn-side,
    Where I and my love were wont to gae!
I leant my back unto an aik,
    I thought it was a trusty tree;
But first it bow'd, and syne it brak—
    Sae my true love did lichtly me.

"O waly waly, but love be bonny
    A little time while it is new;
But when 'tis auld, it waxeth cauld,
    And fades awa' like morning dew.
O wherefore should I busk my head?
    Or wherefore should I kame my hair?
For my true love has me forsook,
    And says he'll never lo'e me mair."[43]

MARY DALY listened now to every leaf that rustled in the wind.
Her heart leaped wildly at each footfall. But Dennis did not come
all that day, nor yet the next.

Then the girl grew sick and faint in heart, yet would not own to
herself that she was afraid, nor what she feared. Still, she crawled
out of bed, although hardly, as yet, fit to move, for she was almost
desperate.

She said to herself, she could *not* bear it. Dennis never had been
unkind before; she was ashamed in her heart to distrust him; she
was sure he did not mean to hurt her, *but she could not bear it.*

And so she went down the lane.

A weak, white creature she looked, but so lovely with her blue-
black hair and eyes like forget-me-nots! No wonder the men's

---

[43] From '*Waly, Waly*', an anonymous 17th century Scotch ballad.

heads had so many a time turned to look after her through all the country round.

Then, turning the corner, Mary met young Ryan face to face!

There was an old ash-tree there which had a seat of its knotted roots on which he sat, bent forward, with his head in his hands. There they two had said good-bye; there kissed on parting.

Mary gave a strange cry, and he got up slowly, came close, and looked her in the face; but never touched her or said a word more than herself. The girl put out her hands to implore; the tears were washing down her hollow white cheeks; she crept up to him, but he spurned her back. "Lass," he said, "ye'll maybe mind now what I told you at parting. I hear tell that ye no minded it whilst I was away. There's queer and bad stories going about ye. Take up with McConnell, if ye like, but never come nigh me that ye can help it. I wouldn't willingly hurt ye! *but I'll not be answerable* for what I might do if I'm—if I'm worse tormented."

At that the dumb girl only wailed; but it was a wail as if she had never before known sorrow like to this one. She clasped her hands round Dennis Ryan's arm and fell down with weakness upon her knees. He shook her off as if she had been a viper; and went on again between his teeth. "Do you want me to do you some bodily harm? I liked ye once too well for the good of my soul, Mary Daly; I'm feared ye'd come round me again if I gave ye the chance; but I swear that from now, till the breath is out of my body, there shall never one word more be spoken betwixt me and you."

How the sick girl got back home her good angel that doubtless was beside her alone knew—but she was ill again after that dreadful hour for long days. She knocked even feebly at death's door, hating life; but it would not open, and she lived.

When the blessed summer came—the summer when she had expected to have been Dennis Ryan's happy wife, down in the warm farmhouse in the hollow—Mary Daly was, indeed, better again, but like a mere wasted image of her former self, having come back as if with reluctant steps from the land of sickness. She was better again, and able to go about, but alone up in the solitary cottage where many a little cherished possession had been parted with to defray that long illness. And down in the farmhouse below … was an ugly bride!

Dennis Ryan had got married in haste. People said it was lest he might again fall under the spell of that young Witch of Windy Hill, when the latter recovered; for as uncanny, unnatural, unfilial, little less than a witch, so poor young Mary was now shunned. She was even accused of having an evil eye, and many a milk-pan soured that hot summer was put down by careless housewives to her having passed by on the road. But for the minister and his protecting kindness some harm, even in these more enlightened times, might have been done her.

Dennis Ryan's wife was the niece of the carpenter's wife, once before spoken of as having a fancy for Ryan and his farm; and being rich herself, as the saying goes, she owned the "grazing of many a goose on the hillside."

That summer passed; and yet two more. The girl in the cottage on Windy Hill was still living all alone; but in the farmhouse were children's voices.

About the same time that Dennis Ryan's bride had been brought to the farm, McConnell, the blacksmith, came up to the cottage on Windy Hill, and said he, "Mary Daly, now that Ryan is married on another woman, ye'd better take up wi' me, lass; will ye marry me, and sail for New York next week? God knows, ye were hardly treated!"

But she would not do it.

So John McConnell left the cottage, and soon after went to America; and poor Mary's only friend on earth was gone. What passed in the dumb girl's mind during the terrible lonely years that followed no human soul knew. Alone she lived; alone she worked.

THE WITCH OF WINDY HILL

Sometimes the awful loneliness upon the hill so overpowered her, poor Mary thought she should go mad. But this fear and feeling passed away as soon as ever the smallest event—a bird's song, or the grateful look in a dumb animal's eyes, came to brighten her easily brightened life. It was like the life almost of a girl hermit. At first, for long, it was terrible, even to the girl herself; then easier, blessed! She seemed to herself at the latter end like one kept apart for a special purpose, but what, as yet, her spirit knew not.

In the wintry nights, nevertheless, when the wind howled under the door, she shuddered thinking of how her father's body had swung upon the gallows; of how her mother had died without a soul by her in the cottage; of how her lover was married and happy beside another woman down there. She remembered how Dennis had said his heart would break if she ever cared for another. Ah! it is not mostly the one who says so whose heart breaks. The man's was whole, but the woman's was hurt past curing.

But, however this bitter trial and these thoughts worked in her heart, the dumb girl grew always meeker and kinder, giving help to all the neighbours she could, though often repulsed, often finding ingratitude; offering to nurse the sick, though often scorned; till once when she saved the carpenter's wife from death by her long devotion (so said the doctor), the country folk "gave in," as was their manner of expressing they at last acknowledged that the witch of a dumb girl, Mary Daly, had begun to mend her ways a good deal. "Dear knows! the change in her for the better was wantit!"

But never, from the day he swore it, had Ryan broken his oath of not speaking to Mary—never!

And as weeks, months, and years rolled by, she said in her heart every day, "If only he would meet and tell me to-day he knew now it was all untrue, why, I think still I could, be in a way happy. And I would be glad to die then; but till I hear those words it seems hard."

THE WITCH OF WINDY HILL

The children at the farm got, as years went on, to love the dumb woman up on the hill-top above, she was so gentle and loving to them. At first, their mother had made them afraid of the witch. But their mother was harsh, and Mary was all gentleness, so in time they overcame their fears, and would toddle up the lane to see her. One, a crippled little creature, fell into a deep flax-hole once, and was near drowning, when Mary Daly jumped in and saved its life; but lost hold of the bank herself in trying to clamber up, and was all but dead when pulled out. Mrs. Ryan had hated her former rival till then, but for that she thanked her, weeping.

Next day Dennis Ryan made as though he would have spoken a word, as he came by the garden patch where Mary was digging out potatoes. The poor creature's heart beat like a bird's; her breath left her; but he passed on.

Then she said to herself: "I am failing, and shall die without being righted by him; but he is a strong man, and will outlive me for years."

CHAPTER V

"There is lyf without ony death,
And there is youth without ony elde:
And there is all manner wealth to welde;
And there is rest without ony travaille;
And there is pees without ony strife,
And there is all manner of lyving of lyfe;—
And there is bright somur ever to see,
And there is never winter in that countrie;
And there is more worship and honour
Than ever had king or emperour;
And there is great melodic of angeles songe,
And there is preysing Him among;
....
As these a man may joys of hevene call;
As quitte the most sovereigns joye of all,
To the sight of Goddes bright face,
In whom shineth all manners grace."[44]

At that time came the cholera in Ireland; it was a terrible year; as if the plague had come again. Around the neighbourhood of Windy Hill it raged with unusual violence. The hospital in the neighbouring small town[45] was full to overflowing; the dead carts could not ply fast enough; the sick and dying lay in every cottage, and some—awful to think of!—deserted in their hour of need by the fears of those around them.

Then Mary Daly seemed to know at last what the especial mission was, the call to which long before had seemed borne in upon her spirit! She arose like an angel of healing, and without

---

[44] Lines from 'Heaven' by Rolle, a 14th century Augustinian hermit.
[45] The old hospital in Newtownards was originally built in 1841 as the Newtownards Poor Law Union Workhouse. It was known as the 'Fever Hospital' until 1932.

fear, with even enthusiasm, went down from her home on the high hill, where no infection ever came, to minister to all alike who needed help. For weeks she went from house to house denying herself almost rest, ready and glad to waste her own life if only she could save those of others.

And so she nursed several till the fame of her powers of healing went abroad, and spread and spread till the miraculous charm once attributed to her as of evil was now turned to seem one of good; and the imagination of many a patient was so cheered when Mary Daly, being sent for in hot haste, crossed the threshold, that they recovered courage to overcome the disease.

And still Mary herself never took the cholera.

Almost at the end of the epidemic, when fears were abating and the worst was over, but few occasional cases breaking out here and there, it happened that one of Dennis Ryan's children at the farm sickened. Mary Daly had come home, and was terribly grieved at the news. And yet she hardly dared to go down to the farm, and face Ryan against his will, to nurse the child.

Mrs. Ryan, however, solved the difficulty by appearing herself up at the cottage an hour later. She came to beseech Mary to save the rest of the children by taking them in to the cottage with herself till danger was over; but when the dumb woman inquired by signs after the sick little one, the mother's jealousy awoke, and she declared she could nurse it well herself, and would rather none other touched it.

So Mary Daly received Dennis Ryan's children to her poor home and hearth. But that very night her favourite, the little crippled girl, was taken with cramps, and the first signs of the terrible cholera, while sleeping in Mary's arms in her own bed.

For two days the dumb woman nursed the child, till it seemed as if she had forcibly kept back its passing soul; then she went down the hill to tell the mother of its safety.

Mrs. Ryan met her with a white hard face. "You saved the

child I gave you, but the one I kept with myself is dead; and its father too!" said she.

Mary Daly threw up her arms, and staggered against the wall. Dead! The last chance was gone—now!

Dead—dead—dead! and never had said the word she had waited for.

In she went and saw the dead man lying. A shiver came over her as she gazed on the corpse, but still she took the clammy hand in hers a moment; then went away out, and crawled up the hill again.

She had said in her heart to him then: "Ye know the truth now, Dennis; but O, that ye had known it living! and had said one word of kindness! Ochone! I could have died so easy."

The children came about her knees, but Mary Daly sat unheeding them, and never stirred; and they thought she looked very strange.

By evening a figure darkened the threshold. It was Mrs. Ryan, come up to see her fatherless children—all that was left to keep her heart warm in this world, as she cried.

She was a mother, and took them in her lap, and wept over them, but she had other woman's feelings too; and suddenly putting them away, she went up and took the dumb woman's hands.

"Lass! lass! ye're deein'!—my dead man has smit[46] ye with the cholera!" she cried. And the other looked back a "Yes" out of her filming eyes. "And, O woman! it's upon my mind since morning I should have telt[47] ye the message Dennis left for ye when the breath was leavin' him. 'Mary Daly! Mary Daly!' says he, 'if I could only see her, and say I've known two years back it was all lies what they told about her; but I was too proud to break my word.'"

A sound came that startled Mrs. Ryan with a horror as of something supernatural. The dumb girl had raised herself with a

---

[46] *deein'* = dying; *smit* = infected.
[47] *telt* = told.

great gasp. The joy on her face drove back the cold dew of death, and brought the red again in a sweet faint flush to her cheek. Her eyes lit up with an ecstasy of gladness. Her tongue was unloosed after its long bondage, and with the sudden shock of that happiness she cried out, as plainly as she had spoken in her childish days, "At last!—at last! God be thanked!"

What all the sorrows heaped on sorrows could not effect joy had done. The good doctor's prophecy, so long pondered on by poor Mary with deep yearning for its fulfilment had come true; and the dumb spake.

She had before wondered that all her pain had never forced a cry of utterance from her powers of speech, which she well knew had but lain sealed, as it were, like river- waters under the power of icing cold. But pain comes naturally to men and women, and there is hope beyond; perfect joy overfills the soul.

The dumb woman never spoke again: as if in that one soul-utterance she had said all she needed, but lay smiling in a weak daze, with her eyes seeming to be seeing happiness, only happiness in some sweet future before their dim gaze.

And thus smiling, she grew weaker and weaker; and so while still she lay smiling, that night her soul passed away from her body that lay in the poor little cottage on the top of Windy Hill.

Many and many a one came to see the last of the witch, as they had called her; and now, when too late, the tide of public feeling turned and ran strong in her favour. The neighbours recounted poor Mary's good deeds, and bewailed her. It was not "the ignorant folk that had so miscalled her," they all said to each other, forgetting that none among them but had, by repetition of an idle nickname and foolish tattling, caused her to be so cruelly shunned for long.

Yet while looking with awe on that white face, so blessed in its expression, who could doubt but that poor Mary had forgiven them all, and found peace and perfect bliss at last.

THE WITCH OF WINDY HILL

So they buried her on the selfsame day as Dennis Ryan, and in a grave beside his, although that was merely by chance. His widow might have said a word against it, but they showed her there was room on his other side for herself, and she was silent.

It is a good many years since then, and poor Mary's grave has long been green, and speckled with white daisies in summer-time. But still often enough, when by the evening firesides, under straw roofs, gossips speak of the terrible year of the cholera, some one among them is sure to tell any chance stranger of the wonderful devotion and courage showed to the sick by a dumb woman; one who in her youth had always been known as the Witch of Windy Hill.

AN OLD MAID'S MARRIAGE

AN OLD MAID'S MARRIAGE;

OR,

FINDING A HUSBAND AT HARE AND HOUNDS

IF you want to know how a regular old maid—such a "regular old maid," as everybody called me—came to be married lately, I'll try and tell you something about it.

Well, for the last ten or twelve years of my life (there is a frank admission on the score of age already for you!) I have spent two months every autumn with some old friends in the north of Ireland. I am a creature of habit, so are most of my friends, and this has been a habit I believe we mutually liked. They call me now over there an "institution."

For most of the other months of the year, by the way, I am likewise visiting; a month yachting with one friend, a month at German baths with another; a month in the dear Highlands, besides innumerable smaller visits. Between times I really have a *pied à terre* to which I can retire with dignity. It is a flat in London; tiny rooms, but pretty. It is not much of a home; and indeed I am so little there, some unkind people hardly credit me with having one. But still, believe me, it is a great thing to have a den, a spot of earth for your very own; the remembrance of it supports one's pride, gives a sense of shelter, security, possession. Well, but to come back to the north of Ireland.

Of all my yearly visits this was one of the pleasantest, and I freely declare and will maintain that however detestable the climate may be there at other times of the year, it is really warmer in October and November than most other places which I know. On this especial visit I had been in the house a week or two before many other visitors arrived. A pleasant little party, however, was asked for the county ball week by the Lawtons. The Lawtons were my hosts; they and their pretty niece, an orphan heiress. Ida

AN OLD MAID'S MARRIAGE

Lawton had hitherto been alone in the house with myself; and a very good time we had of it too.

Being one of those people who are expected to make themselves universally agreeable, and being very fond of doing so (when it is not particularly disagreeable to me), I interpret my *rôle* in life somewhat after this fashion, with much satisfaction to myself. On a brisk October morning, nobody at breakfast having apparently much idea of how the day is to be spent, or possessing much self-will at that often stupidest of meals, I cry in a cheerful, all-alive fashion: "What a delicious morning it would be for a ride!"

Very likely Miss Ida rises to the bait, and languidly observes:

"Well, yes—I think it would be. Will you come out with me if we have nothing better to do?"

And by the time we come in, after a rousing canter, she is heartily convinced I have been one of the most pleasant of companions. If she seems bent upon painting, or "cutting out holes in white calico in order to stitch them up again," as some gentlemen call embroidery[48] she loves doing all the lovely blessed morning, I am equally ready to fall back on making some similar observation about a walk; and if it is taken, may be seen tramping with Sir Hugh round the farm, giving an opinion on fat beasts, oil-cake, turnips, and coming home round the coverts by a short cut through innumerable brambles and thickets. Or else I am, thirdly, still most willing, if my lady feels inclined to leave her housekeeping accounts and innumerable correspondence, to trot with her round the gardens or down to the schools. Lastly and finally, if none of the three care for a morning's outing, and really have some vague plans of their own, and express no such pressing desire for my society indoors as leads me to abandon selfishness—why, I hope I can amuse myself in my own company

---

[48] Ayrshire whitework. The type of drawn thread work and white-on-white embroidery common in the Ards was known as 'Ayrshire Lace'.

by doing a constitutional gaily in solitude round shrubberies and drives. I hope also I have tact enough to see what *is* wanted of me, if anything, and good nature enough to do that little cheerfully.

Give and take is my daily motto. It is surprising how good-natured people are in doing a great deal for me, just because I do a little for them in a pleasant way, and conscience often accuses me of being really very selfish, only that nobody else seems to have found me out.

All this is to show how I generally spend my time with the Lawtons year after year, and get on fairly well, though such a "regular old maid." When first I began my yearly visitation there, however, I was young enough, though orphaned, and living in the big world "on my own account."

"And why you never were married is a mystery to me, Mary Smith," Lady Lawton often says. "Why was it?"

"I'm sure I don't know; except that I perhaps am not a marrying woman," generally replies the plain object of her plain remarks. "You don't know: I don't know: nobody knows. It is one of those odd things that never happen just because there is no especial reason against it ... I believe that I always wanted the people in the days of my youth that couldn't afford to have me, and now in the days of my old age, like a female Major Pendennis, I can't afford to have anybody that *does* want to take me. There is your perpetual curate here, in his house by the bog—and the rich brewer who has persecuted me for the last three winters in Foxshire, when I go for Christmas to the Grandeesons."

"Oh, impossible—you could never settle down here as our curate's wife; and the brewer drops all his H's," cries my lady in horror. "So a female Pendennis old maid I must remain, you see." "Well, luckily, I never saw or heard that you had an especial fancy for anybody. Your heart was never broken, to judge by all appearances, ha! ha! ha!" And both my lady and Miss Ida look up from their dainty five-o'clock teacups to scrutinize my cheerful hardened visage with a sort of soft wondering smile as if I was a true female rarity.

"Ah! how can either of you tell?" is my mock-sorrowful reply, and perhaps there once may have been some truth, however little, in what is implied as I shake a lugubrious head. "I have ever smiled!—but it may have been at times with a false and forced lightheartedness! How do you both know that there may not be some beloved image still enshrined within this bosom." "There is the afternoon post," and Ida jumping up, rudely interrupts the flow of my rhodomontade[49].

"How strange!—how very pleasant!" exclaims my hostess, after reading a letter in silence.

"Fancy, Ida, here is a hurried line from your uncle's old friend Colonel Fletcher. He says he only came home from India a week ago, on business; is obliged to come over to Ireland—(what on earth brings him over here I wonder!)—and as he will be passing our neighbourhood would like to stop and see us for a day. He will probably come on Wednesday evening."

"And be here with the rest of our party; that will suit admirably well," says calm Miss Ida. "What is he like?"

"O, a very pleasant man. I last saw him two years ago, but he was then very good-looking still. *You* will like him immensely, for you always like men of a certain age."

"So do both Minna and Kate O'Donnel," laughed Ida Lawton.

Quite by accident at that moment I nearly upset my teacup, and not wishing the other two to remark my awkwardness, took no part in the conversation.

"Well, then you and Minna will have to pull caps for him," laughed my lady. "But, on the whole, I think you had *better* leave him to Minna; for I won't have him flirted with by you—you pretty little puss! He is too old a man for that, and he really ought

---

[49] *rhodomontade* = rodomontade, vain boasting, rant.

to be married—he ought indeed! Minna is a good sensible girl that would just suit him—"

"What a terrible matchmaker you are, aunt," cried Miss Ida. *I* never said one word; my tea was too hot—I mean a crumb had got in my throat.

"A matchmaker—not a bit! I am only anxious for the good of such a pleasant man, who doesn't know apparently what would be good for himself. Perhaps he never saw any ladies all these years in India. Let me see! … We must send him in to dinner that night, so that Minna sits beside him; then of course we must keep him on for a fortnight. Minna has a little fortune, which will just suit him, as he can't have very much of his own: indeed, so has Kate O'Donnel, but she is rather young for him."

"*Rather*—I should think. And is not Minna rather too young also? Colonel Fletcher must be quite old in comparison with either of those two girls," observes the third person in the party, rather grimly.

My lady put up her eyeglasses, in order mildly to stare me out of such a suggestion.

"My dear Mary, you forget that a man's age is never anything in comparison with a woman's. Colonel Fletcher can't be much more than forty-five, and Minna is three or four and twenty, *good;* and if she took a fancy to him it would do very well, for he is a very fine-looking man still. Every one thinks him a handsome man; don't you? Oh—of course—I was forgetting, you never saw him—"

"Yes, I think I did meet him once … here, in this very house, in 186— , " I replied with a fine air of carelessness.

"What? then!—eight or nine years ago; in the dark ages. I wonder you can even remember so far back."

And Lady Lawton, humming an air to herself, rises and goes off to acquaint Sir Hugh with the news, while I retired upstairs. In the privacy of my bedroom I went straight to my looking-glass, a thing I have given up of late years doing oftener than is strictly necessary. And I looked a good long time in it; likewise unusual. Lady Lawton's words came back and made me feel very bitter, "A man's age is never anything in comparison with that of a woman's!" Quite true: just so. Colonel Fletcher had been several years older than myself once, but he is still considered young enough for Minna O'Donnel, that excellent, stupid little girl, while I—am a regular old maid!

It is a burning shame, I thought to myself. There ought to be a new law of nature made allowing women to be considered young as long as men. Have we got so much more amusement in our quiet lives that we can afford to retire early? Here am I, now—I don't feel old, not a bit old; almost could cheat myself into thinking it was only the other day that Captain Fletcher (as he then was) asked me to go out riding with him for the last time. And what a pleasant ride on a sad autumn day; what a bitter-sweet memory I always had of that ride afterwards!

No matter: now he has come back, and I have withered into a regular old maid; but he, who was then a handsome detrimental, has apparently grown into being quite a marriageable man. All this feminine fuming and indignation against nature's inexorable laws was uncalled-for and foolish every one may think.

But then, you see, in those dark ages to which Lady Lawton so carelessly referred, I had—I had—well—*known* Colonel Fletcher better than she thought.

CHAPTER II

ON the day when Colonel Fletcher was expected, the writer of this confession indulged during part of the fine afternoon, that might have been much better spent, in an absolute revel of morbidity, an utter abandonment to imaginary melancholy. It is quite a luxury, let me tell you; and one not to be indulged in too often.

But that day I said to myself that I didn't care—nothing mattered, nobody mattered, I would be delightfully melancholy for once, and indulge my whim, as all the rest of the world did round me *much* oftener than myself.

My whim was to tramp alone up and down a solitary walk under dismal Scotch firs[50] at the very farthest end of the demesne, thinking about Colonel Fletcher's coming arrival that very evening. I had it all sketched out. We would meet on the stairs, where—by the way—we last said good-bye. He would make way for me as for a stranger, with a half-bow, politely. I should bow in return; utter his name; perhaps offer to shake hands. Then when he, of course looking utterly astonished, and entirely forgetful of my personality, had gazed with blank bewildered civility at my stoutened person and well-worn complexion, I should say with firm cheerfulness, "Don't you remember Mary Smith?—" Whereupon, of course also, he would stare very likely with a muttered "Bless my heart; you don't say so!" (Perhaps that exclamation would be too like an *old* gentleman, however!) Anyway, he would try to look as if he was not astonished, and yet show me plainly that he was very much so; that, in fact, if I had not told him my name and declared I was that bygone comely Mary Smith, he might have been beside me for hours without guessing it.

After which, and a few commonplaces, hoping I had been well lately, or some such banality, he would pass on to dress for

---

[50] Scots pines.

dinner; and having time during his toilet to tell himself that I had altered frightfully, while his glass would doubtless assure him that he had not "much," not nearly so much! he would, on coming downstairs, devote himself to Minna O'Donnel, and calmly seem oblivious of the existence of the present old person whom they called Miss Smith.

It is extremely agreeable, as I before remarked, to indulge in such brown studies, and weep tears (unshed ones) over one's age and disappointed little fond hopes, or at least, ideas; to imagine the *What might have been!* Is there any pity deeper to a selfish person than the *pitié de soi même?*

Sometimes, I have often, on the other hand, cheered and flattered myself by brighter day-dreams, in which fancy has pictured quite delightful scenes as happening for my especial benefit, not romantic ones though—pooh! I am past all that. Going out for a drive with Lady Lawton to their market-town, in which lives a wonderful old miser with no relations, a retired butterman, I have highly amused her by imagining how we might drive by accident over that miser, or, better still, find him in a fit by the roadside, the said fit being probably brought on by inanition. Out of the carriage would spring, of course, that helpful person Mary Smith, pick up the miser's form, convey him to the nearest shelter, nurse him there with all a woman's tender care and un-selfishness of purpose, and finally—utterly to my astonishment, and this is *really* meant—be rewarded with the inheritance of the butterman's savings.

After which, being an extremely wealthy maiden lady, I should keep a fine steam yacht, five hundred tons at least, and go round the world probably; or else I should have a house in town, a villa on Lake Como, a deer forest in Scotland, for I love everything relating to sport; or else—

The one only drawback is, that none of these dreams ever have come true. I never have met that forlorn miser; my mind misgives me at times that I never shall.

As to that little arrangement of my morbid soul about the How and WHEN of meeting again with my old l—,— my old acquaintance, Colonel Fletcher, you may guess beforehand it could not happen precisely according to my programme; no such little arrangements in one's own mind ever do.

"Mary Smith—Mary! is that you?" called Miss Ida, disconsolately, through the trees just now; as if it could be any one else, when she saw me plainly.

"Well, and what do you want?" I inquired, with a hearty manner hastily assumed. The young lady drew her arm through mine and was plainly disposed to be low in spirits, on which, according to some secret love of opposition in nature, mine made a defiant attempt to rise.

"I have been looking for you everywhere, dear, to help me to entertain those old ladies. Aunt Emily has left them on my hands, and they have all gone in to do acrostics till tea-time. And I hate acrostics."

"O well, let us go in, and I'll give them lights enough—false ones, no doubt; but that will only give them the pleasure of crowing over me. I hate acrostics too, but never mind—come on."

"Oh yes, dear, thank you so much, Mary; but don't let us go in to them just yet. You are always so cheery, it does me good to be with you, and I do feel so depressed today."

"Poor Ida! what is the matter? what has gone wrong? Nothing amiss, I hope." I began thinking of a most promising love affair of hers, in which the gentleman, though absent hunting at present, was everything that could be wished as to fortune, family, and all the rest of it, and very devoted.

"Oh, no; not exactly. Only I am so bored with old Mrs. Hummingtop; and my new dress requires taking in, so I can't wear it to-night—and Kate O'Donnel is making such a set on the one man I really like in the house. Haven't you noticed it?"

AN OLD MAID'S MARRIAGE

The expected party had arrived since two days at the Lawtons, and the gentleman referred to, a good-looking young guardsman, was at that moment playing a lawn-tennis match in the asphalte court against Kate O'Donnel. Kate played remarkably well. Ida always had a figurative hole in her racket.

"But what should it matter to you—to an engaged girl—whether she sets her cap at him or not? Nonsense, Ida, you are as good as settled for in life; don't be a dog in the manger."

"Ah but, Mary, you don't understand how low one gets without a little attention now and then." (O, don't I? well, I ought to! ironically reflects her companion.) "Of course, Theodore likes to have his hunting, and I don't object to his amusing himself away from me with it, as we are not to be married till next spring; but then, I want a little fillip dreadfully too, just because I do miss him very much, and Kate O'Donnel need not have fixed on the very one man I most like here," observes the spoiled child.

(N.B.—Here comes in a moral reflection. I have remarked several spoiled children who never grew out of that spoiling, and expected strangers to carry on the agreeable process for their benefit till they reach any age. One old lady of nearly eighty was the worst-spoiled child that ever I knew, retaining all the little affectations of that past age, and imagining that her caprices and crossness had still the charm of sunshine and shade.)

To come back to our strayed muttons! I went indoors, and, as I had promised, *did* acrostics with Mrs. Hummingtop, a drowsy old dame from a neighbouring county, invited each year by the Lawtons because—she always had been invited before. There were also some other not very agreeable people. A travelling lady of title, as I called her, one Lady Sarah Brown, the impecunious widow of an unhappy half-pay general. Report said she had worried him into a better world. Lady Sarah spent all her autumns, and as much of the whole year as she could decently manage, in visiting country houses. Like myself, you will say; not a bit of it. Mine were *bonâ fide* invitations, but she (I knew this for a fact) constantly made a practice of writing to such people as the Lawtons, saying she heard there was to be a ball in their neighbourhood, and that their neighbours, the So-and-so's, had kindly asked her to pay them a visit (date of said visit carefully not mentioned), could dear Lady Lawton kindly shelter her for that ball-week, as she feared the So-and-so's would be unable to keep her? Lady Lawton would make up her mind to refuse, but be over-ruled by Sir Hugh's good-nature, who would tell her not to be unkind. Lady Sarah, on receiving a coolly-expressed yes for answer, forthwith writes off to the So-and-so's that dear Lady Lawton having given her a warm invitation for their county ball, she will find herself in the So-and-so's neighbourhood; could they give her house-room during the preceding or following week for some gaiety or other, as, most unfortunately, she fears the Lawtons will not then have room for her?

Having come for a week, Lady Sarah seldom leaves before a month.

I was almost forgetting to mention that this estimable feminine travelling title owns an invalid daughter; one who ought to be living quietly at home, poor soul, and who would gladly do so. But no! Lady Sarah without a daughter to take about would have no decent excuse to gad to balls and parties, so the unhappy Mary Anne, when suffering agonies of indigestion or pangs of neuralgic headache, is dragged down to heavy dinners, or out in the carriage to county hops, being far older and more faded than myself; and when they return to their temporary host's home about five of a miserable morning, Lady Sarah owns, over soup in the hall, that she "is half dead; but it is a positive matter of duty to give Mary Anne all possible chances."

It was these persons and a few similar old fogies, that made the heavy element in our party assembled for dinner that night.

It must be remarked that Colonel Fletcher had arrived; that

no doubt he had been hurried upstairs just in time to dress. But I never saw him arrive, as it was after dressing time then; and, it need hardly be observed, that I did *not* meet him on the stairs. Instead, there was not a living soul to be seen, except, presently, Sir Hugh, who crossed the hall below, and called to me to come downstairs, begging to know why I was dawdling—my usual manner of descent being much brisker.

So downstairs, feeling all over a regular old maid, I dutifully hurried, feeling, likewise, especially ugly, as pride and self-ridicule had prevented me from taking even as much pains as usual in fixing my hair "and things;" and I meekly ensconced myself behind a large table, one of those useful tables it is hard to get round, well piled with all the library books, the English newspapers come by the evening post, and an enormous épergne.

I had made my small private calculations that Colonel Fletcher would have to take me in to dinner. There was a sucking Honourable for Lady Lawton, and Sir Hugh would be obliged to give his arm to Lady Sarah, while an old fogey of a general would prose with Mrs. Hummingtop. I was the one of all the young ladies (with a note of admiration, at being nominally among them!) who must infallibly get Colonel Fletcher.

What was Lady Lawton doing with those slips of folded paper; while Ida whispered to her about them with an air of fuss?

"O, Mary dear," says Lady Lawton with a confidential smile, as much as to hint I understood and would warmly help the furtherance of her little plans.

"We thought, as you younger people don't stand upon precedence or ceremony and that sort of thing, that it would be amusing for you all to draw lots as to who takes in who to dinner."

Smash number two of another of my illusions! really, really, I will give up imagination and day-dreaming. Nobody could quite guess that I felt very small, however, I hope.

And just then—in came Colonel Fletcher.

AN OLD MAID'S MARRIAGE

The room was not very brightly lit before dinner; still the instant that rather tall gentleman, in evening dress, entered the further door, I, who had been wondering what changes there would be in his face, seemed to see them all in a moment, and feel as if they were exactly right and just what I had expected and foreknown. And yet a moment before the door-handle turned I had known nothing about his once plentiful fair hair having become decidedly thin on the top of the head and a trifle grey about the sides, though with his colour it did not much show. He had always had a thick reddish moustache of the shade that mostly goes with fair hair, and that was as thick and reddish as ever, and his eyes seemed as cheerful, his carriage as upright as eight or nine years ago—really.

As Colonel Fletcher came towards the universal point of attraction, the fireplace, Lady Lawton met him, renewing the hospitable professions she had already made on his arrival; then she began introducing all the guests that stood near, especially Minna O'Donnel.

I was behind the big table, you must remember; and unperceived, naturally, not being meant to be the future Mrs. Fletcher. After the Colonel was able to look round from the circle of new acquaintances, all of whom he was perforce first occupied with, his eyes took a calm searching sweep of the remainder of the room, fell on me behind the table and well behind the épergne—"Ah, Miss Smith, how do you do; how are you?" he exclaimed, coming cheerfully forward and holding out his hand to give mine a hearty grasp. "You have not forgotten me, I hope?"

Was ever the delicate distress of a tender fancy more rudely and healthily shaken? I was not forgotten or changed out of all knowledge.

I was not the person to cry, with firm cheerfulness, "Don't you remember me?" on the contrary, mine was the limp answering handshake, quite a feeble reply to so hale an old friend. In fact

I—had nothing on earth to make myself miserable about.

"I thought you had forgotten me—you did not seem to recognize me when I looked at you, I fancied," said Colonel Fletcher, gazing again straight at me.

"Oh—oh—yes, indeed I did. Only I was not quite sure whether you remembered me, as it is some time—so long, I mean, since we met."

"It is a long time certainly; a long time!" reiterated Colonel Fletcher, "but still, of course, I remembered you. What made you think I should not?"

"O, because—"

"Colonel Fletcher, will you come and draw your lot?" called her ladyship, and away the Colonel had to go, before I could say anything of a properly demure, old-maidish flavour as to changed features.

And the lot Colonel Fletcher drew was Minna O'Donnel.

My lady and Ida must have shuffled all the lots with cleverness.

The O'Donnel girls were nice fresh blondes, whose good looks struck one the more, because, being very similar, and dressed alike to the very spots upon their veils of a morning, and their lockets and bracelets at night, seeing one was the same as seeing the other, and thus, doubly seen, their faces grew upon people's liking—our only other girl, properly speaking, being the beauty, Ida Lawton. She is, to my mind, perfectly lovely, with her pale sweet refined face, soft brown hair, and lustrous brown eyes; naturally, all our gentlemen would vie to be the lucky drawer of the lot that held her name.

Of course I drew back, knowing quite well that whoever got none of the young creatures must take me, and they were shuffling rather suspiciously with the papers. After all, though one be rather hardened and weather-beaten instead of velvety-complexioned, yet, thank goodness! one may still be agreeable. Lads who might be my nephews, often beg of me to dance with them, and though

AN OLD MAID'S MARRIAGE

I am well aware they call me "a dear old thing" behind my back (some persons of even more than my age might think the term derogatory), they tell me many a trouble—poor boys—and it does give me immense pleasure to be confided in. Well, we had the Rev. Algy Vernon (a delightful parson, and *certain* to be a bishop); a pleasant little sailor, a flag-lieutenant; Major Fletcher, the bronzed soldier, and two guardsmen, with good looks, good fortunes, and very likely good hearts! (I should not have grumbled had my escort been either—or both.)

Well, Miss Ida was drawn in lot by the "only gentleman" she cared to speak to, in the absence of her fiancé. It was really a shame, since he plainly preferred Kate O'Donnel, and the lots were manipulated in some occult manner; how selfish very young girls are, to be sure! No matter—Miss Ida's "only vice-loves" were so frequently changed that very likely she would prefer the Reverend Algernon to-morrow, who was plainly sighing in vain for her. He fell to my share to-night; and it may be now remarked occupied a large portion of dinner-time in longing glances towards her, and in trying to draw me out as to Miss Lawton's pursuits and likings, artfully veiling these inquiries under cover of asking how I spent my time (much he cared!) during my long visits to the house.

As we sat down at dinner, Colonel Fletcher came beside me, but before I had time to reflect that there might be small mercies yet in store for the disappointed, came a call from the bottom of the table. "Colonel Fletcher, would you mind moving up a little and leaving a place beside you. We expect Lady Dorothy Fitzerle—and she is a little late in arriving."

What a detestable thing it is (sometimes) when you are all settled down at dinner to be sent moving round again; just, probably, when one has undone a napkin and fingered a bit of bread!

No matter once more! If there is a young person who most of all other lively beings runs me a race in good spirits, and is always trying to get the best of it—a race in which the emulation makes us all the better friends—that is the Lady Dorothy in question. So before the fish was handed, I had settled into my usual state of blissful content, and by the time the last entrée arrived, had forgotten all inclinations to bend forward for a sight of the tip of Colonel Fletcher's nose, or to bend back to be rewarded by a glimpse of his close-cropped hair. These human phenomena had again become quite as ordinary as the physical features of other folk. It seemed so truly ridiculous at my age to have been disturbed in mind at seeing again a gentleman I had known in former years, a fair-reddish man not very unlike other men, that I quite laughed at myself, and the Reverend Algy's lugubrious face infected me more with hilarity, so that at last he too thawed and we became extremely merry.

You must all distinctly understand that there had been no tender passages, strictly speaking, in bygone days between Colonel Fletcher and myself!

No; he had seemed to like me, and I knew I had liked him. Everybody else thought it was a mere passing flirtation, if they ever remarked it; and no doubt so it was. The truth is, in those days being young and foolish, and not understanding the full meaning of a full purse—but the absence of intentions in an empty one—I had rather expected that Captain Fletcher would have asked me a certain question!

And he didn't; that was the whole of it.

He looked quite tender unspoken words on saying goodbye for one second; looked away the next; gave me a nothing- particular of a parting shake of the hand. But that was the whole story.

"What a capital cook the Lawtons keep!" says my reverend friend in a hugely comforted, confidential tone.

"Yes: eating is a fine art here," I answered; at my time of life the fine arts are a solid consolation for imaginary ills.

When the gentlemen came into the drawing-room after din- ner that night, and all we ladies turned our faces to the door like sunflowers to the sun, it so happened, I remember, that Colonel Fletcher did not come with the rest. It afterwards appeared that Sir Hugh had kept his friend back to have a chat, and to press him to stay on longer than for a mere day. Also I do remember that, when he did enter, on passing by my sofa he lingered.

"I hope that now at least I may have a little chat with you, and renew our recollections of old times," he observed quite diffidently, as this time he found me able to look him in the face with all the cheerful briskness of a regular old maid.

Just then Lady Lawton came swimmingly down the long room to us. "O, Colonel Fletcher, we have been waiting for you, hoping that you would make a fourth at whist with us. Miss O'Donnel is to be your partner—she plays *so* admirably for such a young girl—unless,"—with an arch smile at my old-maidenly features,—"unless, of course, that you prefer staying to talk to Miss Smith."

"I am ready to do whatever you wish, Lady Lawton," replied the Colonel gallantly, as of course he ought; but at the same time he blushed visibly all over his honest face.

I remember wondering what on earth he was blushing about, and reflecting that fair men do blush so much more readily than dark ones; however, as their complexion is generally of a fine brick-red hue it shows considerably less. Lady Lawton never saw this, however; she was airily preparing to swim back with her prize. "And Mary, of course, will join the young people in the billiard-room; that is what you always like best, isn't it, dear?" she observed looking over her shoulder.

Without a thought of having missed much, I do assure you, the Mary in question accordingly went off to make a sort of public jester of herself for the benefit of the young folks, to be positively a mental buffoon; for when one has once gained a reputation for good spirits it is terribly incumbent to keep it up.

What would Colonel Fletcher have said? was all I thought.

Then most placidly, aided by good sense, told myself it would have been probably nothing more than that he had been in India ever since we parted, and that it was very hot there. After which, having received graciously a few similarly original remarks from myself, he would without doubt have civilly risen and gone to gaze on fairer forms.

So it was with equanimity that I occasionally peeped back into the hushed and darker library, where the whist players were intent over their game.

With not equal equanimity, however, as we were all preparing to say good-night, I found Colonel Fletcher once more beside me and gazing straight at my face; it being just that weary time of night when wrinkles tell most dreadfully and we old ones look fagged. "Well, Miss Smith, I hope you enjoyed the game that you and the rest of the young people had together … I am afraid it made me feel what an old fogey I really am, when Lady Lawton kindly asked me to play whist," he said in a low tone.

I stared up at him amazed. Either he was clean stark staring mad, or else he was rather too ironical.

"You don't suppose for a moment, I hope, that I am so foolish as to class myself among the young people—at my age, Colonel Fletcher! and as to whist being reserved for the old fogies, what nonsense! Why you had a quite young girl for a partner."

"Miss O'Donnel? oh, yes, I fear I have not been grateful enough to our kind hostess, then," said this strange man; adding, "But, Miss Smith, will you tell me one thing—why did you think I should not remember you? You said so— before dinner."

"Because Father Time is not kind to feminine beauty; because I have grown fat and faded," I replied, with an awkward laugh.

Colonel Fletcher became of a redder hue again, and declared with a warmth that really did me good, though I did not believe him one bit,—"How absurd! that is really too absurd! … Of course, every one knows years do change some people a little. A battered old soldier—like me, for instance—does not look any the better for it. But for you to say so is—is most unnecessary."

"Can you tell me honestly that I am not a great deal older-looking than when you last knew me? that I am not terribly changed for the worse?"

"You are—certainly—a little older-looking; you are *not* terribly changed for the worse," replied my unflinching friend in slow accents.

"When you first saw me this evening, surely your first thought must have been, what changes there were in my face! ... Say so openly, Colonel Fletcher; and you have no idea how I shall respect you. I never cared for flattery."

"When I first saw you this evening, Miss Smith, I did remark at once whatever changes there are in you. I will confess that I was even prepared to look for some, knowing such changes must happen. But afterwards, now—it almost seems to me as if there are none; perhaps because they are only becoming to you."

"Well I never was pretty, so if time has mellowed me, it is a comforting reflection."

Colonel Fletcher was just about to say something, what, nobody ever knew, when at that moment, like fate, down swept Lady Lawton upon us.

"What is this I hear?" she reproachfully exclaimed. "Hugh tells me he cannot persuade you to stay longer than to-morrow with us. O fie! Colonel Fletcher."

"Business, you see, Lady Lawton," pleaded her guest, with many thanks for her kind hospitality. "What can one do if business intervenes? You see I am not at all sure about my business. I might be obliged even to leave you to-morrow afternoon."

"What, and not stay one more night! I don't believe in your business. I very often do not believe in the excuses of gentlemen about their business," laughed her ladyship; then gazing round at Sir Hugh and me who stood near, "It is really most mysterious business that brings Colonel Fletcher over to Ireland at this time of year, and only allows him to pay us such a flying visit. He ought to be made to explain it."

That was evidently a false move on her part, for Colonel Fletcher looked extremely uncomfortable, and hummed and hawed, and pulled his moustache, so that even Lady Lawton, who is rather impulsive, perceived she had been indiscreet; and that her guest could not be expected to reveal his private affairs to gratify her curiosity.

So to put him out of embarrassment she gaily exclaimed, "Well, I cannot prevail on this obstinate man! Perhaps the young ladies may have more influence with him. Ida! Miss O'Donnel! will you all give your help."

False move number two! Colonel Fletcher again positively reddened, though, unless any one was watching him as keenly as myself, it might not have been perceived. And as Lady Lawton spoke of appealing to the young ladies, his eye by haphazard met mine. Decidedly, thought I sagely, he must have discovered her ladyship's little plan for his future happiness.

In the hair-brush club held later in Miss Ida's room by several of the young ladies, Colonel Fletcher was voted delightful, so fine-looking, so chivalrous in manner, and really not at all—old. Upon which I, yawning, stepped away, and when they made an outcry about it, I declared, at my venerable age that sleep was necessary.

And so it was indeed, for I remember that I did not sleep by any means soundly that night.

CHAPTER III

COMING downstairs on the following morning (at that convenient moment when prayers *ought*, in the nature of things, to be over and breakfast almost ready), a shout hailed me from the wide hall below, and peeping over the balusters I spied everybody busily tearing up paper into tiny fragments, with piles more in waste-paper baskets.

"Come down here and help, you lazy old thing!" cried Lady Dorothy—that one of our young lady guests who had got my place at dinner the night before. "We are all going to run a paper-chase this morning." Lady Dorothy was elegantly seated *à la turque* upon the floor; she is a red-headed little English body, owning a perfect complexion, very high birth, and very high spirits: nobody skated better in hard weather; while, as to hunting, to see her out with some celebrated packs was a sight some folk never forgot.

"Of course she calls me 'an old thing;' everybody may, for it's true," I soliloquized in descending. "I'm *not* as young as I was! but that's everybody's luck." (However, I meant to revenge myself by calling her "Dolly," which she hates, when we visited each other's rooms that night, and telling her in the unvarnished language of honest affection what a plain little chit she is, and how much I wonder that any men should fancy her—as, between ourselves, they do!).

Some of our gentlemen came trooping down the shallow stairs just then, got up in knickerbockers, strong boots, and heather-coloured stockings; so Sir Hugh, our handsome host, began making arrangements. He was to run hare, knowing his own country best, and as his wife afterwards said, "so thoughtlessly—just like a man," he gallantly asked Lady Dorothy, the general favourite of the bachelors, to accompany him, while the rest might "sort themselves," as the Manchester clergyman said to fifty couples whom he had just finished marrying at a time, and who had somehow all got mixed.

I don't think the little lady quite liked it, but she smiled with good grace, and told our hostess she would not run off with Sir Hugh; although he was so pleasant, it was quite a temptation.

The sorting accordingly began. To my secret entertainment, the Reverend Algernon at once made two strides across the room, and besought to be allowed to escort Miss Ida Lawton.

If there is anything good going a clergyman is sure to get it! as the naval lieutenant profanely remarked behind me.

The latter speaker at once himself "went for" Lady Lawton, by way, no doubt, of settling the vexed question as to whether the navy takes precedence of the army.

The two guardsmen naturally turned to the O'Donnel girls, who seemed thus predestined for them.

"Oh—but Colonel Fletcher!" murmured my lady, as she stood beside me, glancing at Minna: then recollecting herself, "However, it doesn't matter, since he *is* going to-day."

At that very moment, while I stood unsought, as might be expected, but cheerfully determined to run by myself as well as anybody, the subject of her soliloquy came in—having apparently been out for a morning ramble—and heard what was going on.

And so, seeing me standing apart, that good-natured Colonel Fletcher, who never likes to see any one in the background because they have lived a few more years than others, gave quite an eager pleased look, and offered in his cheery way to take charge of me. "Agreed," cried I politely; only mindful that he was a compeer of mine own. "We old people will beat these young ones yet."

At eleven o'clock the start was to be, and whichever lady was first in at the death, or gained soonest the farm-gate in the demesne wall where the hare (if alive) was to finish, would win a dear little gold compass. (Each vowed that its possession must be compassed! A small joke goes a great way in a country house.)

AN OLD MAID'S MARRIAGE

We assembled accordingly, our own sex being arrayed in short stout petticoats, homespun bodices, and upper skirts, strong boots, chamois gloves, and tall walking-sticks (no such encumbrances as jackets, since light apparel was much to be desired).

Such a warm dark October morning as it was!

There were masses of clouds piled apparently on the tops of all the surrounding hills, signs that we in our eagerness and heyday of spirits completely disregarded.

The hares were to start from a certain field beyond the lodge-gates, we hounds remaining inside the demesne till they had had a fair start of fifteen minutes. Then came the hue and cry.

Lady Lawton first spied the scent behind a hedge and was away foremost down the hill with her sailor, every one following.

Over a brook we went in splendid style, being fresh, up another hill, down the far side and across some meadows with horrible treacherous banks and thorny hedges. In front loomed a high, craggy hill, and with eagle-eyes we all strained our eyes to note every bush and stone upon its face. Nothing moving save a goat could be descried. They had not had time to get to the top as yet, and we must certainly have viewed our hares upon the side. No; we lose the scent at times, and make false casts and draw breath, but finally the paper leads us skirting the hill-base through a brown soaking bog all cut with deep trenches. Woe to the luckless one who jumps *in,* and to the wight who must pull her out. Struggling through with miry feet, the trail leads up the back of that great horrible hill! A general exclamation of indignation and wrath bursting at the same moment from the throats of even the most distant couples, showed all knew the truth! Those wily hares went up the back lest we should spy them, and had doubled.

Up we climbed silently; no running now!

The Colonel offers me an arm, and inwardly I utter a pious thanksgiving, that, though stout and short of figure, I am not short of *breath.*

AN OLD MAID'S MARRIAGE

A cold blast seemed to cut the skin on our faces; but delicate cheeks and I parted company long ago, and any red from exertion is perhaps an improvement upon tallow colour. Down that hill all the couples raced, and I was in (owing to lack of breath, truly unspeakable) joy, having beaten most; but the last drop was too frightful! Jumping first, the tall Colonel seemed far below poor me, wavering on the top. He called out that I must spring, stretched up his arms. It seemed *too* ridiculous, but—that compass!

With one despairing jump *at* him, somehow the next moment we found ourselves on our noses in the wet grass!

Quick as might be, we both scrambled up and trotted on, trying to look dignified, for one O'Donnel, and her attendant guardsman, were close behind, and would have laughed unmercifully. "Luckily," said I, "we have neither of us much beauty to spoil."

On, on again, in a jogging fashion, and sadly different now from our first light-heeled pace. We must have gone three Irish miles[51]. (An Irish mile means an English one and a "bit." "But how much that 'bit' is, as our other guardsman, who had just come up with the eldest O'Donnel, sadly remarked, "no man knows!") And now, to our secret fears, a drizzle of rain began; the black clouds grew blacker, but no one would utter the dismal forebodings all felt.

Just then the scent stopped short at a wide deep stream, with no possible crossing-place visible up its banks for ever so far; and on the opposite edge fluttered the tell-tale paper. A cry of execration burst from each heart, for a wide plank lay upon the other side—the enemy had pulled away the bridge!

It was a vile, a detestable trick, we all agreed, gazing ruefully at the black turbid bog-water, that was good five feet deep and

---

[51] An Irish mile is equivalent to 1.27 statute or 'English' miles. The statute mile of 5,280 feet became law in 1592. In Ireland, however, the old mile of 6,720 feet continued in local use in the 19th centuries.

exceedingly unsavoury!

Our best jumper had to lead the forlorn hope, and nerving himself to the uninviting width, he went at it—lit on the far side, broke down the hollow edge with his weight, and fell back with a splash into the water—(I felt so glad it was not my Colonel). Getting out and shaking himself, the little sailor, however—for it was he who had jumped—gallantly seized the plank for us to troop across, and then still valiantly ran on, though dripping with every step. The sky was darkening still more ominously, and one seemed to feel rain, rain, rain in the air. That a heavy shower was coming—and a soaking one, too—who could doubt? But how far from home we were, or where we were, who could tell?

We jumped into a lane and ran heavily, drearily down it after the scent.

Two men drove by in a cart, and we called out to ask had they seen Sir Hugh, and which way had he taken; but they only flogged their old mare and passed us in a jolting canter. An old farmer ploughing turned to gaze steadily at the horizon, never heeding the queries we halloaed over the hedge. For Irish people, even the most stolid Northerns, this was certainly remarkable conduct. We all asked each other in vain what it could mean. There are monks of La Trappe in the south of Ireland, but surely no such community could be here unknown to us, or could count these sturdy peasants among its members.

"I'll make him answer," said Colonel Fletcher, and he ran to a man who was clipping a hedge, but got never a word in reply to his questions.

"Did—you—see—Sir—Hugh—running by with a young—lady?" absolutely yelled my companion at last in his ear; but still the man went immovably on—clip, clip, clip!

"He hasn't heard one syllable, one might think," said my friend, blankly.

Suddenly the peasant looked up in grim affirmation and an

absolutely defiant nod.

"Ye're right there, sorr, niver a wurred."

"All stone deaf like yourself in this part of the country?" as grimly inquired the Colonel.

"We are so," assented the other, apparently thinking he had the best of it; and grinning with a sly twinkle in his eye which we could not understand, and yet a very serious, even reproving expression, as stolidly he turned again to his hedge.

This little interlude had belated us; even the languid Ida, the slowest of all, with the Reverend Algy, had gone by, and down came the rain in earnest—soaking, blinding, driving in white wreaths of vapour before the breeze.

"Come and take shelter," cried the Colonel.

"No—I won't," I gasped back, though the rain seemed singing in my ears. "We cannot be far from the end now— cannot be far from home now. Is it not better to run on—any way—till we—join—the rest?"

"I am afraid those are the Ballykillycocky woods in front there," answered my far from reassuring companion.

The Ballykillycocky woods, three miles from the Lawtons' demesne—woods at the very name of which all English visitors to those parts either laughed or shuddered, or else declared that the natives were playing on their credulity by inventing such a barbaric appellation.

At the sound of that name now, and thoughts of our distance still from friendly shelter, my heart sank down into my muddy heavy boots, and a big sigh followed.

"So far!—Have we all that long way still to go, and the rest all gone on in front?"

"Do you mind being alone with me very much, then? Is my society so very disagreeable to you?" asked Colonel Fletcher, keeping easily at my side as I panted on in the jog-trot to which we were now getting accustomed.

"Of course not—what a silly idea! Why should I mind it?"

But somehow, when this question had been put and answered, I felt that the idea of going so far home had suddenly received an access of agreeability that was quite remarkable.

There was a barn for holding straw standing with its door half open by the side of the lane.

"Come in here for shelter," now said my companion in a tone of authority, against which I no longer felt pleased to rebel. There was not much room for any one beside ourselves in the little space left by the piled straw, but we found that a little shock-headed urchin in very tattered garments had been before us, and now gazed with big astonished eyes at the gentlefolk.

As my dress was luckily almost waterproof, no great harm was to be dreaded from our wetting, so I sat down on a fallen straw-truss, and with my accustomed geniality tried to render myself agreeable by discussing all the probabilities of the ending of our chase, and kindred topics.

No use! Colonel Fletcher shifted from one foot to the other, and, though answering most civilly, was plainly uninterested as to which of our party should gain the compass. He kept gazing nervously from the open door to my self-possessed person, and regarding the little gossoon[52] in especial with a most unfavourable expression. The latter had drawn closer and closer to us, and was now staring hard and straight at our faces alternately, with an apparent resolution to get our features by heart.

"That young ragamuffin ought to be at school. What plagues all boys of that age are!" exclaimed my fellow-hound now with unamiability.

"There must be a cottage belonging to this barn, and very likely he belongs to the cottage," I remarked with a logical air.

"There is. I saw one just round the corner of the lane as we

---

[52] *gossoon* = boy.

came in here."

"O, then—what a pity we did not run on! Most likely all the others are there taking shelter."

"You would have got ever so much more wet. This is not such a bad place, is it, to wait in? … But perhaps," with a stiff tone, "you are regretting the society of the rest of our party—or of *some* of them."

The tone of this rather than the words raised a vivid blush long a stranger to the cheeks of his hearer, who was at once still more attentively gazed at by the juvenile Pat, as she heartily denied the soft impeachment.

"Well," replied the Colonel, with a suddenly pleased air, turning to the boy, "there is a way of soon finding out whether they are there or not. Here, sir—there is a sixpence for you. Run on to the cottage, and see if there are any ladies and gentlemen there too for you to stare at."

"But, poor child! he will get all wet," I exclaimed with womanly pity.

The boy, who was preparing to dart from the threshold like a loosed arrow, paused one moment.

"Am I till[53] come back and tell yer?"

"No, don't;" and as the urchin sped away, Colonel Fletcher turned to me with a guilty smile, yet one that told lurking triumph. "You seemed so anxious about his health that it seemed a pity to endanger it again. Now he can get his clothes dried at his mother's fire."

(There were really so few garments on the poor little individual in question, that this observation seemed superfluous.)

But Colonel Fletcher, now having got rid of our small bogie, seemed very little better able to talk, but looked so persistently at the door with a lugubrious face and nervous expression, that

---

[53] *till* = to.

I quite pitied him, and remember now that I said, with an air of positive certainty no less than commiseration:

"I know what is the matter with you. You want to be back at the house as fast as possible in order that you may see after this business of yours."

"So that is what you think. Do you believe you can read the expression of my face so well?" (with a rather satirically nervous smile, as I afterwards read it to be).

"Yes, that is what I do think, Colonel Fletcher. I am so sorry for your disappointment in being kept so long here with me. But will your business really call you away this evening?"

"I don't know—yet. Perhaps you can help me to tell, Miss Smith."

"I!—(in astonishment). But I know nothing about it; and nothing of any business."

"Well, at least I may tell you something about this of mine;" and Colonel Fletcher, with a sort of nervous great quietness took a seat beside me.

"You may remember that when we were both here some years ago—when I first met you—that I was not at all well off; very poor in fact. Well; some two or three months back a distant relation of mine died, and in the most unexpected way left me a small fortune."

"Really! I had never heard so; but I congratulate you on your good luck," was my answer, as he paused rather abruptly, and gave me a sudden look. "So I suppose you were obliged to come home from India to see about it. Was not that it?"

"Not quite precisely. I came home from India at once because I had long ago made up my mind that if such an event happened, I should ask some one to share it with me. ... So I wrote to Sir Hugh that business brought me to this part of the country. ... And now shall I succeed, Miss Smith? Do you think it possible? For—if not—I must certainly go away this evening again."

AN OLD MAID'S MARRIAGE

We were not very romantic persons either of us; we were past babbling noisily of feelings that, perhaps, were all the deeper for that; one at least likes to think so. And therefore it was that the Colonel's speech may seem tame to read, however differently it sounded with voice, look, and gesture, all clothing it with meaning. But that it did not seem at all dull or blunt or commonplace to me, of that one may be certain.

And now what did I say? What could such a regular old maid say?

I declare I shall not tell; and however much they did and still do plague me, nobody shall know one word more of what happened then between us—*there!*

All I shall say further is, that when the rain was over—indeed, a little time past—and some faintly clear October sunlight stole out, it shone on two persons with exceedingly happy faces, emerging from the hospitable barn in a very leisurely manner. And in an equally leisurely manner we were going down the road side by side, when a loud hail made us start.

That wall!—those woods!—that well-known excitedly-tired-looking group of people! Why surely we were not at Ballykillycocky at all, but back without knowing it at the farmgate of our host's home, and the great paper-chase had been ended without us; Lady Lawton herself having won the prize.

How they did laugh at us, to be sure! We were quite unmercifully chaffed, until towards evening, when Colonel Fletcher, seeking Sir Hugh in his study, informed the latter that his guest's business had now become of that nature that he preferred to stay; while I at the same time found means to have a very private chat with her ladyship in the boudoir for a quiet quarter of an hour.

She *was* very much astonished; rather unflatteringly so.

"What! you?—" was her first exclamation. But afterwards she nobly and amply made up for that unpremeditated expression by kind remarks, such as—she "always had guessed something;" she "was not at all surprised;" these ever increasing in number and certainty, till at last her ladyship convinced herself with satisfaction that the match was all of her own making, and that she had foreseen it "all along."

As to her congratulations and those of all the rest of my friends in the household, *nothing* could have been warmer (italics are such a comfortable way of expressing one's superabundant feelings without trouble).

The young people were a little unmerciful, certainly, and rushed at me all at once, asking leave to be bridesmaids— "as if such a regular old maid would have bridesmaids!" I replied with ridicule; further declaring that to spite them all I would be married only in private, and be dressed in a travelling costume of hodden gray[54].

"O, and what about all the farmers and peasants who would not answer our inquiries? It seems, that they actually imagined Sir John and Lady Dorothy were *running away!* and though thinking this very wrong, nothing would induce them to betray their landlord. After such devotion, who need talk of the bad feeling of the tenantry, in spite of all the agitators and the Land League;" so cried Lady Dolly with admiring fervour.

And before the evening was over, when Colonel Fletcher was standing beside me, Lady Lawton came up, and in the most solemn manner before everybody presented me with the little gold compass, as a keepsake of the day when at hare and hounds I found a husband.

---

[54] *hodden* = homespun, coarse grey woollen cloth.

CARROWDORE CONNECTIONS

CARROWDORE – CROMMELIN CONNECTIONS

by *Mark Thompson*

Carrowdore Castle, the childhood home of May Crommelin was built in a rustic gothic style by her grandfather (Nicholas Delacherois-Crommelin) in 1819, on the site of an old farmhouse previously owned by their family.

The unusually wide Main Street of Carrowdore (the 'Ballyboly' of *Orange Lily*), leads straight towards the main ('Upper') gothic gate and gate-lodge of Carrowdore Castle among the trees of the 'Plantin'. From 1927 until the year 2000 the street would be filled with motorbike riders and spectators for the annual 'Carrowdore 100' road race.

This 'Upper Ludge' is now demolished, but a similar 'Lower' gate at the far end of the 'Plantin' remains.

The row of cottages in this photo taken from the far end of the 'plantin' near the 'Lower' gate of Carrowdore Castle included my grandfather's home. The children are his brother and sister (Henry and Rhoda Wilson). In 1860 all 3 houses were owned by Nicholas Delacherois-Crommelin and rented to the Adams family. By 1879 two of the houses were listed as "free for 17 years". The family tradition is that the Crommelins allowed them to live rent-free, as one of them had nursed a Crommelin girl back to health from a life-threatening illness. This theme of this story is reflected in *Orange Lily*.

A grand-daughter of William Adams (Mary Kerr) inherited the houses and they were still listed as "free" in 1930. Mary Kerr was the mother of Lizzie Kerr who married Hugh Wilson. The Wilsons and the Adams families attended the 'United Free Church of Scotland' at Ballyfrenis.

Mary and Lizzie Kerr.

Ballyfrenis baptismal certificate.

CARROWDORE CONNECTIONS

Main Street Carrowdore, showing a girl and older lady "flooerin". White-on-white embroidery was an important cottage industry in the Ards and is accurately described by May Crommelin in *Orange Lily* and *The Witch of Windy Hill*.

An Orange Arch in Main Street, Carrowdore. May Crommelin's grandfather, Nicholas Delacherois-Crommelin of Carrowdore Castle, was a leading County Down Orangeman in the early 1800s. He was instrumental in establishing the Carrowdore Lodge in 1823, was County Grand Master for 30 years and Worshipful Master of the Carrowdore Lodge from 1837 to 1849. As the heroine of *Orange Lily* ('Lily Keag') was the fictional daughter of the local Worshipful Master, it seems that May was writing about 'Orange Lily' with some authority! Indeed, May's uncle, Frederick Armand Crommelin, (who was to inherit Carrowdore Castle when May's father — and Frederick's older brother, Samuel — died in 1885), was also Worshipful Master of the Carrowdore Orange Lodge from 1891 to 1901 and had donated the land for an Orange Hall to be built in Main Street in the late 19th century.

The importance of "Mr. Crommelin" to the Orange tradition in the Ards is celebrated in no fewer than 2 verses of the traditional Orange ballad, *The Hills o Carrowdore* and the last lines perhaps echo how 'Orange Lily' and her boyfriend 'Tammy Cowltert' spent one particular 'Twalth Day'.

THE HILLS O CARROWDORE

Come-al-ye loyal Orangemen, wherever you may be
I hope ye'll pay attention, and listen ontae me
For while I sing these verses, I hope wi me ye'll join
Tae commemorate King William at the Battle o the Boyne

Now the Orangemen o Newtonards, still loyal tae their cause
They dae inten' tae hae their rights in spite o Acts an Laws
They met on that Twalth mornin as they'd aft-times done before
And the fifes and drums King Williams Sons, before their masters bore.

There was Ballywalter Heroes an boys frae Greba toon
Cloghey, Ballyhalbert tae, an the Lower Ards o Doon
The colours that were on the hill they numbered half a score
They were met by loyal brethren frae the toon o Carrowdore

There was Ballyblack and Ballyhay and Bangor Nummer Three
Likewise Groomsport and Crawfordsburn an also Donaghadee
They hoisted up their flags that morn, they coontit fifty four
They were met by loyal brethren frae the hills o Carrowdore

Noo the speeches frae the platform, weel they soondit in oor ear
An first was Mr Crommelin, wha occupied the chair.
He toul us o oor forefaithers wha did King William join
Wha focht an gained the victory at the Battle o the Boyne

Sae here's tae Mr Crommelin, wha gien tae us the grun
A splendid platform he pit up — it coast him monys a pun.
We need tae sing his praises noo, an will for evermore
For the honour he did show us on the Hills o Carrowdore

Noo Carrowdore's a village that's encircled by the sea
Three miles frae Greba toon an four frae Donaghadee
There was monys a friend was there that day, not met for years before
An maybe niver will again, on the Hills o Carrowdore

Sae noo ye're free tae see the flags come babbin doon the fiel'
For loyal sons o William, they niver yet did yiel'.
Each boy he had his ain sweetheart, the yin he did adore
An wi fifes an drums King William's sons went hame frae Carrowdore.

CARROWDORE CONNECTIONS

Carrowdore Parish Church was built on land donated by Nicholas Delacherois-Crommelin in 1843, and completed in 1859. The enclosure of the Delacherois-Crommelin family is to the east of the church, and the grave of the poet Louis MacNeice is nearby. This was not only the church of the 'castle ladies' in the Orange Lily story, but of the 'church-clergyman' ('Reverend Redhead'), and indeed Lily Keag ('Orange Lily') herself. The fact that most of the local Ulster-Scots community were Presbyterian is not brought out in the story.

CARROWDORE CONNECTIONS

According to the 1901 census, 75% of the population of Carrowdore Parish of almost 2,000 was Presbyterian, and less than 20% Church of Ireland. Carrowdore Presbyterian Church was built in 1843, the same year as the Church of Ireland (Christ Church) building, and again on land donated by Nicholas Delacherois-Crommelin just behind Main Street—where there had been an earlier Meeting House since 1828. Today the church is combined with the old United Free Church of Scotland congregation of Ballyfrenis, just east of Carrowdore, on the Millisle Road. In 1901, the 'other' denominations included less than a dozen Roman Catholics, and about 100 'Christian Brethren', Unitarians and adherents of the United Free Church of Scotland..

CARROWDORE CONNECTIONS

Ballyfrenis United Free Church.

Building work on Ballyfrenis Presbyterian Church began in 1846 (since the 1930s this congregation has been merged into Carrowdore Presbyterian). It was originally a 'Seceder' or 'Covenanter' congregation of the Associate Presbytery of Ireland, which in 1858 joined the United Free Church of Scotland. Ballyfrenis remained in the Ayr Presbytery of that church until the 1920s, being by then the only Presbyterian church in Ireland still belonging to a Scottish rather than an Irish Presbytery. The building is now a private house. My mother's family (the Wilsons of Ballyrawer and Islandhill, also known to some of the older generation as 'Blacktoon') were members of this church.

GLOSSARY

Descriptive Ulster-Scots Glossary: *Orange Lily* and *The Witch of Windy Hill*

The language used by May Crommelin to represent the speech of many principal characters in these novels is rich in Ulster-Scots vocabulary and idiom. This includes spellings which would be regarded as 'markers' of Ulster-Scots speech such as '*breid*' and '*heid*' for 'bread' and 'head'; '*gie*' and '*hae*' for 'give' and 'have'; '*dochter*' and '*almichty*' for 'daughter' and 'almighty'; and '*couldna*' and '*dinny*' for 'couldn't' and 'don't'. Although she modified her spellings to accommodate an English and American readership, the text reveals she had an intimate knowledge of the local language of her early years spent around Carrowdore and the townland of Ballyboley, in the middle of the Ards peninsula, County Down, where *Orange Lily* (1879) is set. She was careful to emphasise that, although the Ards folk were in general of *'mingled Scotch and Irish breeding'*, those of Carrowdore belonged to *'the fairer-haired, purer Scotch race which King James had planted'*. This meant that (to her) their speech was also distinctive: *'Tom Coulter, or "Tammy Cowltert," as his name was generally pronounced by those who spoke as broad as their Scotch ancestors did'*. In *The Witch of Windy Hill* (1880), May Crommelin describes this 'distinctive' speech as 'Scotch': *'In the North of Ireland … where … Protestants and Presbyterians and Scotch-speaking descendants of Scotch-bred colonists abide'*.

However, even back in the 19th century, the effect of schooling on the local Ulster-Scots speech was noted: *'the schoolmaster's denunciations of the Ballyboly dialect had taken effect upon the speech of both. Lily's anxiety for self-improvement made her keep the door of her lips with constant care, so that she even spoke quite pretty to the baby, said her doting father. But Tom used English, it is to be feared, rather as the English once talked French, because it was considered modish so to do, and relapsed into broad northern pronunciation in all his moments of thoroughly vulgar enjoyment'.* Sometimes, of course, 'Or'nge Lily' would 'forget hersel': *'It's owre ocht—it's beyant the beyants!" she gurgled; forgetting the schoolmaster's withering sarcasms upon "broad pronunciation"'.* This 'correction' of local speech in the classroom is a recurring theme : *'the scene changed to the school-house again, and Lily was observing with grave contempt—"You do speak so broad, Tom; say path, not kash." Whereupon the Misses Alexander, the schoolmaster, and all the children gave full chase after Tom, crying out—"Spell kash! spell kash!'*

The following glossary includes some perfectly transparent 'English' words where these are shared with Ulster-Scots, but are commonly used in the local vernacular with a slight shift in meaning in preference to the 'usual' English form, for example: **allow, alloo**—admit, concede (*"I did **allow** you were right, about not fighting this night,"*). This gives some indication of the subtlety and variety of the Ulster-Scots vocabulary used. It is the author's restrained but confident use of Ulster-Scots grammar and idiom in the dialogue of the local characters that demonstrates her famil-iarity with the everyday speech of her native community. Among many examples that could be quoted, we find *'at the drink'* used in place of 'drinking alcohol', and *'tha'* used for 'the' (as in mod-ern Ulster-Scots) to emphasise how Tom Coulter was unable to pronounce the definite article ('the') properly in the classroom.

Philip Robinson

GLOSSARY

aboot — about

acquent — familiar, acquainted

affronted — ashamed, disgraced

afore — before

against — in exchange for *(… I offered to swap a moss-cheeper's nest and three eggs against another boy's book)*

ailed — upset

ails — troubles, is wrong with

allow — admit, concede

Almichty — Almighty

anent — concerning

answer — suit *(… if I had but ten pounds more to buy a beast at the morrow's fair, it would answer me well)*

as — that

at the drink — drinking alcohol

ay — yes

aye — always

back side — far side, rear

bad scran — bad luck (to you)

bairn — baby

bar — except

barring — except

bating — beating

be'd to — had to

betwixt — between

bidden – commanded

bide — live

blatheration — foolish talk

blathers — nonsense

bogie — spectre

bonny — pretty

bools — pot-hooks *(… pots on the bools (or pot-hooks), which fasten these to the crane)*

brae — hill

bravely — well

breid — bread

broad — broad dialect

brogues — shoes

bumming — buzzing

call — (a) right *(… a matter in which "wee-men had no call to interfere —")*

came to words — quarrelled

can'le — candle

cassel — castle

certain sure — certain

champit — mashed

chid — chided, scolded

childer — children

chin-cough — whooping cough

church-clergyman — Episcopalian clergyman

clawk — clock

clever — utter

clocking — brooding (hen)

clod — throw (stones)

clout — hit

colley-dog — collie

conduck — conduct

convoy — escort *(… Let me convoy you back, Miss Keag)*

coort — court

coorting — courting

couldna — couldn't

cowld — cold

Cowltert — Coulter

cowpit — threw down

GLOSSARY

craiv — beg *(… but i doo not craiv a Peneworth)*
crature — person
creaive — beg
creepie-stool — low stool
cried — called
crowl — an undersized person
da — father
Dan'l — Daniel
darred — challenged
daunder — stroll
daundered — confused
daundered on — wandered on
daured — dared
deave — bewilder
deed — indeed
deein — dying
deil a hait! — not at all
deith — death
denner — dinner
dinna — don't
dinny — don't
discourse — talk
dishabilities — casual clothes
dispepshur — dyspepsia
disremember — forget
divarting — entertaining
divil a — not a
do be — am, is, are
dochter — daughter
done — did
douce — tidy, pleasant, comfortable
dulse — edible seaweed
dummy — a deaf-mute person

GLOSSARY

dumbfoundered — astounded
durst — dared
fairing — gift from a fair
fallow — fellow
farl — quarter of flat griddle bread
feared — afraid
flesh-meat — meat
flit — move house
flitting — emigrating
flowering — embroidery
foortherin — fumbling
for — wanting to
forbye — besides
free —friendly
frighted — frightened
fustling — fidgeting
gapes — a disease in poultry
gawk — fool
gey and — very
gie — give
gi'ed — gave
goodman — husband
goodwife — wife
gosson — boy
got married on — married
grup — grip
hae — have
happed — wrapped
har'ly — barely
head-rig — top and final ridges ploughed
heartsome — cheering
heartsomest — most cheering
heerd tell — heard

GLOSSARY

heid — head

hie — hurry, rush

hodden — coarse, homespun grey woollen cloth

Hoots! — Gosh!

hould — bet, promise

hould — hold

hould yer whisht! — be quiet!

hunnered — hundred

hurted — hurt

i' — in

ijit — idiot

ill — bad

immejently — immediately

imperent — impudent

in a tremmle — trembling

in course — of course

Injin — Indian

insense — explain, cause to understand

jeer — mimic in a hurtful way

kash — path through bog (… *Tom; say path, not kash."* *Whereupon the Misses Alexander, the schoolmaster, and all the children gave full chase after Tom, crying out—"Spell kash! spell kash!)*

knowe — knoll, hillock

lass — girl

lassie — girl

lassies — girls

let on — intimate (… *Deed is it! Only don't let on to the rest*)

let on — yelled (…*I misdoubt that it was fairly broken; though she let on" (yelled) "as much as if it was*)

griddle — flat-iron plate for open-hearth bread-making

lint-flowers — flax blossom

lint-hole — flax dam

GLOSSARY

linties — linnets
logie — dry, warm storage hole
looking-glass — mirror
lump of a girl — teenager
Majempsy — McGimpsey
many's the day — often
marched — bordered
Marget — Margaret
married on — married to
mesel — myself
mind — look after
mind — remember
minded — remembered
misdoubt — suspect
misrested — suffering from loss of sleep
morn — morning
moss — peat bog *(… drowning in the moss (bog).)*
moss-cheeper — meadow-pipit
my lone — alone (by myself)
naething — nothing
naw — no
neardest — nearest
nearhand — nearly
newuns — news, unusual behaviour *(… well, this is new-uns!"*
  (or something new), "exclaimed her step-mother …)
niver — never
no — not
noan — none
nor — than
not can — not be able to
o' — of
o't — of it
och — but, oh!

GLOSSARY

Och, anee! anee! anee! — alas!

ochone — alas!

ocht — any(thing)

offered — attempted *(… "He kissed ye; and I never even offered* to do it!" [*Attempted])*

on the top of — after *(… Ay, he darred me there, on the top of" (after) "we'r hymn-practice)*

ony — any

or'nge — orange

orfant — orphan

orphant — orphan

ould — old

ouldest — oldest

over anything — exceptionally

own — admit

owning — admitting

owre ocht — best of all, exceptional

pad — path

pains — rheumatism

party — sectarian

peat-reek — peat smoke

press — cupboard

purty — pretty

put upon — take advantage of

quare — fine

quare and — very

quaw — marsh

queer and — very

quern — hand-mill

quieted — pacified

quit — finish (work, school)

quoth — said

ram-stam — run headlong

GLOSSARY

reg'lar — regularly
releegious — religious
retail — repeat (gossip)
rick-me-tick — amount *(… he offered to lend me what would pay off the whole rick-me-tick!)*
Sabbath — Sunday
scarred — frightened
scatterment — dispersal
schuil — school
Scotch — Scottish
Scotch fir-trees — Scots Pine
scrawls (*recte* **scraws**) — layer of sod or turf including grass and roots *(… as much ground as would sod a lark … his allusion being to the fresh scrawls or sods that are daily placed in the cages of caught larks")*
shandhrydan — rickity conveyance
shough — ditch
shure — sure
Shusy — Susan
sitch — such
skelp — slap
smiddy — smithy
smit — infected
smithereens — tiny pieces
sned — cut the tops off
something — a little *(… Lill did feel something vexed that it was true)*
sonsie — pretty, loveable
sonsy — pleasant
sorr — sir
sough — rumour
spells — spellings
squandering — spoiling

stanes — stones
steam-coach — train
stirabout — porridge
stirring — constantly moving
stooks — stacks of sheaves
stop — stay
strand — beach, shore
subjeck — subject
such an' a — such a
suckit — sucked
sunder — separate
swalled — swelled
swarree — church hall entertainment with refreshments *(… besides the more frequent entertainments of school house concerts, meeting-house "swarrees" to enjoy tea and cake and hear moral addresses)*
Tammas — Thomas
Tammy — Tom
telled — told
telt — told
terrible — very
tha — the ('… Saint John th*a* Bap-tist was a good man an' a … pro-phet an' he … pre-ched in *tha* wil-der-ness of Ju-de-a')
that — so
the cowld — a cold
the day — today
the dear knows — God knows
the Lord be thankit — thanks be to God
the morrow — tomorrow
The quality — Gentry
the schooling — education
thegether — together

GLOSSARY

theirselves — themselves
them — those
think long — feel homesick
thinking long — homesick, yearning
thole — endure
thon — that
threshed — thrashed (beaten with a stick)
throng — busy
throughother — untidy
till — to
till-iron — crow-bar *("There's a till-iron" (crowbar) "there needs sharpening. I'll maybe be taking it to the smiddy about the time you'd be coming back,")*
timorsome — timid
tory — rogue, rascal
tould — told
travalin — walking
tryst — agreed meeting, appointment
trysted — pledged
Twalfth — Twelfth
twelvemonth — year
unbeknownst — unknown
want — do without
warrant — guarantee
water-hole — pool
we'r — our
wean — child
weddingers — bride and groom *(… what has become of the weddingers—of the bride and groom?)*
wee — small
wee lass — young girl
wee while — short time
wee-thing — little

GLOSSARY

whaled — beat
what for? — why?
wheen — several
while — time
whiles — sometimes, at times
Whinny Knowe — gorse-covered hill
whins — gorse
whullabaloo — hullabaloo, commotion
wimmen — women
winsey — woollen and linen interwoven cloth
word — news
wrack — sea-weed
wrang — wrong
wummun — woman
wunner — wonder
wurred — word
wynd! — turn left (horse command)
ye — you
yer — your
yez — you (plural)
yun — one

OTHER TITLES FROM ULLANS PRESS

 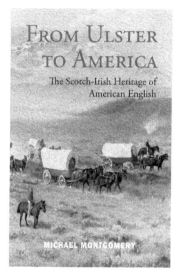

The Hamely Tongue: A personal record of Ulster-Scots in County Antrim James Fenton (978-1905281237)

'This is the standard 'picture' of modern Ulster-Scots in a form that makes compulsive reading for anyone … The book gives a heartening insight into what is now a now fast-disappearing language and culture. An absolute treasure.'

From Ulster to America: The Scotch-Irish Heritage of American English Michael Montgomery (978-1905281282)

'This book recounts the lasting impact they [the Ulster-Scots] made on the development of the English language of the United States from the eighteenth century to the present day. It documents nearly four hundred terms and meanings … that were contributed to American English by these eighteenth-century settlers from Ulster.'

TITLES FROM BOOKS ULSTER

Fighters of Derry: Their Deeds and Descendants, Being a Chronicle of Events in Ireland during the Revolutionary Period, 1688–91   William R Young   (978-1910375082)

'William R. Young's *Fighters of Derry* has for decades been one of the most overlooked works on the Siege of Derry and as a local genealogical resource … '

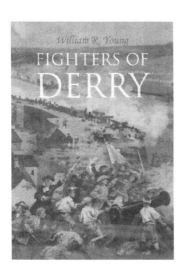
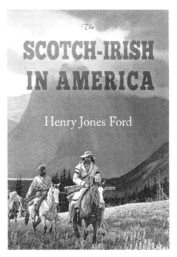

The Scotch-Irish in America   Henry Jones Ford

(978-1910375495)

'[*The Scotch-Irish in America*] … tells the story of how the hardy breed of men and women, who in America came to be known as the 'Scotch-Irish', was forged in the north of Ireland during the seventeenth century.'

www.booksulster.com

www.uuhf.co.uk

The United Ulster History Forum was formed in 2007. We are pleased to support this new edition of *Orange Lily* published by the Ulster-Scots Language Society and the Ulster-Scots Academy.

The focus of the work of the United Ulster History Forum is on military history. We collect memorabilia from both world wars and other past conflicts such as the Boer War and the 1798 Rebellion of the United Irishmen.

The Forum regularly holds displays and exhibitions of photographs, letters and other memorabilia about the lives and times of the people who were involved in wars of the past.

For the past few years we have been conducting visits to the battlefields on the continent and explaining and showing the people of today the events of the past.

Find us on

Printed in Great Britain
by Amazon